Sous Vide Cookbook for Everybody

500+ Best Sous Vide Recipes of All Time.

|With Nutrition Facts and Everyday Recipes|

Legal & Disclaimer

The information contained in this book and its contents is not designed to replace or take the place of any form of medical or professional advice; and is not meant to replace the need for independent medical, financial, legal or other professional advice or services, as may be required. The content and information in this book has been provided for educational and entertainment purposes only.
The content and information contained in this book has been compiled from sources deemed reliable, and it is accurate to the best of the Author's knowledge, information and belief. However, the Author cannot guarantee its accuracy and validity and cannot be held liable for any errors and/or omissions. Further, changes are periodically made to this book as and when needed. Where appropriate and/or necessary, you must consult a professional (including but not limited to your doctor, attorney, financial advisor or such other professional advisor) before using any of the suggested remedies, techniques, or information in this book.
Upon using the contents and information contained in this book, you agree to hold harmless the Author from and against any damages, costs, and expenses, including any legal fees potentially resulting from the application of any of the information provided by this book. This disclaimer applies to any loss, damages or injury caused by the use and application, whether directly or indirectly, of any advice or information presented, whether for breach of contract, tort, negligence, personal injury, criminal intent, or under any other cause of action.
You agree to accept all risks of using the information presented inside this book.
You agree that by continuing to read this book, where appropriate and/or necessary, you shall consult a professional (including but not limited to your doctor, attorney, or financial advisor or such other advisor as needed) before using any of the suggested remedies, techniques, or information in this book.

TableofContent

Aromatic Chicken
Chicken Wings
Mediterranean Chicken
Duck a la Orange
Chicken Thighs with Herbed Rice
Mirin Teriyaki Wings
Fried Chicken
Sticky DuckWings
Ginger Marmalade Chicken
Honey Dredged Duck Breast
Lemon Grass Chicken Dish
Waldorf Chicken Salad Sous
Vide Poached Chicken Rare
Duck Breast Moroccan
Chicken Salad Korean
Chicken Wings Panko
Crusted Chicken Clementine
Chicken Breast Chicken &
Melted Leeks Moroccan
Chicken Meal Spicy Adobo
Chicken Ginger DuckBreast
Greek Meatballs
Jamaican Jerk Chicken
Bacon Wrapped Chicken
Chicken Caprese Stuffed
Cornish Hen Chicken
Mint PeaFeta
Duck Breast with Calamansi Sauce
Chicken Roulade
Pheasant Breast
TurkeyMeatballs
Thai Green Curry Noodle Soup
Chicken Parmesan Balls
Chicken & Avocado Salad
Sweet Chili Chicken
Lemon Grass Salad
Coconut Chicken

Cherry Manhattan
Lavender Syrup
Thyme Liqueur
Pineapple Rum
Vodka Lemon Meyer
Rosemary & Lemon Vodka
Bloody Mary Vodka Coffee
Liquor
Honey Ginger Shrub
Cherry Bourbon
Raspberry Cordial
Bacon Vodka Spiced
Rum
Mulled Wine Hot
SpicedCider
Mint Julep & Coconut Sugar
Grand Marnier
Red Wine Plum Shrub
Sous Vide Classic Creamy Eggnog
Tomato Shrub
Strawberry & Rhubarb Shrub
Rhubarb & Thyme Syrup
Chili Agave Liqueur
Bourbon Grape & Ginger Beer Cocktail
Sous Vide Gin
Limoncello Vodka Cocktail
Swedish Rosemary Snaps
Strawberry Basil Shrub
Drambuie
Bacon Infused Bourbon
Lemongrass Syrup Thai
Basil Drink Jalapeno
Vodka

Chicken Stock
Cinnamon-Apple Flavored Balsamic Vinegar
Strawberry & Blueberry Coulis
Summer Corn Salsa
Grand Marnier Cranberry
Sauce Lemon Ginger
Marmalade Meyer Lemon
Infused Olive Oil

Introduction

Dear reader, welcome to my SOUS VIDE cookbook. I am so grateful that you can download and purchase this cookbook, I hope you will be happy with it.

I am writing this book to share with you the benefits of using the sous vide machine and the amazing sous vide recipes. The recipes are filled with so many nutrients that are important for your body.

This book is aimed to reach readers who seek to find and enjoy meals full of nutrients. Many foods out there lose their nutrients while they are being prepared. With sous vide machine, the food retains all its nutrients, and this ensures that you remain healthy throughout. The book aims to reach readers who want to lose weight. The sous vide recipes use little or no fat or salt, and this helps in weight loss.

This book aims to solve the problem of undercooked food. Many people out there have no option but to eat food that is undercooked because that is what is available for them to choose from. With sous vide, the food is well cooked, and there is no problem of undercooking.

As a reader, you can expect to find a lot of information about sous vide cooking. This information will help you in preparation for the sous vide meals. You should also expect to find amazingly delicious sous vide recipes that are well prepared.

So, what are you waiting for? It is time to discover a completely new way of healthy cooking! Enjoy cooking!

Chapter 1: The Sous Vide Basics

What is Sous Vide?

Sous Vide, is a cooking art that uses exact temperature control to produce consistent, high-quality meals. Sous vide is a French term that means "under vacuum." The process involves placing food in vacuum sealed bag and cooking it in a water bath using a very precise temperature. This makes it impossible for any other cooking method to produce the same quality of food.

A Brief History of Sous Vide Cooking

The origin of the technique of Sous Vide cooking dates to the mid-1970s when a very famous chef named Georges Pralus developed the technique with a hope of minimizing costly shrinkage and creating an optimal environment for cooking foie gras.

The news of this cooking technique spread like wildfire and was eventually picked up by another chef named Bruno Goussault.

Having understood the potentiality and delicacy of Sous Vide cooking, Bruno started to serve food prepared by Sous Vide to the first-class guests of Air France. The individuals who were lucky enough to taste the Sous Vide prepared meals were left completely mesmerized.

Once Bruno realized the true potential of this cooking technique, he went on to introduce it to the general audience. Despite reaching a mass popularity, it still was a very expensive technique for normal people to afford and it took about 2 years of evolution before it completely broke the barriers and became one of the "Best" cooking techniques ever made. This reputation has also led to the creation of a more affordable device, using which people of every budget are now able to enjoy the delicacies of Sous Vide meals right from their own kitchen.

The Science Behind The Sous Vide Cooking

You begin by placing the food you want to cook in a vacuum seal bag then remove air from inside the bag using a vacuum sealer or water displacement method.

The vacuum sealer has a fan quite similar to that in a vacuum cleaner, which pulls air from the bag and prevents more air from entering it. The plastic of the sealing bag typically conforms to the shape of the food sealed inside it.

Afterwards, you need to seal the air from the vacuum sealer to prevent more air from getting in. This is achieved by using a heated sealing surface, which presses the bag shut and applies some heat to the bag to melt the plastic slightly, which creates a secure airtight seal which can't be pulled apart simply.

Now that the foods are sealed, you heat the water bath next. This process requires a device that allows a stable temp of water, so the more even the heat is and the greater the volume, the better. Ideally, slow cookers and rice cookers such as the Admiral craft RC-E50 are used in this process.

We'll use 72-hour short ribs as a good example of sous vide cooking. When you cook meat at a low temperature, it turns the connective tissue into tender mouthwatering deliciousness – reason being that firm collagen proteins of the meat begins to denature and change into softer gelatin. When you cook the meat at high temp, it causes the muscle fibers of your meat to toughen. Since browning of steak is caused by high heat when the short ribs are done cooking, you will have a pale and soft piece of meat because as mentioned earlier, sous vide involves low temp. The browning is usually done after sous vide. The meat would cook for 72 hours at 55 degrees C after which you get your skillet as hot as you can then remove your cooked meat from the water bath. Open your vacuum sealed bag, oil the skillet then add the meat immediately. Turn the steak with tongs until it is nicely browned on each side and voila, you have perfectly cooked steak.

The Advantages of Sous Vide Cooking

Accuracy

Traditional cooking methods don't allow you to control temperature and heat, so you end up having burnt food on the outside but raw on the inside, most especially when grilling. This is what makes sous vide different. It allows you to cook food in a precise temperature at a specific duration, producing very accurate results. It gives you more control over your cooking times. You can prepare your food and vacuum seal it up to a day in advance and leave it to cook slowly in the water oven. It also gives you the pleasure of coming back and serving up your meal whenever you are ready to eat. The best part is that you can even sous videovernight.

Predictability

In Sous Vide, you will know exactly when to stop cooking the food because you have set it a time and temperature. You will not guess whether the inside is cooked well by simply looking at the food externally.

No More Burnt, Chewy Or Undercooked Food

It is not uncommon to end up with food where a piece is cooked on the outside but still raw on the inside when pan-frying. In such instances, cooking the food until it is very well done on the inside means that the outside can easily end up overcooked or even burnt.

This problem never arises with sous vide cooking where the food cooks evenly all the way through at a low temperature and can be later on seared or browned.

It is nearly impossible to overcook food in a water bath.

Great Quality Delicious Food

Sous vide cooked food is utterly delicious and infinitely more appealing, the reason being that since the food is placed in a vacuum sealed bag, it does not lose its form or dehydrate while cooking. The original flavor, weight, aroma and natural color of the food is not lost. It also means that you can utilize forgotten or cheaper cuts of meat to youradvantage.

Other than that, sous vide produces food in the texture that it is meant to be eaten. Gone are the days of soggy asparagus and chewy chicken – sous vide vegetables retain their color and crunch and the meat is moist and tender.

Range

You can cook your favorite food using the Sous Vide technique according to the type of readiness that you prefer. Everyone in the family gets to enjoy the meal according to their individual preferences.

Time

Preparing good food is very time-consuming especially when using the traditional methods. It requires a lot of effort and attention that you cannot do anything else. Because Sous Vide is a precise cooking method, the food is cooked to the exact temperature and you don't have to worry about it being overcooked. You can do other things and just check the food you are cooking because once it reached the exact temperature the precision cooker will hold it.

Adventure

What better way to enjoy your kitchen that to try something new? Sous vide is definitely something worth experiencing, and believe me, once you've tried it, you'll never go back to the old ways of cooking ever again! Adventure time in the kitchen, why not?

Portioning

Because sous vide requires that you place a single meat in each vacuum-sealed bag, you don't worry about portioning later on. You just take off the bag and put it portion for plating unlike in stove cooking where you put all the food together and portion them later.

Wow Factors

Surprise your family or friends with a precisely cooked meal any random day of the week. The inviting appearance, the tenderness, and the tastiness of the meal you cooked will be too obvious. They will enjoy their food for sure and of course, admire the inner chef inyou!

The Health Benefits of Sous Vide Cooking

Little Or No Salt Or Fat Is Needed

Unlike in frying, grilling, or any other conventional way of cooking food, Sous Vide does not require extra salt or fat. Moreover, vacuum-sealing means that the vitamins and minerals of the food are kept, which is more beneficial to your body. No MSG or artificial flavors needed to enhance the taste.

No More Undercooked Or Burnt Food

Undercooked food can be harmful when eaten as they can contain bacteria like E. coli, Salmonella, and others, which may cause diarrhea, vomiting, and food poisoning among others. On the other hand, eating burnt food often can increase your risks for cancer as they tend to be carcinogenic. This is the great thing about Sous Vide. It allows you to cook your food, avoiding it to be undercooked or burnt.

Extended Shelf Life

When you cooked your food through conventional ways, you can still put in the fridge and reheat a day or so later. However, Sous Vide food, since they are locked or vacuum-sealed have a longer shelf life. In addition, you don't need to worry about its accumulating bacteria in the fridge. This means that meal cooked in Sous Vide is safer to keep and recooklater.

What Do You Need To Sous Vide?

Below is a list of the basic equipment that you need to get started:

Food-Save Sous Vide Bags

Resealable plastic bags or Ziploc bags made from either polypropylene, low-density polyethylene, or food-grade high-density polyethylene are the safest kinds of plastics that you can use in Sous Vide. Most of the popular Ziploc, resealable, or Sous Vide bags are made from these plastics.

Sous Vide Precision Cooker

You can own a Sous Vide precision cooker under $100, which is one of the key things you need to succeed in this cooking method. It is simply clipped to the pot, set to your preferred temperature, and then just hit the play button for that magical result! You can browse for available brands online and get the one you wish.

Large Pots

Large, stainless steel pots are other sous vide essentials. This is where you will cook the vacuum-sealed food, by filling it with water.

Water Containers

As you will cook in a water bath, you obviously need water containers in Sous Vide. The minimum depth of water in Sous Vide is 2.5 inches so choose Sous Vide containers that can hold a higher volume of water.

Cast Iron Pans

You will need one cast iron skillet after cooking the meat using the Sous Vide technique because you would like to add a crisp, brown look to the food, and the better way to do it is with a hot pan. It will not only make the food look tastier but actually adds textural contrast and flavor.

Grills and Torches

Sears would make the sous vide-cooked meat look more appetizing. In order to add this final touch, you will need grills and torches, and using these tools can help to put on texture, flavor, and color contrast to your final output.

Step By Step Guide To Sous Vide

1. Heating a water bath with a Sous Vide cooker in it, which is set at a particular temperature.
2. Preparing your food, seasoning it, oiling it, etc. as you willdesire.
3. Placing the food in a sealable vacuum bag, releasing air from the bag, and sealingit.
4. **Tip**: Water Displacement Method: This process helps you release air efficiently from the bag when sealing it. Place the ingredient-filled bag halfway in the water bath, and air will naturally be released from the bag. Then sealit.
5. Placing the food in the water bath to cook for a desiredtime.
6. Searing the food with heat, ifdesired.

FAQs of Sous Vide

Is It Safe Cooking With Sous Vide?

Yes. Sous vide cooking is safe for everyone who wants to cook.

Can I Sous Vide Without a Sous Vide Circulator?

No. The circulator is precise and its hands-off ease-of-use is a good quality that is important in cooking with sous vide. Cooking without a circulator will most probably lose the good taste of cooking with the sous vide machine. Therefore, it is good to stick to using the sous vide circulator.

Must I Have a Vacuum Sealer?

No. You do not have to buy a vacuum sealer. It is an important tool but it is not a must- have. A zipper-lock plastic bag of high-quality works just ok.

What Is The Importance Of Covering The Pot When Cooking Sous Vide?

Covering is important in preventing evaporation. The need to refill water several times will also be cut. Covering is also important in bringing the temperature up back fast after ingredients have been added.

What Is The Correct Volume Of Water In The Bath?

You need water in which you will immerse what you will cook fully. You also need to remember the displacement principles- leave some space that will be occupied by the displace water after you immerse what to cook.

How can I remove air bubbles without having to put the hands into the hot water?

The water is not usually that hot. However, to avoid the heat, fill cold water into a separate container and seal. After sealing, put the bag into the hot water bath.

What Should I Do When My Bag Floats On Water Other Than Sink Into The Water?

Sous vide works by immersing into a hot bath and therefore when the bag floats, it is not right. Here are tips to deal with a floating bag:

Get a big binder clip and clip it at the bag's bottom and then fix a spoon that is heavy into the clip's mouth.

Put inverted steamer basket on the floating sous vide bag and then add more weights such as pie weights or heavy spoons.

Conclusion

Sous Vide certainly is not just a trend in the kitchen. It is not also something that only professional chefs and restaurateurs can do. Your family can also enjoy Sous Vide-cooked food in the comfort of your home and feel like they taste pricey meals straight from a fine dining restaurant!

I hope you enjoyed reading this cookbook and that I was able to cover everything you need to know about Sous Vide including the equipment you need, the most popular Sous Vide machines in the market and its health benefits, etc.

Sous Vide is truly an artful skill that is worth mastering. If it is your first time don't fear to fail the results you want to achieve. You will definitely get better while getting experience with this cookbook! The key is patience, the right information, andconsistency.

Experiment regularly and soon you will become an expert in Sous Vide cooking. The 600recipes in this book gives you a wide variety to experiment yourcooking.

Chapter 2: Eggs & Dairy

Omelette

Prep time: 10 minutes, Cook time: 20 minutes, Serves: 4

Ingredients:

- 8 medium eggs
- 1 cup heavy cream
- ½ cup cottage cheese
- 1 cup chopped tomatoes
- 1 cup baby spinach
- 3 tablespoons chopped smokedham
- Salt and pepper, to taste

Instructions:

1. Fill and preheat Sous Vide cooker to 167°F.
2. In a bowl, whisk eggs with heavy cream, cottage cheese, salt, andpepper.
3. Fold in remaining ingredients.
4. Pour ½ cup omelet in a Sous Vide pouch. Remove the air from bag and sealit.
5. Submerge bags into water and cook 20minutes.
6. Remove the bags from the water bath andopen.
7. Serve and enjoy.

Nutritional Value Per Serving:

Calories 175, Carbohydrates 4.8 g, Fats 21.1 g, Protein 17.2 g, Fiber: 0.8 g

Crispy Sous Vide Egg Yolks

Prep time: 10 minutes, Cook time: 65 minutes, Serves: 4

Ingredients:

- 4 + 1 egg
- 4 tablespoons all-purposeflour
- 1/3 teaspoon bakingpowder
- ½ cupbreadcrumbs
- ½ teaspoon finesalt
- ¾ teaspoon black truffle salt
- Salt and pepper, to taste

Instructions:

1. Fill and preheat Sous Vide cooker to148°F.
2. Cook four eggs 60 minutes. Let the eggs cool in cold water 10minutes.
3. Carefully peel the eggs, and let the egg white dripsout.
4. Reserve egg yolks.
5. Heat 1-inch oil in a skillet over mediumheat.
6. While the oil is heating, whisk flour, baking powder, and salt in abowl.
7. Beat remaining egg in a smallbowl.
8. Dredge egg yolks through flour and dip into beaten egg. Finally, roll inbreadcrumbs.
9. Fry in heated oil until goldenbrown.
10. Drain the egg yolks on a paper towel. Sprinkle with black trufflesalt.
11. Serve.

Nutritional Value Per Serving:

Calories 160, Carbohydrates 16.3 g, Fats 6.3 g, Protein 9.5 g

Herbed Scrambled Eggs

Prep time: 10 minutes. Cook time: 40 minutes. Serves: 4

Ingredients:

- 8 large eggs
- ¼ cup heavy cream
- ½ cup grated cheese, as you wish
- 1 teaspoon chopped basil
- 1 teaspoon chopped tarragon
- Salt and pepper, totaste

Instructions:

1. Set your Sous Vide cooker to 170°F.
2. Whisk the eggs in a bowl with basil, tarragon, salt, andpepper.
3. In a separate bowl, whisk heavy cream with cheese. Fold the cheese mixture into eggs and stir to combine.
4. Pour the egg mixture into the vacuum bag. Seal the bag with a vacuumsealer.
5. Place the bag into Sous Vide cooker, and cook 20 minutes. After 20 minutesremove from the cooker, and massage the eggs to help ensure evencooking.
6. Cook 10 minutes more.
7. Serve hot with whole-grain bread and freshly slicedtomatoes.

Nutritional Value Per Serving:

Calories 227, Carbohydrates 1.3 g, Fats 17.4 g, Protein 16.3 g

Salty Custard

Prep time: 10 minutes. Cook time: 30 minutes. Serves: 4

Ingredients:

- 8 large eggs
- 2 cups chicken stock
- 2 teaspoons sesame oil
- Salt and pepper, to taste

To garnish:

- Soy sauce, chopped green onion

Instructions:

1. Fill and preheat Souse Vide cooker to 180°F.
2. In a blender, blend eggs, chicken stock, sesame oil, salt, and pepper until smooth.
3. Strain through a fine-mesh sieve to remove any froth.
4. If needed, strain again and transfer into the vacuum bag.
5. Seal the bag and submerge into the water bath.
6. Cook 20 minutes. Remove from the water bath and shake or massage gently.
7. Cook 10 minutes additional.
8. Remove from the water bath and place into ice-cold bath 20 minutes.
9. Serve in a bowl, and top with a splash of soy sauce and chopped green onion.

Nutritional Value Per Serving:

Calories 169, Carbohydrates 1.1 g, Fats 12.5 g, Protein 12.9 g

Egg Soufflé with Avocado and Toast

Prep time: 10 minutes, Cook time: 50 minutes, Serves: 4

Ingredients:

- 8 large eggs
- ¼ teaspoon salt
- ¼ teaspoon black pepper
- ½ cup grated parmesan
- 1 tablespoon olive oil

Additional:

- 1 sliced avocado
- Toasted bread

Instructions:

1. Fill and preheat Souse Vide cooker to 172°F.
2. In a bowl, beat eggs with salt and pepper.
3. Fold in parmesan and olive oil.
4. Divide the mixture among four 4oz. jars.
5. Attach two-part canning lids "fingertip tight." Do not over tight because the pressure will not be able to escape and the jar will shatter.
6. Submerge jars in water bath 50 minutes.
7. Remove jars from water bath. Loosen outer edge with a knife. Invert soufflé onto toasted bread. Serve with avocado slices.

Nutritional Value Per Serving:

Calories 216, Carbohydrates 5.3 g, Fats 24 g, Protein 14.7 g

Eggs with Roasted Peppers

Prep time: 15 minutes, Cook time:1 hour, Serves: 6

Ingredients:

- 6 large eggs
- ½ cup grated Gouda cheese
- ¼ cup cream cheese
- 3 roasted peppers, peeled andseeded
- Salt and pepper, to taste

Instructions:

1. Set the cooker to 172°F.
2. In a food blender, blend eggs, Gouda cheese, cream cheese, salt, andpepper.
3. Slice the peppers into thin strips.
4. Place the peppers in the bottom of six 4oz. Jars, making sure they go up the sides abit.
5. Pour the egg mixture. Attach two-part canning lids "fingertiptight."
6. Submerge in a water bath and cook 1hour.
7. Remove the jars from a water bath. Slide a knife around the peppers and eggsand remove carefully, or invert onto aplate.
8. Serve with warm bread.

Nutritional Value Per Serving:

Calories 158.3 Carbohydrates 6.1 g, Fats 10.7 g, Protein 9.4 g

Crispy Bacon and Eggs

Prep time: 10 minutes, Cook time: 1 hour, Serves: 2

Ingredients:

- 4 large sized egg yolks
- 2 slices, British style bacon rashers cut up into ½ inch by 3-inch slices 4
- slices of crisp toasted bread

Instructions:

1. Prepare your Sous Vide water bath by dipping your immersion cooker and raisingthe temperature to 143°F
2. Gently place each of your egg yolks in the re-sealable bag and seal it upusing immersion method
3. Submerge it underwater and let it cook for about 1hour
4. In the meantime, fry your bacon slices until they arecrisp
5. Drain them on a kitchentowel
6. Once the cooking of the eggs is done, serve by carefully removing the yolks fromthe bag and place them on top of yourtoast
7. Place a slice of bacon on top andserve!

Nutritional Value Per Serving:

Calories 467, Carbohydrates 6 g, Fats 35 g, Protein 32 g

Egg Devils for Any Meal

Prep time: 15 minutes, Cook time: 1 hour, Serves: 4

Ingredients:

- 8 pieces, large eggs
- 3 tablespoons, mayonnaise
- 1 tablespoon, Dijon mustard
- Just a pinch, sugar
- Kosher salt
- Ground black pepper

Instructions:

1. Prepare your Sous Vide water bath by dipping your immersion cooker and raisingthe temperature to 170°F
2. Carefully use a slotted spoon and submerge the eggsunderwater
3. Let them cook for 1 hour
4. Once the timer is off, use the slotted spoon to transfer the eggs to an ice waterbath
5. Let them chill for about 20minutes
6. Peel the eggs and cut them up in halflengthwise
7. Carefully remove the yolk and mash it with Dijon, mayonnaise,sugar
8. Season with some pepper and salt
9. Pip the mixture into the halves andserve!

Nutritional Value Per Serving:

Calories 165, Carbohydrates 9 g, Fats 9 g, Protein 12 g

Orange Yogurt

Prep time: 10 minutes, Cook time: 4 hours, Serves: 4

Instructions:

- 4 cups milk
- ½ cup Greek yogurt
- 1 tbsp orange zest
- ½ tbsp lemon zest

Instructions:

1. Pour the milk into a pan and heat it to 180°F.
2. Cool it down to the room temperature.
3. Preheat the water bath to 113°F.
4. Mix in the yogurt, add the orange and lemon zest and pour the mixture into canning jars.
5. Cover the jars with the lids and cook in the water bath for 3 hours.
6. When the time is up, cool down the jars to the room temperature and then refrigerate before serving.

Nutritional Value Per Serving:

Calories 99, Carbohydrates 6 g, Fats 3 g, Protein 12 g, Fiber 5g

Apple Yogurt with Raisins

Prep time: 10 minutes. Cook time: 4 hours. Serves: 4

Ingredients:

- 4 cups milk
- ½ cup Greek yogurt
- ½ cup sweet apples, peeled, cored and chopped into small pieces 1
- tsp cinnamon
- 4 tsp small raisins
- 2 tbsp honey

Instructions:

1. Pour the milk into a pan and heat it to 180°F.
2. Cool it down to the room temperature.
3. Preheat the water bath to 113°F.
4. Mix in the yogurt, add the apples, cinnamon, honey, raisins, and pour the mixture into canning jars.
5. Cover the jars with the lids and cook in the water bath for 3 hours.
6. When the time is up, cool down the jars to the room temperature and then refrigerate before serving.

Nutritional Value Per Serving:

Calories 99, Carbohydrates 6 g, Fats 3 g, Protein 12 g

Spiced Frozen

Prep time: 10 minutes, Cook time: 24 hours, Serves: 8

Ingredients:

- 4 cups milk
- 3 tablespoons yogurt
- ½ cup light honey
- ¼ cup fine sugar
- 1 teaspoon vanilla paste
- ½ teaspoon cinnamon
- ¼ teaspoon nutmeg

Instructions:

1. Preheat your Sous Vide cooker to 115°F.
2. Heat the milk in a saucepan, until it reaches 180°F. Insert a candy thermometer to see the precise temperature.
3. Pour the milk into a canning jar and chill until reaches 120°F.
4. Stir in the yogurt, vanilla, and spices.
5. Seal thc jar with lid (not too tightly) and cook 24hours.
6. Remove the jar from the cooker.
7. Allow cooling completely.
8. Churn the yogurt in ice cream machine according to manufacturerdirections.
9. Serve with fresh fruits.

Nutritional Value Per Serving:

Calories 162.2, Carbohydrates 30.3 g, Fats 2.6 g, Protein 4.4

Perfect Sous Vide Eggs with

Prep time: 10 minutes, Cook time: 45 minutes, Serves: 4

Ingredients

- ½ lemon, juiced, zested
- 1 whole avocado, pitted and the skin removed, sliced thinly
- 4 tablespoons, butter at room temperature
- 4 slices of thick cut bread or Ciabatta bread
- 4 whole eggs
- Maldon sea salt to taste

For garnish:

- Arugula micro greens
- Queso fresco, crumbled
- McCormick Sriracha seasoning

Instructions:

1. Preheat your precision cooker to 147°F
2. Lower the eggs carefully into preheated water bath in a sous vide bag of yourchoosing and cook for 45 minutes. Place the cooked eggs into a paper towel lined plate using slotted spoon.
3. Spread butter on each bread slices on both sides then use the extra butter to grease a large pan. Heat the pan on medium high heat then add extra butter to the slices ofbread. Toast the bread for about 2 minutes per side until golden brown on bothsides
4. Remove the toast and place on a serving platterand spread theavocado slices on each toast slice.
5. Squeeze the lemon over the top then finish with zest. Sprinkle the top with maldonsea salt.
6. Crack the eggs on the paper towel then carefully transfer them using a spatula or a slotted spoon to each toast. Sprinkle with crumbled queso and srirachaseasoning.
7. Garnish with micro greens and serve immediately.

Nutritional Value Per Serving:

Calories 376, Carbohydrates 26 g, Fats 16 g, Protein 32 g

Ham and Manchego

Prep time: 5 minutes , Cook time: 1 hour , Serves: 6

Ingredients

- 1 cup, chopped ham
- ½ cup, Manchego cheese
- ½ cup, heavy cream
- 6 pieces, eggs
- Pepper, taste
- Salt to taste
- Butter for brushing

Instructions:

1. Place the cheese, heavy cream and eggs in a blender and process until smooth.Season with pepper and salt.
2. Brush the interior of the canning jars (bottles) with butter then place the chopped ham inside.
3. Add in the egg mixture then cover the jars and cook in a water bath with yourprecision cooker set to 170°F for 1 hour.

Nutritional Value Per Serving:

Calories 343, Carbohydrates 25 g, Fats 11 g, Protein 36 g

Egg and Bacon Salad

Prep time: 25 minutes , Cook time: 1 hour , Serves: 4

Ingredients

- 1 small watermelon radish, sliced thinly using a mandolin 1
- small radicchio, cored, sliced thinly
- 1 small endive, cored, slicedthinly
- 4 cups, baby mesclun
- 2 tablespoons, bacon fat
- ¼ cup, olive oil
- Freshly ground black pepper and kosher salt to taste
- 1 small shallot, minced
- 1 teaspoon, Dijon mustard
- ½ tablespoon, honey
- 1 tablespoon, lemon juice
- 2 tablespoons, champagne vinegar
- 4 ounces, slab bacon cut into lardons
- 4 eggs

Instructions:

1. Preheatyour water bath to 145°F with a sous vide immersion circulation following the manufacturer's directions. Add in the eggs in a sous vide bag and cook for 1hour.
2. Meanwhile, heat the bacon lardons in a medium skillet over medium heat and cook until all the fat has rendered and the bacon is golden brown, 10 to 12 minutes. Transfer the bacon to aplate lined with paper towel then set aside 2 tablespoons ofbacon fat for the dressing.
3. Whisk together the mustard, honey, pepper, salt, shallot, lemon juice and vinegar ina small bowl.
4. Streamin the bacon fat and olive oil and then proceed to whisk until it has emulsified before setting it aside until you are ready totoss.
5. Toss together the reserved bacon, radish, radicchio, endive, and the mesclun withthe vinaigrette in a large bowl then divide the mixture among 4bowls.
6. Remove the eggs carefully from the water bath once they are done cooking thencrack and open into a small bowl. Strain any loose albumen using a slotted spoon while you slide an egg into each salad.
7. Season the eggs with a little pepper and salt thenserve.

Nutritional Value Per Serving:

Calories 481, Carbohydrates 38 g, Fats 21 g, Protein 35 g

Eggs Benedict

Prep time: 25 minutes , Cook time: 1 hour, Serves: 4

Ingredients

- 4 slices, Canadian bacon
- 4 eggs
- 2 English muffins
- Fresh parsley, chopped
- Butter
- Hollandaise
- ½ shallot, diced 1
- teaspoon, water
- 1 teaspoon, lemon juice
- 1 egg yolk
- 4 tablespoons of butter
- Salt to taste
- Pinch, cayenne

Instructions:

1. Preheat your water bath to 148°F
2. Add all the hollandaise ingredients to a large Ziploc bag then place the bag in the water bath to remove air through water displacement. Seal the bag and place it in the water bath
3. Add 4 eggs into the same water bath in another Ziploc bag ordirect.
4. Cook for an hour.
5. Sear the Canadian bacon until done, over mediumheat.
6. Slice the 2 English muffins in half then toastthem.
7. If need be, place the seared bacon and toasted muffins into an oven preheated to250°F to keep warm as you finish making the sauce.
8. Remove the hollandaise from the Ziploc bag once done cooking and pour into your blender. Blend until the mixture becomes smooth light yellow on medium speed – this is because the mixture will be quite separated when you remove it from the water bath.
9. Crack the poached eggs with a spoon and do away with the excess egg whites orplace in a bowl.
10. Place each of the poached egg onto each muffin slice, which is topped withbacon.
11. Top generously with hollandaise sauce and choppedparsley.

Nutritional Value Per Serving:

Calories 433, Carbohydrates 25 g, Fats 21 g, Protein 36 g

Egg and Bacon Breakfast Ramen

Prep time: 10 minutes , Cook time: 5-10 minutes , Serves: 1

Ingredients

For chili oil

- 1 tablespoon chili flakes
- 2 cloves, garlic, minced
- 1 tablespoon, oil

For the soy dressing

- ½ teaspoon, dashi granules
- 1 teaspoon, sugar
- 1 tablespoon, sesame oil 1
- tablespoon, rice vinegar 1
- tablespoon, mirin
- 1 tablespoon, soy sauce
- 2 cloves, garlic, minced

For the noodles

- 1 slow poached egg
- 3 slices, pork belly or crispy bacon
- 1 portion, thick ramen noodles
- Garnish
- Toasted black sesame seeds
- Katsuobushi
- Sliced green onions
- Seaweed strips

Instructions:

1. In a small pan, heat the oil over medium low heat. Add the chili flakes and garlic and cook until the mixture has heated up and is sizzling (take about 2 minutes). Keep the heat low to avoid burning – you want the chili flakes to release their spice and the garlic mellow. Remove from pan and set aside to cool.
2. In a small bowl, mix the soy dressing and set aside. Cook the noodles according to the manufacturer's instructions and drain well then toss with the soy sauce. In a shallow bowl, place the cooked noodles and top with the poached egg and the sous vide pork belly. Garnish with the seaweed strips, toasted black sesame seeds, green onions and katsuobushi. Serve with a significant amount of chili oil.

Nutritional Value Per Serving:

Calories 426.1, Carbohydrates 25 g, Fats 18.9 g, Protein 39 g

Chapter 3: Poultry

Duck Leg Confit

Prep time: 10-12 hours, Cook time: 12 hours 10 minutes, Serves: 2

Ingredients:

- 2 duck legs
- 1 tbsp dried thyme
- 2 big bay leaves,crushed
- 6 tbsp duck fat
- Salt and pepper to taste
- Cranberry sauce for serving

Instructions:

1. Preheat your Sous Vide machine to 167°F.
2. Mix the bay leaves with salt, pepper and thyme, and season the duck legs withthe mixture.
3. Refrigerate overnight.
4. In the morning, rinse the legs with cold water and carefully put them into thevacuum bag.
5. Add 4 tbsp duck fat, seal the bag removing the air as much as possible, put it intothe water bath and set the cooking time for 12hours.
6. Before serving, roast the legs in 2 remaining tbsp of duck fat untilcrispy.
7. Serve with cranberry sauce.

Nutritional Value Per Serving:

Calories 529, Carbohydrates 15 g, Fats 37 g, Protein 34 g,

Caramelized Chicken Teriyaki

Prep time: 10 minutes, Cook time: 1 hour 40 minutes, Serves: 2

Ingredients:

- 2 chicken fillets
- 1 tbsp ginger juice
- 3 tsp sugar
- ½ tsp salt
- 2 tbsp Japanese Sake
- 2 tbsp unsweetened soy sauce

Instructions:

1. In a small bowl, mix the ginger juice with salt and 1 tspsugar.
2. Rub the chicken and leave it overnight tomarinate.
3. In the morning, carefully put the chicken into the vacuum bag and preheat yoursous vide machine to 140°F.
4. Seal the bag removing the air as much as possible, put it into the water bath and set the cooking time for 1 hour 30 minutes.
5. Mix 2 tsp sugar with sake and soy sauce and boil in a small skillet or saucepan until the sauce thickens a bit.
6. Pour half of the sauce over the cooked chicken breasts and torch the glaze untilit caramelizes.
7. Chop the fillets and serve over white rice, drizzling with the remaining liquid half of the sauce.

Nutritional Value PerServing:

Calories 522, Carbohydrates 32 g, Fats 18 g, Protein 58 g

Chicken Breast with Lemon and French Herbs

Prep time: 10 minutes, Cook time: 3 hours 2o minutes, Serves: 2

Ingredients:

- 2 chicken breast fillets
- Salt and pepper to taste
- 1 tsp olive oil

For the sauce:

- 1 onion, sliced
- 2 garlic cloves, minced
- 1 tbsp olive oil
- 1 tbsp unsalted butter
- 1 cup button mushrooms, coarselychopped
- 2 tbsp white wine
- ½ cup chicken broth
- 1 cup cream
- Salt and pepper to taste

Instructions:

1. Preheat your sous vide machine to 145°F.
2. Carefully put the chicken breasts into the vacuum bag. Add the butter, salt, pepperand halved garlic cloves and seal the bag removing the air as much aspossible.
3. Put it into the water bath and set the cooking time for 3hours.
4. While the chicken is cooking, make thesauce.
5. Heat olive oil in a medium skillet, and cook the chopped onion for about 2-3minutes.
6. Add the butter and minced garlic and cook for 2 moreminutes.
7. Add the chopped mushrooms and cook at the medium heat until the liquidevaporates.
8. Add the white wine, cook until the liquid almost evaporates and add the chickenbroth and cream.
9. Continue cooking until the sauce thickens, add salt and pepper if needed. Set thesauce aside.
10. Remove the cooked chicken from the sous vide machine and roast it in a skillet onboth sides until light brown. Add the sauce and wait just till it heats to the desired temperature.
11. Serve with mashed potato.

Nutritional Value Per Serving:

Calories 261, Carbohydrates 12 g, Fats 9 g, Protein 33 g

Chicken Breast with Mushroom Sauce

Prep time: 10 minutes, Cook time: 3 hours 20 minutes, Serves: 2

Ingredients:

- 2 chicken breastfillets
- 2 tbsp lemon juice
- Salt and pepper to taste
- French herbs seasoning to taste
- 1 tsp olive oil
- 1 tsp butter

Instructions:

1. In a small saucepan, mix the olive oil with the lemon juice and the herbs and set aside for an hour to marinate.
2. Preheat your sous vide machine to 145°F.
3. Carefully put the chicken breasts into the vacuum bag and seal it removing the air as much as possible.
4. Put it into the water bath and set the cooking time for 3hours.
5. Heat 1 tsp butter in a frying pan and sear the cooked fillets for about 1 minute oneach side until golden.

Nutritional Value Per Serving:

Calories 252, Carbohydrates 16 g, Fats 8 g, Protein 29 g

Italian Chicken Marsala

Prep time: 10 minutes, Cook time: 2 hours 20 minutes, Serves: 2

Ingredients:

- 4 chicken breast fillets, bones and skin removed
- Salt and pepper to taste
- 1 cup all-purpose flour
- 1 tbsp olive oil
- 1-pound porcini mushrooms, chopped
- 1 cup dry red wine
- 1 cup chicken broth
- 3 tbsp freshly chopped parsley

Instructions:

1. Preheat your sous vide machine to 140°F.
2. Carefully put the chicken breasts sprinkled with salt and pepper into the vacuumbag, and seal it removing the air as much aspossible.
3. Put it into the water bath and set the cooking time for 2hours.
4. When the time is up, remove the chicken breasts from the bag, dry them withkitchen towels and dredge them in theflour.
5. Heat olive oil in cast iron skillet and brown the fillets over the medium heat until golden. Set aside.
6. Put the chopped mushrooms in the skillet and sauté for 5 minutes. Add the wineand chicken broth, simmer for 10minutes.
7. Pour the sauce over the chicken breasts and serve sprinkled with the freshlychopped parsley.

Nutritional Value Per Serving:

Calories 304, Carbohydrates 15 g, Fats 12 g, Protein 34 g

Aromatic Chicken

Prep time: 20 minutes, Cook time: 1 hour 30 minutes, Serves: 4

Ingredients:

- 1 cup chicken stock
- 1 tablespoon chili sauce
- 1lb. boneless chicken breasts
- 2 cloves garlic, minced
- 1 good pinch salt
- 1 lemon, thinly sliced
- 4 sprigs basil
- 1 tablespoon olive oil

Instructions:

1. Combine chicken stock and chili sauce in a bowl. Add the chicken breasts andcover with a clean foil.
2. Marinade 45 minutes.
3. In the meantime, heat the Sous Vide cooker to146°F.
4. Pat dry the chicken with papertowels.
5. Combine the garlic and salt until you have a paste. Spread the past over chicken breasts and top the chicken with lemon.
6. Place the chicken breasts into Sous Vide bag and add-in remainingingredients.
7. Vacuum seal the bag and submerge chicken inwater.
8. Cook the chicken 1 hour 30minutes.
9. Heat grill pan to high.
10. Remove the chicken from the cooker and open thebag.
11. Arrange the lemon slices on a grill pan and top withchicken.
12. Grill the lemon and chicken for 3 minutes perside.
13. Serve.

Nutritional Value Per Serving:

Calories 300, Carbohydrates 14 g, Fats 12 g, Protein 34 g

Chicken Wings

Prep time: 20 minutes, Cook time: 7 hours, Serves: 4

Ingredients:

- 12 chicken wings
- ¼ cup vegetable oil
- 4 sprigs thyme
- 2 teaspoons crushed red pepper flakes
- Salt, to taste

Instructions:

1. Preheat Sous Vide cooker to 167°F.
2. In a Sous Vide bag, combine the chicken wing with remainingingredients.
3. Shake gently to coat the chicken and vacuum seal thebag.
4. Submerge in water and cook 7 hours.
5. Remove the bag with chicken fromcooker.
6. Heat some oil in a largeskillet.
7. Place the wings into a skillet and cook until the skin iscrispy.
8. Serve.

Nutritional Value Per Serving:

Calories 351, Carbohydrates 8.6 g, Fats 19.8 g, Protein 34.7 g

Mediterranean Chicken

Prep time: 10 minutes, Cook time: 90 minutes, Serves: 2

Ingredients:

- 2 chicken breast fillets
- ½ cup sun-dried tomatoes, packed in oil
- 2 tablespoons oil, from the sun-dried tomatoes
- Salt and black pepper, to taste
- 1 sprig basil
- 1 tablespoon olive oil

Instructions:

1. Preheat the Sous Vide Cooker to 140°F.
2. Season the chicken with salt and pepper.
3. Heat the olive oil in a skillet. Add chicken breasts and cook for 1 minute per side.
4. Transfer immediately into Sous Vide bag, and add remaining ingredients.
5. Vacuum seal the bag and submerge in water.
6. Cook the chicken 90 minutes.
7. Remove the bag with chicken from the Cooker.
8. Open the bag and transfer the chicken to a warmed plate.
9. Serve.

Nutritional Value Per Serving:

Calories 400, Carbohydrates 17.8 g, Fats 21.7 g, Protein 33.4 g

Duck a la Orange

Prep time: 20 minutes, Cook time: 2 hours 30 minutes, Serves: 2

Ingredients:

- 2 5oz. duck breast fillets, skinon
- 1 orange, sliced
- 4 cloves garlic
- 1 shallot, chopped
- 4 sprigsthyme
- 1 teaspoon black peppercorns
- 1 tablespoon sherry vinegar
- ¼ cup red wine
- 2 tablespoonsbutter
- Salt, to taste

Instructions:

1. Preheat Sous Vide cooker to 135°F.
2. Place the duck breast fillets into a Sous Videbag.
3. Top the breasts with orange slices, garlic, shallot, thyme, andpeppercorns.
4. Vacuum seal the bag and submerge in water.
5. Cook the breasts 2 ½ hours.
6. Remove the bag from a water bath. Open the bag and remove thebreasts.
7. Heat a large skillet over medium-high heat. Sear the duck, skin side down, for30 seconds. Place the breasts aside and keep warm.
8. In the same skillet, add sherry vinegar and wine. Add the bag content and bringto simmer. Simmer 5 minutes.
9. Stir in the butter and simmer 1 minute.
10. Serve the duck with prepared sauce.

Nutritional Value Per Serving:

Calories 446, Carbohydrates 15.1 g, Fats 27.4 g, Protein 34.5 g

Chicken Thighs with Herbed

Prep time: 30 minutes, Cook time: 4 hours, Serves: 10

Ingredients:

- 4 chicken thighs
- 2 tablespoons salt
- 4 cups water
- 1 tablespoon paprika powder
- 2 tablespoons vegetable oil 2
- tablespoons butter

Peppers:

- 4 red bell peppers, seeded, quartered
- 3 tablespoons olive oil
- 1 sprig thyme
- Salt, to taste

Herbed rice:

- ¾ cup long grain rice
- 2 cups water
- 1 teaspoon salt
- 1 bunch parsley, chopped
- 1 bunch chives, chopped

Instructions:

1. Make the chicken; heat Sous Vide cooker to150°F.
2. In a large bowl, combine salt and water. Add the chicken thighs into a bowl andcover with a clean foil. Refrigerate 4 hours. Remove the chicken, rinse, and patdry.
3. Combine the butter and paprika and top the chicken. Place the chicken into Sousvide bag and vacuum seal.
4. Cook in the Sous Vide cooker 4hours.
5. Make the peppers; combine the peppers with olive oil, thyme, and salt in a SousVide Bag.
6. Vacuum seal the peppers and cook in Sous Vide cooker for 30 minutes at186F.
7. Make the rice; vacuum the rice with water, salt, and herbs. Cook in the SousVide cooker 60 minutes at203°F.
8. Heat vegetable oil in a skillet. Add chicken and cook until the skin iscrispy.
9. Remove the peppers from the bag and cook in the same skillet with chicken, for1 minute. Spread the rice on a plate. Top with chicken and bellpeppers.

Nutritional Value Per Serving:

Calories 317, Carbohydrates 14.8 g, Fats 13.5 g, Protein 34.1 g

Mirin Teriyaki Wings

Prep time: 10 minutes, Cook time: 45 minutes, Serves: 4

Ingredients:

- 1.5lb. chicken wings, sliced into flats and drumettes
- Salt and freshly ground black pepper
- 1 teaspoon teriyaki sauce
- 1 tablespoon hoisin sauce
- ½ teaspoon mirin
- ¼ teaspoon minced fresh ginger
- Vegetable oil, for frying
- Wasabi for garnish

Instructions:

1. Set the Sous Vide cooker to 140°F.
2. Season chicken wings, lightly with salt and pepper.
3. Place wings in a zip-lock bag and seal using immersion watertechnique.
4. Place the bag in a water bath and set the timer to 45minutes.
5. Meanwhile, prepare the sauce; combine teriyaki sauce, hoisin sauce, mirin and ginger in a bowl.
6. When the timer goes off, remove the bag and take the chickenout.
7. Pour around 2-inches of oil in large pan and heat over medium-highheat.
8. Fry wings for 1-2 minutes and transfer to bowl with prepared sauce; toss tocombine.
9. Serve wings on a platter, with wasabi paste.

Nutritional Value Per Serving:

Calories 323, Carbohydrates 2.4 g, Fats 12.8 g, Protein 49.4 g

Fried Chicken

Prep time: 15 minutes, Cook time: 2 hours, Serves: 8

Ingredients:

- 3 lb. chicken drums 1
- tablespoon finesalt

Coating:

- 3 cups all-purpose flour
- 1 tablespoon onionpowder
- 1 teaspoon garlicpowder
- ½ tablespoon dried basil
- 1 tablespoon salt
- 2 cup buttermilk

Instructions:

1. Preheat Sous Vide cooker to 155°F.
2. Season chicken with salt.
3. Place the chicken drums in Sous Vide bags. Vacuumseal.
4. Submerge in water and cook 2 hours.
5. Heat 3-inches oil in apot.
6. Remove the chicken from bags and patdry.
7. Combine all dry breading ingredients in a large bowl. Place buttermilk in a separate bowl.
8. Dredge chicken drums through flour, buttermilk, and flouragain.
9. Fry chicken in batches, until golden andcrispy.
10. Serve warm with fresh salad and favoritesauce.

Nutritional Value Per Serving:

Calories 362, Carbohydrates 39.6 g, Fats 10 g, Protein 28.4 g

Sticky Duck Wings

Prep time: 20 minutes, Cook time: 2 hours, Serves: 6

Ingredients:

- 3lb. duck wings
- 1 tablespoon mustard
- ½ cup honey
- 1 tablespoon soy sauce
- ¼ cup ketchup
- 1 tablespoon hot sauce
- 2 tablespoons Cajun spice blend
- ¼ cup butter
- Salt and pepper, to taste

Instructions:

1. Preheat Sous Vide cooker to 150ºF.
2. Cut the wings into portions and rub with Cajun blend. Season with some saltand pepper.
3. Transfer the wings into cooking bags and addbutter.
4. Vacuum seal the wings and submerge inwater.
5. Cook the wings 2 hours.
6. Preheat your broiler.
7. Combine remaining ingredients in abowl.
8. Remove the wings from the cooker and toss with preparedsauce.
9. Arrange the wings on baking sheet and broil 10 minutes, basting with anyremaining sauce during thattime.
10. Servewarm.

NutritionalValue PerServing:

Calories 316, Carbohydrates 27 g, Fats 16.1 g, Protein 15.8 g

Ginger Marmalade Chicken

Prep time: 7 minutes, Cook time: 4 hours, Serves: 4

Ingredients

- 2 lbs. bone-in skin-on chicken
- 4 tablespoons marmalade
- 2 tablespoons minced ginger
- Salt and pepper

Instructions:

1. Prepare your water bath using your Sous Vide immersion circulator, and raisethe temperature to 170°F
2. Season the chicken with salt and pepper
3. Put the ingredients (including the chicken) in a heavy-duty, resealable bag andseal using the immersion method
4. Submerge the bag and cook for 4 hours
5. Transfer the cooked chicken to a baking dish
6. Heat the broiler to a temperature of 500-degreesFahrenheit
7. Arrange a rack, making sure it is 20 cm away from the heatsource
8. Place the baking dish to the broiler and broil for 10 minutes untilcrispy
9. Remove and serve!

Nutritional Value Per Serving:

Calories 804, Carbohydrates 29 g, Fats 48 g, Protein 64 g

Honey Dredged Duck Breast

Prep time: 7 minutes, Cook time: 3 ½ hours, Serves: 3

Ingredients

- 1 x 6 oz. boneless duck breast
- ¼ teaspoon cinnamon
- ¼ teaspoon smoked paprika
- ¼ teaspoon cayenne pepper
- 1 teaspoon honey
- Salt and pepper

Instructions:

1. Prepare your water bath using your Sous Vide immersion circulator and raisethe temperature to 134.9°F
2. Remove the duck breast from the packaging and pat dry using a kitchentowel
3. Score the skin of the duck breast using a crosshatch pattern - do not cut theflesh, sprinkle some saltover
4. Take a medium sized frying pan/skillet and place it on your stove overmedium-high heat
5. Put the breast in the pan and cook for 3-4 minutes, making sure the skin side isfacing down
6. Remove the breast from your pan and set it on asurface
7. Add the paprika, cayenne pepper and cinnamon in a small bowl and mixeverything well
8. Spread the mixture over the duck breast and season, add some additional saltand pepper
9. Now put the breast in a heavy-duty, resealable bag with a teaspoon ofhoney andseal the bag using the immersion method and submerge itunderwater
10. Cook for about 3½ hours and take it out oncedone
11. Pat dry and place in a frying pan over high heat to sear for about 2 minutes, makesure you keep the skin side facing down
12. Flip it and sear for another 30 seconds, allow to rest andserve!

Nutritional Value Per Serving:

Calories 307, Carbohydrates 25 g, Fats 15 g, Protein 18 g

Lemon Grass Chicken Dish

Prep time: 5 minutes, Cook time: 45 minutes, Serves: 3

Ingredients

- 1 lb. chicken breast
- 1 stalk, fresh lemon grass,chopped
- 2 tablespoons fish sauce
- 2 tablespoons coconut sugar
- ½ teaspoon salt
- 1 tablespoon chili garlic sauce

Instructions:

1. Prepare your water bath using your Sous Vide immersion circulator and raisethe temperature to 150°F
2. Cut the chicken into bite size portions and put them in abowl
3. Chop the lemon grass and place in ablender
4. Add the fish sauce, sugar, and salt and blendwell
5. Pour the marinade over your chicken and mixwell
6. Insert skewers into thechicken
7. Keep repeating until all the chicken has beenused
8. Place the skewered chicken in a heavy-duty, resealable bag, seal them usingthe immersion method and submerge and cook for 45minutes
9. Remove the bag transfer it to a water bath tochill
10. Remove the chicken from the bag and slice it up even more if youprefer
11. Brush with chili-garlic sauce
12. Sear the chicken on a skillet over medium heat and thenserve

Nutritional Value Per Serving:

Calories 305, Carbohydrates 34 g, Fats 9 g, Protein 22 g

Waldorf Chicken Salad

Prep time: 15 minutes, Cook time: 2 hours, Serves: 4

Ingredients

- 2 skinless chicken breasts, boneless
- ½ teaspoon ground black pepper
- 1 tablespoon corn oil
- 1 Granny Smith apple, cored anddiced
- 1 teaspoon lime juice
- ½ cup red grapes, cut in half
- 1 stick rib celery, diced
- 1/3 cup mayonnaise
- 2 teaspoons Chardonnaywine
- 1 teaspoon Dijonmustard
- 1 tablespoon kosher salt
- 1 Romaine lettuce head
- ½ cup walnuts, toasted and chopped

Instructions:

1. Prepareyourwater bath usingyour Sous Vide immersion circulator, and increase the temperature to 145°F
2. Take the chicken and season it with black pepper and salt. Put the seasonedchicken breast and corn oil in a large, resealable bag and seal using the immersionmethod
3. Cook for 2 hours and then remove thebag
4. Put the apple slices in a large-sized bowl, add the lime juice, and toss themwell.
5. Add the celery and red grapes and stirwell
6. Put the mayonnaise, Dijon mustard, and Chardonnay wine in a small bowl and mixwell
7. Pour the whole mixture over the fruits and give them a nicetoss
8. Remove the chicken breast from the plastic bag and discard theliquid
9. Dice the breast and place in a medium-sizedbowl
10. Add some kosher salt and tosswell
11. Put the seasoned chicken in with the rest of the salad and tosswell
12. Dived your romaine lettuce amongst the salad bowls, spoon the salad on top ofthe lettuce, and garnish with some walnuts
13. Serve!

Nutritional Value Per Serving:

Calories 416, Carbohydrates 34 g, Fats 16 g, Protein 34 g

Sous Vide Poached Chicken

Prep time: 45 minutes, Cook time: 6 hours, Serves: 4

Ingredients

- 1 whole bone-in chicken, trussed
- 1-quart low sodium chicken stock
- 2 tablespoons soy sauce
- 5 sprigs fresh thyme
- 2 dried bay leaves
- 2 cups thickly sliced carrots
- Salt and pepper as needed
- ½ tablespoon olive oil
- 2 cups thickly sliced celery
- ½ oz. dried mushrooms
- 3 tablespoons unsalted butter

Instructions:

1. Prepare your Sous Vide water bath using your immersion circulator and raisethe temperature to 150°F
2. Add the soy sauce, chicken, stock, herbs and veggies in a heavy-duty zip bag andseal using the immersion method and cook for 6hours
3. Remove the chicken and strain theveggies
4. Pat dry and season with the olive oil, pepper andsalt
5. Roast in your oven for 10 minutes at450°F
6. Simmer the cooking liquid in a largesaucepan
7. Once done, turn off the heat and whisk in thebutter
8. Carve the chicken, making sure to discard theskin
9. Divide the veggies and chicken between the platters and serve with the sauce ontop

Nutritional Value Per Serving:

Calories 442, Carbohydrates 17 g, Fats 26 g, Protein 35 g

Rare Duck Breast

Prep time: 10 minutes, Cook time: 2 hours, Serves: 2

Ingredients

- 2 duck breasts
- ¼ cup olive oil
- 4 sprigs thyme
- Salt and pepper

Instructions:

1. Prepare your Sous Vide water bath using your immersion circulator and raisethe temperature to 135°F
2. Transfer the duck breast to a hot pan and sear them for 1-2 minutes perside
3. Place in a zip bag with the olive oil andthyme
4. Cook for 2 hours
5. Sear them again for 1-2 minutes in a hotpan
6. Allow them to rest andslice
7. Sprinkle with salt and pepper andserve

Nutritional Value Per Serving:

Calories 476, Carbohydrates 18 g, Fats 24 g, Protein 47 g

Moroccan Chicken Salad

Prep time: 10 minutes, Cook time: 60 minutes, Serves: 2

Ingredients

- 6 chicken tenderloins
- 4 cups pumpkin, cubed, roasted
- 4 cups rocket tomatoes
- 4 tablespoons sliced almonds
- Juice of 1 lemon
- 2 tablespoons olive oil
- 4 tablespoons red onion, chopped
- 2 pinches paprika
- 2 pinches turmeric
- 2 pinches cumin
- 2 pinches salt

Instructions:

1. Prepare your water bath using your Sous Vide immersion circulator and raisethe temperature to 140°F
2. Add all the spices and chicken in a zip-bag. Coat the chickenwell
3. Seal using the immersion method and cook for 60minutes
4. Sear for 1 minute on each sideafterwards
5. Put the remaining ingredients in another bowl and tosswell
6. Top them up with the chicken andserve!

Nutritional Value Per Serving:

Calories 302, Carbohydrates 16 g, Fats 18 g, Protein 19 g

Korean Chicken Wings

Prep time: 15 minutes, Cook time: 2 hours, Serves: 3

Ingredients

- 12 chicken wings
- Salt and pepper
- 1 cup Korean fried chicken batter
- ½ cup water
- ½ cup soy sauce
- ½ mincedonion
- 4-5 garlic cloves, minced 2
- teaspoons ginger powder 2
- tablespoons brownsugar
- ¼ cup mirin
- Sesame seeds
- Cornstarch slurry
- Olive oil

Instructions:

1. Prepare your Sous Vide water bath, using your immersion circulator and raisethe temperature to 147°F
2. Season the wings with pepper andsalt
3. Put the wings in the Sous Vide zip bag and seal using the immersion method andcook for 2 hours
4. Once the cooking is done, take the bag out of the water and remove the wings,transfer the wings to a kitchen towel and drythem
5. Pre-heat the oil to475°F
6. Mix ½ cup of Korean fried chicken batter mix, and ½ cup of water in abowl
7. Put the other ½ cup of batter mix onto anotherplate
8. Drench the wings in the wet batter, then dredge them through the drybatter
9. Flash fry for 1-2 minutes until golden brown andcrispy
10. Mix all the ingredients for the sauce and heat over a saucepan untilboiling
11. Add the wings to the sauce and coatwell
12. Garnish with sesame seeds andserve!

NutritionalValuePerServing:

Calories 467, Carbohydrates 15 g, Fats 27 g, Protein 41 g

Panko Crusted Chicken

Prep time: 30 minutes, Cook time: 1 hour, Serves: 4

Ingredients

- 4 boneless chicken breasts
- 1 cup panko bread crumbs
- 1 lb. sliced mushrooms
- Small bunch of thyme
- 2 eggs
- Salt and pepper
- Canola oil

Instructions:

1. Prepare your water bath using your Sous Vide immersion circulator, and increase the temperature to 150°F
2. Season the chicken with salt, and thyme
3. Place the breast in a resealable bag and seal using the immersion method and cook for 60 minutes
4. Then, place a pan over medium heat, add the mushrooms and cook them until the water has evaporated
5. Add 3-4 sprigs of thyme and stir
6. Once cooked, remove the chicken from the bag and pat dry
7. Add the oil and heat it up over medium-high heat. Add the eggs into a container and dip the chicken in egg wash until well coated.
8. Add the panko bread crumbs in a shallow container and add some salt and pepper. Put the chicken to bread crumbs and coat until well covered.
9. Fry the chicken for 1-2 minutes per side and serve with the mushrooms

Nutritional Value Per Serving:

Calories 405, Carbohydrates 71 g, Fats 5 g, Protein 19 g

Clementine Chicken Breast

Prep time: 30 minutes, Cook time: 2 hours 30 minutes, Serves: 2

Ingredients

- 1½ tablespoons freshly squeezed orange juice
- 1½ tablespoons freshly squeezed lemon juice
- 1½ tablespoons brown sugar
- 1 tablespoon Pernod
- 1 tablespoon extra-virgin olive oil
- 1 tablespoon whole grain mustard
- 1 teaspoon fennel seeds
- 1 teaspoon kosher salt
- ¾ teaspoon freshly ground black pepper
- 2 chicken breasts, bone in, skin on
- 1 medium-sized fennel bulb, trimmed, thinly sliced up
- 2 clementines, unpeeled, cut into ¼ inch thick slices
- Chopped parsley for garnishing

Instructions:

1. Prepare your water bath using your Sous Vide immersion circulator and raisethe temperature to 146°F
2. Put the lemon juice, orange juice, Pernod, olive oil, fennel seeds, brown sugar,mustard, salt and pepper in a large bowl, give it a goodmix
3. Putthechicken breast, slicedclementineand sliced fennel in a large, resealable zip bag and add the orange mixture
4. Seal using the immersion method and cook for 2½hours
5. Setthe broiler to high heat. Preparea broiler safe baking dish andline it with aluminum foil
6. Once cooked, take the bag out from the water bath and transfer the contents tothe baking sheet
7. Broil for 3-6 minutes to charslightly
8. Transfer the juice from the bag into a small saucepan and simmer for about5-10 minutes
9. Put the chicken and vegetables on a platter and drizzle the sauce allover.
10. Sprinkle with parsley and fennel fronds andserve!

Nutritional Value Per Serving:

Calories 305, Carbohydrates 34 g, Fats 9 g, Protein 22 g

Chicken & Melted Leeks

Prep time: 15 minutes, Cook time: 45 minutes, Serves: 4

Ingredients

- 4 x 6 oz. skinless chicken breast
- Salt and pepper as needed
- 3 tablespoons butter
- 1 large leek, cleaned and sliced crossways
- ½ cup panko
- 2 tablespoons choppedparsley
- 1 oz. cheddar cheese
- 1 tablespoon olive oil

Instructions:

1. Prepare your water bath using your Sous Vide immersion circulator and raisethe temperature to 145°F
2. Take the chicken breast and season it generously on both sides with salt and pepperand put in a zip bag
3. Seal using the immersion method and cook for 45minutes
4. Take a skillet and add 2 tablespoon of butter over medium heat, allow the butter toheat up and add the leeks
5. Stir to coatthem
6. Season with salt and pepper
7. Then, lower down the heat to low and cook for additional 10minutes
8. Put a clean skillet over a medium heat. Put in a tablespoon ofbutter
9. Add the panko and toast, and stir well until the panko ishot
10. Spoon the panko mixture from the skillet into a separate bowl and add thecheddar cheese and chopped up parsley, mix well
11. Once the chicken breasts are thoroughly cooked, remove them from the bag and patdry
12. Heat the olive oil over a high heat and sear the breasts for 1minute
13. Serve each breast on the melted leek, and top with the toasted panko/cheesemix

Nutritional Value Per Serving:

Calories 797, Carbohydrates 11 g, Fats 61 g, Protein 51 g

Moroccan Chicken Meal

Prep time: 15 minutes, Cook time: 1 hour, Serves: 2

Ingredients

- 6 chickentenderloin
- 4 cups pumpkin, cut into cubes, roasted
- 4 cups rocket lettuce
- 4 tablespoons sliced almonds
- Juice of 1 lemon
- 2 tablespoons olive oil
- 4 tablespoons red onion, chopped
- 2 pinches paprika
- 2 pinches turmeric
- 2 pinches cumin
- 2 pinches salt

Instructions:

1. Prepare your water bath using your Sous Vide immersion circulator, and raisethe temperature to 140°F
2. Put the chicken and the seasoning in a heavy-duty, resealablebag
3. Seal it using the immersion/water displacementmethod
4. Submerge the bag and let it cook for about 60minutes
5. Once done, take the chicken out from the bag and sear the tenderloins in a very hotpan, allowing 1 minute per side
6. Put all the remaining ingredients in a serving bowl and toss themwell
7. Cover the chicken with your salad andserve!

Nutritional Value Per Serving:

Calories 305, Carbohydrates 34 g, Fats 9 g, Protein 22 g

Spicy Adobo Chicken

Prep time: 5 minutes, Cook time: 2 hours, Serves: 2

Ingredients

- 2 chicken leg quarters 2
- garlic cloves,crushed
- ¼ teaspoon whole black peppercorns
- ½ tablespoon molasses
- ¼ cup dark soy sauce
- Salt as needed
- 1 tablespoon canola oil
- ½ Worcestershire sauce
- 1 bay leaf
- ¼ cup white vinegar

Instructions:

1. Mix the soy sauce, Worcestershire, peppercorns, molasses, garlic, bay leaf and salt.
2. Add the chicken legs in a Sous Vide bag with the marinade and refrigerate for 12hours or overnight.
3. Prepare your Sous Vide water bath, using your immersion circulator, and raisethe temperature to 165°F
4. Submerge the chicken and cook for 2hours
5. Remove the chicken legs from the bag and air dry for 10-15minutes.
6. Sear over medium heat in a nonstick pan with canolaoil
7. Add the sauce from the bag to the pan and keep cooking until you have reachedthe desired consistency
8. Serve the chicken with sauce!

Nutritional Value Per Serving:

Calories 322, Carbohydrates 33 g, Fats 14 g, Protein 16 g

Ginger Duck Breast

Prep time: 20 minutes, Cook time: 2 hours, Serves: 2

Ingredients

- 2 boneless duck breasts
- Kosher salt andpepper
- 1-inch fresh ginger, peeled, sliced thinly
- 2 garlic cloves, thinly sliced
- 1½ teaspoons sesame oil

Instructions:

1. Prepare your water bath, using your Sous Vide immersion circulator, and raisethe temperature to 135°F
2. Season the duck breasts with pepper and salt
3. Put the breasts in a zip bag and add the ginger, sesame oil andgarlic
4. Seal using the immersion method, and cook for 2hours
5. Remove the duck and discard the garlic, ginger and cookingliquid
6. Place the duck breast in a cold, non-stick skillet and put it over a highheat
7. Cook the breast with the skin side down for about 30 seconds, flip, and cookfor another 30 seconds
8. Then place the breasts on a cutting board to rest for 5minutes
9. Slice the breasts and serve with your desired sidedishes

Nutritional Value Per Serving:

Calories 373, Carbohydrates 19 g, Fats 25 g, Protein 18 g

Greek Meatballs

Prep time: 20 minutes, Cook time: 2 hours, Serves: 4

Ingredients

- 1 lb. ground chicken
- 1 tablespoon extra-virgin olive oil
- 2 garlic cloves, minced
- 1 teaspoon fresh oregano,minced
- 1 teaspoon kosher salt
- ½ teaspoon grated lemon zest
- ½ teaspoon freshly ground black pepper
- ¼ cup panko bread crumbs
- Lemon wedges for serving

Instructions:

1. Prepare your Sous Vide water bath, using your immersion circulator, and raisethe temperature to 146°F
2. Add the garlic, olive oil, chicken, oregano, lemon zest, salt, and pepper in amedium-sized bowl
3. Mix well everything using your hands and gently mix in the panko breadcrumbs
4. Form the mixture into 14 balls
5. Put the balls in a resealable bag and seal using the immersionmethod
6. Submerge the bag and cook for 2 hours
7. Remove the bag and transfer the balls to a baking sheet (lined withfoil)
8. Set your broiler to high heat
9. Broil the balls for 5-7 minutes until they turnbrown
10. Serve with lemon wedges

Nutritional Value Per Serving:

Calories 473, Carbohydrates 43 g, Fats 21 g, Protein 28 g

Jamaican Jerk Chicken

Prep time: 5 minutes, Cook time: 3 hours 10 minutes, Serves: 3

Ingredients

- 2 lbs. chicken wings
- 2 tablespoons jerk seasoning
- ¼ cup fresh cilantro for garnishing, chopped

Instructions:

1. Prepare your Sous Vide water bath using your immersion circulator, and increase the temperature to 145°F
2. Put the chicken and jerk seasoning in a resealable, heavy-duty plastic bag and sealthe bag using the immersion method
3. Carefully transfer the bag under the pre-heated water bath and allow to cook for about 3 hours
4. Once done, take the bag out from the water and remove the wings, pat the wingsdry with kitchen towel
5. Heat up your grill to high, and put the wings underit
6. Lower down the heat of your grill to medium and cook the chicken until crispyand slightly brown
7. Remove from the grill and add some jerk paste
8. Garnish with chopped cilantro
9. Serve

Nutritional Value Per Serving:

Calories 439, Carbohydrates 34 g, Fats 23 g, Protein 24 g

Bacon Wrapped Chicken

Prep time: 15 minutes, Cook time: 3 hours, Serves: 2

Ingredients

- 2 chicken breasts
- 2 strips bacon
- 2 tablespoons Dijon mustard
- 1 tablespoon grated parmesan cheese
- ½ teaspoon salt

Instructions:

1. Prepare your water bath using your Sous Vide immersion circulator, and raisethe temperature to 145°F
2. Season the chicken with salt and spread Dijon mustard on bothsides
3. Sprinkle with parmesan cheese
4. Wrap the bacon around the chicken breast and place in a zipbag
5. Cook for 3 hours
6. Remove the chicken and pat dry
7. Sear until crispy
8. Serve!

Nutritional Value Per Serving:

Calories 281, Carbohydrates 5 g, Fats 21 g, Protein 18 g

Chicken Caprese

Prep time: 5 minutes, Cook time: 45 minutes, Serves: 2

Ingredients

- 2 chicken breasts, boneless,skinless
- Salt and pepper asneeded
- 2 teaspoons unsalted butter
- 4 cups lettuce
- 1 large tomato, sliced
- 1 oz fresh mozzarella, sliced
- 2 tablespoons red onion,diced
- Fresh basil leaves
- 1 tablespoon extra-virgin oliveoil
- 2 lemon wedges forserving

Instructions:

1. Prepare your Sous Vide water bath, using your immersion circulator, and raisethe temperature to 145°F
2. Season the chicken with pepper and salt
3. Add them in a large zip bag and seal using the immersion method and cook for45 minutes
4. Once cooked, remove the chicken from the bag and discard the cookingliquid
5. Place a large skillet over a medium/highheat
6. Add the butter and allow to heat
7. Add the chicken breasts and sear until they turn goldenbrown
8. Transfer to a servingplatter
9. Divide the lettuce among the breasts and top up with tomato, red onion, mozzarella,and basil
10. Season with pepper and salt and then drizzle the olive oil over thetop
11. Serve with lemon wedges

Nutritional Value Per Serving:

Calories 477, Carbohydrates 15 g, Fats 33 g, Protein 30 g

Stuffed Cornish Hen

Prep time: 45 minutes, Cook time: 4 hours, Serves: 5

Ingredients

- 2 whole Cornish game hens
- 4 tablespoons unsalted butter plus 1 tablespoon extra, melted
- 2 cups shitake mushrooms, thinly sliced
- 1 cup leeks, finely diced
- ¼ cup walnuts, coarsely chopped
- 1 tablespoon fresh thyme, minced
- 1 cup cooking wild rice
- ¼ cup dried cranberries
- 1 tablespoon honey

Instructions:

1. Prepare your water bath using your Sous Vide immersion circulator, and raisethe temperature to 150°F
2. Take a large sized skillet and place it over mediumheat
3. Once the skillet is hot, add 3 tablespoons of butter and allow the butter tomelt
4. Add the mushrooms, thyme, leek and walnuts and cook for 5-10minutes
5. Stir in the rice, cranberries and remove from the heat, allow to cool for 10minutes
6. Divide the stuffing between the hencavities
7. Truss the legs together tightly and put the hens in a zipbag
8. Seal using the immersion method and cook for 4hours
9. Remove the hens and patdry
10. Set your broiler to highheat
11. Add the honey and the extra tablespoon of melted butter in a smallbowl
12. Brush the mixture over thehens
13. Broil for 2 minutes and thenserve

Nutritional Value Per Serving:

Calories 764, Carbohydrates 50 g, Fats 32 g, Protein 69 g

Chicken Mint Pea Feta

Prep time: 10 minutes, Cook time: 1 hour 15 minutes, Serves: 8

Ingredients

- 6 chicken breast tenderloins, boneless
- 4 tablespoons extra virgin-olive oil
- Salt and pepper
- 2 cups green peas, blanched
- 1 cup mint, freshly torn
- ½ cup crumbled feta cheese
- 1 tablespoon freshly squeezed lemonjuice
- 2 teaspoons honey
- 2 teaspoons red wine vinegar

Instructions:

1. Prepare your water bath, using your Sous Vide immersion circulator, and increase the temperature to 140°F
2. Put the chicken and 2 tablespoons of olive oil in a zipbag
3. Season with pepper and salt
4. Seal using the immersion method, and cook for 75 minutes
5. Add the peas, feta cheese and mint in a largebowl
6. Whisk the lemon juice, red wine vinegar, honey and 2 tablespoons of olive oil ina small bowl
7. Season with salt and pepper
8. Once cooked, take the chicken out from the bag and chop it into bite sizedpieces
9. Discard the cooking liquid and toss the salad with the chicken and thedressing
10. Serve!

Nutritional Value Per Serving:

Calories 252, Carbohydrates 29 g, Fats 8 g, Protein 16 g

Duck Breast with Calamansi

Prep time: 15 minutes, Cook time: 2 hours, Serves: 2

Ingredients

- 2 duck breasts
- 1 teaspoon ground coriander, gingerpowder
- 1 teaspoon, garlic powder
- Salt and pepper
- 2 tablespoons olive oil

For Sauce

- 1 tablespoon butter
- 1 sprig of thyme
- 1 garlic clove, minced
- 1 small shallot, minced
- 3 tablespoons calamansi juice
- Cooking juice (from the Sous Vide bag)

Instructions:

1. Prepare your Sous Vide water bath using your immersion circulator, and increase the temperature to 134°F
2. Take a knife and score the skin of the duck breast in a cross-hatch pattern and season it with coriander, garlic and ginger powder
3. Place the breasts in a sous vide bag and seal using the immersionmethod
4. Submerge and cook for 2 hours
5. Put some oil in a pan, place it over mediumheat
6. Add the duck and sear until crispy, flip and sear the other side for 1minute
7. Use the same pan for the sauce ingredients. Add all the sauce ingredients and simmer until thickened.
8. Slice the duck and drizzle the sauce over
9. Serve!

Nutritional Value Per Serving:

Calories 368, Carbohydrates 15 g, Fats 16 g, Protein 41 g

Chicken Roulade

Prep time: 30 minutes, Cook time: 1 hour 30 minutes, Serves: 2

Ingredients

- 1 x 8 oz chicken breast
- ¼ cup goat cheese
- ¼ cup julienned roasted red pepper
- ½ cup loosely packed arugula
- 6 slices prosciutto
- Salt and pepper as needed 1
- tablespoon oil forsearing

Instructions:

1. Prepare your water bath, using your Sous Vide immersion circulator, and raisethe temperature to 155°F
2. Drainthe chicken breast ifneeded, andplace it between plasticwrap. Poundit using a mallet or the side of wine bottle, until it gets ¼ inchthick
3. Cut in half and season both sides with pepper andsalt
4. Spread 2 tablespoons of goat cheese on top and top each half with roasted redpeppers
5. Top with half the arugula
6. Roll both breasts like sushi
7. Place 3 layers of prosciutto on your work surface (overlapping eachother)
8. Put the rolled chicken at the base of the prosciutto and roll it all up to enclosethe roulade
9. Place in a zip bag and seal using the immersion method and cook for 90minutes
10. Take out of the bag andsear
11. Slice and then serve

Nutritional Value Per Serving:

Calories 500, Carbohydrates 6 g, Fats 32 g, Protein 47 g

Pheasant Breast

Prep time: 15 minutes, Cook time: 45 minutes, Serves: 2

Ingredients

- 2 pheasant breasts, bonein
- Kosher salt asneeded
- Fresh ground black pepper to taste
- 2 tablespoons unsaltedbutter
- 3 sprigs ofthyme
- 1 tablespoon extra-virgin olive oil

Instructions:

1. Prepare your Sous Vide water bath, using your immersion circulator, and raisethe temperature to 145°F
2. Season the pheasant breast with pepper and salt and place them in a zipbag
3. Add the butter and thyme
4. Seal using the immersion method and cook for 45minutes
5. Once done, remove the pheasant and patdry
6. Discard the cooking liquid
7. Place a large, non-stick skillet over a medium heat and add theoil
8. Once the oil is heated, add the pheasant, skin side down, in theskillet
9. Sear for 2 minutes andserve!

Nutritional Value Per Serving:

Calories 269, Carbohydrates 3 g, Fats 21 g, Protein 17 g

Turkey Meatballs

Prep time: 20 minutes, Cook time: 1 hour, Serves: 4

Ingredients

- 1 lb. groundturkey
- 3 scallions, finely chopped
- 1 large egg, beaten
- 1 tablespoon seasoned breadcrumbs
- 1 teaspoon dried oregano
- Salt and pepper as needed
- ½ cup of pesto (plus 2 teaspoons extra)
- 2 oz. mozzarella, torn into ¼ oz. pieces
- 4 large dinner rolls

Instructions:

1. PrepareyourSous Vide waterbath using your immersion circulator, and increase the temperature to 145°F
2. Add the turkey, egg, breadcrumbs, scallions and oregano in a medium-sizedbowl
3. Mix well and season the mixture with salt andpepper
4. Give it a good mix again to incorporateeverything
5. Form 8 balls, using the mixture, and put a light indent in each, using yourthumb
6. Top the balls using ¼ teaspoon of pesto and ¼ ounce of mozzarellacheese
7. Press well to ensure the pesto and cheese has been engulfed by themeat
8. Shape the ballsagain
9. Place the balls in 2 resealable zip bags and seal them using the immersionmethod
10. Submerge underwater and cook for 60minutes
11. Once cooked, remove the balls and pat dry using the kitchentowels
12. Take a non-stick skillet and put it over a medium heat and heat ½ cup ofpesto
13. Add in the meatballs and stir well to coat them with thepesto
14. Place 2 meatballs in each of the dinner rolls andserve!

Nutritional Value Per Serving:

Calories 781, Carbohydrates 72 g, Fats 29 g, Protein 58 g

Thai Green Curry Noodle

Prep time: 45 minutes, Cook time: 1 hour 30 minutes, Serves: 2

Ingredients

- 1 chicken breast, boneless and skinless
- Salt and pepper as needed
- 1 can coconut milk
- 2 tablespoons Thai Green CurryPaste
- 1¾ cups chicken stock
- 1 cup enokimushrooms
- 5 kaffir lime leaves, torn in half
- 2 tablespoons fishsauce
- 1½ tablespoons palm sugar
- ½ cup Thai basil leaves, roughly chopped
- 2 oz cooked egg noodle nests
- 1 cup cilantro, roughlychopped
- 1 cup bean sprouts
- 2 tablespoons fried noodles
- 2 red Thai chilis, roughly chopped

Instructions:

1. Prepare your water bath using your Sous Vide immersion circulator, and raisethe temperature to 140°F
2. Take the chicken and season it generously with salt and pepper and place it ina medium-sized, resealable bag with 1 tablespoon of coconutmilk
3. Seal it using the immersion method and submerge. Cook for 90minutes
4. After 35 minutes, place a medium-sized saucepan over a mediumheat
5. Add the green curry paste and half the coconutmilk
6. Bring the mix to a simmer and cook for 5-10 minutes until the coconut milk startsto show a beady texture
7. Add the chicken stock and the rest of the coconut milk and bring the mixture toa simmer once again, keep cooking for about 15minutes
8. Add the kaffir lime leaves, enoki mushrooms, palm sugar and fishsauce
9. Lower the heat to medium-low and simmer for about 10minutes
10. Remove from the heat and season with palm sugar and fish sauce, stir in thebasil
11. Once the chicken is cooked fully, transfer it to a cooking board. Let it cool forfew minutes and then cut into slices
12. Serve the chicken with the curry sauce and a topping of cooked eggnoodles
13. Garnishthe chicken with some bean sprouts, cilantro, Thai chilies and fried noodles. Serve!

Nutritional Value Per Serving:

Calories 243, Carbohydrates 21 g, Fats 11 g, Protein 15 g

Chicken Parmesan Balls

Prep time: 30 minutes, Cook time: 45 minutes, Serves: 6

Ingredients

- 1 lb. ground chicken
- 2 tablespoons onion, finely chopped
- ¼ teaspoon garlic powder
- Salt and pepper as needed
- 2 tablespoons seasoned breadcrumbs
- 1 egg
- 32 small, diced cubes of mozzarella cheese
- 1 tablespoon butter
- 3 tablespoons panko
- ½ cup tomato sauce
- ½ oz. grated parmesan cheese
- Chopped parsley for garnishing

Instructions:

1. Prepare your Sous Vide water bath using your immersion circulator, and raisethe temperature to 145°F
2. Mix the chicken with onion, salt, garlic powder, pepper and seasoned bread crumbs ina bowl
3. Add the egg and mix well
4. Scoop out 32 balls
5. Top each ball with 1 cube of cheese and press the meat around thecheese
6. Put the balls in a zip bag and chill for 20minutes
7. Seal the bag using the immersion method and cook for 45minutes
8. Remove the balls from thebag
9. Melt butter over a medium-high heat and add thepanko
10. Cook until golden brown. Warm the tomato sauce
11. Transfer the balls in a serving dish and top with tomato sauce, panko andcheese
12. Garnish with chopped parsley and serve by piercing them with atoothpick

Nutritional Value Per Serving:

Calories 277, Carbohydrates 15 g, Fats 17 g, Protein 16 g

Chicken & Avocado Salad

Prep time: 5 minutes, Cook time: 75 minutes, Serves: 2

Ingredients

- 1 chicken breast
- 1 avocado, sliced
- 10 pieces, halved cherry tomatoes
- 2 cups chopped lettuce
- 2 tablespoons oliveoil
- 1 tablespoon lemon juice
- 1 garlic clove, crushed
- Salt and pepper as needed
- 2 teaspoons honey

Instructions:

1. Prepare your Sous Vide water bath, using your immersion circulator, and raisethe temperature to 140°F
2. Add the breast to a Sous Vide zip bag and seal using the immersion method,submerge and cook for 75 minutes
3. Season the breast with salt andpepper
4. Pan fry 1 tablespoon of olive oil for 30seconds
5. Slice the breasts
6. Add the garlic, lemon juice, honey and olive oil in a smallbowl
7. Add the lettuce, cherry tomatoes and avocado andtoss
8. Top the salad with chicken and season with pepper andsalt
9. Serve!

Nutritional Value Per Serving:

Calories 522, Carbohydrates 13 g, Fats 22 g, Protein 68 g

Sweet Chili Chicken

Prep time: 30 minutes, Cook time: 2 hours, Serves: 2

Ingredients

- 4 chicken thighs
- 2 tablespoons olive oil
- Salt and pepper
- 1 garlic clove, crushed 3
- tablespoons fishsauce
- ¼ cup lime juice
- 1 tablespoon palm sugar
- 3 tablespoons Thai basil, chopped
- 3 tablespoons cilantro, chopped
- 2 red chilies, deseeded, chopped
- 1 tablespoon sweet chili sauce

Instructions:

1. Prepare your water bath using your Sous Vide immersion circulator, and incrcase the temperature to 150°F
2. Cover the chicken thighs with cling film and chill them for awhile
3. Place them in a zip bag along with the olive oil, salt and pepper, and seal usingthe immersion method
4. Cook for 2 hours
5. Once done, heat the olive oil in a pan and chop the chicken into 4-5pieces
6. Dip them in the veggie oil and cook untilcrispy
7. Combine all the above dressing ingredients in a bowl and place to oneside
8. Sprinkle with salt on top and serve with thesauce

Nutritional Value Per Serving:

Calories 706, Carbohydrates 9 g, Fats 54 g, Protein 46 g

Lemon Grass Salad

Prep time: 20 minutes, Cook time: 75 minutes, Serves: 2

Ingredients

- 2 chicken breasts, skinless
- Salt and pepper
- Vegetable oil
- 1 cup unsalted cashews
- 2 tablespoons palm sugar
- 4 red Thai chilis, thinly sliced
- 1 garlic clove, peeled
- 3 tablespoons fish sauce
- 2 teaspoons freshly squeezed lime juice
- 1 cup cilantro, roughly chopped
- 1 scallion, thinly sliced
- 1 stalk lemon grass, white part only slightly bruised and thinlysliced 1
- piece 2-inch ginger, julienned

Instructions:

1. Prepare your Sous Vide water bath using your immersion circulator, and increase the temperature to 140°F
2. Take the chicken and season it with salt and pepper, place the chicken in a zip bagand seal using the immersion method and cook for 75minutes
3. After 60 minutes, heat 1 inch of vegetable oil, in a medium-sized saucepan, to350°F over a medium-high heat
4. Add the cashews and golden fry them for 1 minute, drythem
5. Pound the palm sugar, garlic, and chili in a mortar andpestle
6. Add the fish sauce and limejuice
7. Once the timer has finished, remove the bag from the water bath and take outthe chicken
8. Allow to cool, once the chicken has reached the room temperature, take a knife andcut the chicken in bite-sized pieces and put in abowl
9. Add the dressings and toss
10. Add the cilantro, ginger, lemon grass, scallion, and fried cashews and mixwell
11. Garnish with additional chilis and serve!

Nutritional Value Per Serving:

Calories 482, Carbohydrates 18 g, Fats 26 g, Protein 44 g

Coconut Chicken

Prep time: 10 minutes, Cook time: 1 hour, Serves: 2

Ingredients

- 2 chicken breasts
- 4 tablespoons coconut milk
- Salt and pepper as needed
- For Sauce
- 4 tablespoons satay sauce 2
- tablespoons coconut milk
- Dash, fish sauce

Instructions:

1. Prepare your Sous Vide water bath using your immersion circulator, and raisethe temperature to 140°F
2. Add the chicken in a zip bag and add the salt, pepper and 4 tablespoons ofmilk
3. Seal using the immersion method and cook for 60minutes
4. Once done, mix the sauce ingredients in a bowl and microwave for 30seconds
5. Slice the chicken and arrange on servingplatter
6. Pour the sauce ontop!
7. Serve

Nutritional Value Per Serving:

Calories 938, Carbohydrates 51 g, Fats 50 g, Protein 71 g

Chicken Saltimbocca

Prep time: 15 minutes, Cook time: 1 hour 30 minutes, Serves: 4

Ingredients

- 4 small chicken breasts, boneless, skinless
- 8 sage leaves
- 4 pieces of thinly sliced prosciutto
- Freshly ground black pepper
- 1 tablespoon extra-virgin olive oil
- 2 oz. grated provolone

Instructions:

1. Prepare your Sous Vide water bath using your immersion circulator, and increase the temperature to 145°F
2. Transfer the chicken breast to a very clean flat surface and season with pepper andsalt
3. Top each of the chicken breast with sage leaves and 1 slice ofprosciutto
4. Place them in a zip bag and seal using the immersion method and cook for 90minutes
5. Once cooked, remove the chicken from the bag and patdry
6. Add some oil in a large skillet over a medium-highheat
7. Put the chicken and prosciutto and sear for 1 minute
8. Give the chicken pieces a flip and top each of the pieces with 1 tablespoon ofprovolone
9. Cover the skillet with lid and cook for 30 seconds to allow the cheese tomelt
10. Add the chicken on a serving platter and garnish with sageleaves
11. Serve!

Nutritional Value Per Serving:

Calories 296, Carbohydrates 5 g, Fats 20 g, Protein 24 g

Zucchini Mini Chicken Bites

Prep time: 30 minutes, Cook time: 1 hour 15 minutes, Serves: 2

Ingredients

- 1 chicken breast, boneless, skinless, butterflied
- Salt and pepper as needed
- 3 tablespoons extra-virgin olive oil
- 1 tablespoon pesto
- 1 zucchini, sliced into ¼ inch pieces
- ¼ cup water
- 1 avocado
- 1 cup fresh basil leaves

Instructions:

1. Prepare your Sous Vide water bath using your immersion circulator, and raisethe temperature to 140°F
2. Pound the chicken breast with mallet until it has an even thickness, season with pepper and salt and place in a zip bag
3. Add 1 tablespoon of oil and the pesto and seal using the immersion method andcook for 75 minutes
4. After 60 minutes, heat 1 tablespoon of olive oil in large skillet over amedium-high heat, and add the zucchini and water
5. Cook until the water has evaporated
6. Once cooked, carefully remove the bag from the water bath and take out thechicken
7. Heat the remaining oil over a medium/high heat. Allow it toshimmer
8. Add in the chicken and sear for 2 minutes per side
9. Transfer the chicken on a cutting board and allow it to cool for 5minutes
10. Slice it into pieces, roughly the same size as thezucchini
11. Slice the avocado to the same size
12. Serve by stacking slices of avocado on top of the chicken and topping them with aslice of zucchini and a basil leaf
13. Secure with toothpicks and drizzle olive oil over and thenserve!

Nutritional Value Per Serving:

Calories 251, Carbohydrates 36 g, Fats 7 g, Protein 11 g

Chapter 4: Beef & Lamb

Lamb Shoulder

Prep time: 10 minutes, Cook time: 8 hours, Serves: 10

Ingredients:

- 2 pounds lamb shoulder, bones removed
- 1 garlic clove
- 2 tbsp olive oil
- 2 rosemary sprigs
- Salt and pepper to taste

Instructions:

1. Preheat the water bath to 180°F.
2. Season the lamb shank with salt and pepper.
3. Put the lamb into the vacuum bag, adding rosemary sprigs, olive oil and garlic.
4. Seal the bag.
5. Set the cooking timer for 8 hours.
6. Serve with boiled potatoes pouring the cooking juices over.

Nutritional Value Per Serving:

Calories 225, Carbohydrates 7 g, Fats 13 g, Protein 20 g

Sliced Lamb Shoulder with Jalapeno

Prep time: 10 minutes, Cook time: 8 hours, Serves: 10

Ingredients:

- 2 pounds lamb shoulder, bones removed
- 1 garlic clove
- 2 tbsp olive oil
- Salt and pepper to taste
- Sous Vide Jalapeno Sauce

Instructions:

1. Preheat the water bath to 180°F.
2. Season the lamb shank with salt andpepper.
3. Put the lamb into the vacuum bag, adding olive oil andgarlic.
4. Seal the bag.
5. Set the cooking timer for 8 hours.
6. Slices the cooked shoulder and serve it with the Sous Vide jalapenosauce.

Nutritional Value Per Serving:

Calories 293, Carbohydrates 17 g, Fats 13 g, Protein 27 g

Plain Lamb Shank with Cranberry

Prep time: 10 minutes, Cook time: 48 hours, Serves: 10

Ingredients:

- 1 lamb shank
- 2 tbsp olive oil
- 2 garlic cloves, coarselychopped
- Salt and pepper totaste
- Sous Vide cranberry sauce

Instructions:

1. Preheat the water bath to 144°F.
2. Sprinkle the lamb shank with salt and pepper. Put it into the vacuum bag togetherwith olive oil and garlic.
3. Seal the bag.
4. Set the cooking time for 48hours.
5. Serve with boiled potato and Sous Vide cranberry sauce.

Nutritional Value Per Serving:

Calories 300, Carbohydrates 20 g, Fats 12 g, Protein 28 g

Leg of Lamb with Smoked Paprika

Prep time: 10 minutes, Cook time: 10 hours 20 minutes, Serves: 6

Ingredients:

- 3 pounds lamb leg, bones removed
- 2 garlic cloves
- 1 tsp ground smoked paprika
- 2 tbsp dried oregano
- 1 garlic clove, minced
- 2 tbsp olive oil
- Salt and pepper to taste
- Juice of 1 lemon

Instructions:

1. Preheat your Sous Vide machine to 134°F.
2. Prepare the seasoning: whisk together the minced garlic, olive oil, smoked paprika, salt, pepper and oregano.
3. Spread the mixture evenly over the lamb.
4. Put the lamb into the bag, remove the air and cook for 10 hours.
5. When the time is up, place the lamb under the preheated grill for 4-5 minutes just until it becomes crispy.
6. Slice the cooked lamb and serve it sprinkled with lemon juice.

Nutritional Value Per Serving:

Calories 280, Carbohydrates 18 g, Fats 12 g, Protein 25 g

Garlic & Butter Lamb Chops

Prep time: 10 minutes, Cook time: 3 hours 20 minutes, Serves: 4

Ingredients:

For the lamb

- 4 lamb chops
- 4 thyme sprigs
- 2 tbsp olive oil
- Salt and pepper to taste

For searing

- 2 tbsp butter, melted 1
- garlic clove,minced

Instructions:

1. Preheat your Sous Vide machine to 145°F.
2. Season the lamb shank with salt and pepper.
3. Put the lamb into the bag; add 2 tbsp olive oil and 1 thyme sprig on eachchop.
4. Remove the air and cook for 3 hours.
5. When the time is up, combine the melted butter with the minced garlic, and coat each cooked chop with the butter-garlic mixture.
6. Sear each chop in the preheated cast iron skillet for 20 seconds on each sideuntil golden.

Nutritional Value Per Serving:

Calories 299, Carbohydrates 21 g, Fats 11 g, Protein 29 g

Party Lamb Dips with

Prep time: 3 hours, Cook time: 6 hours 10 minutes, Serves: 4

Ingredients: For the lamb

- 10 lamb short ribs
- Zest of 1 lime
- Juice of 1 lime
- 2 garlic cloves, minced
- 4 tbsp olive oil
- Salt and pepper to taste
- 2 tbsp ground paprika

For the sauce

- Any preferred Sous Vide sauces

Instructions:

1. Whisk together the lime juice, lime zest, minced garlic, olive oil, salt andpepper.
2. Rub the mixture into the ribs and leave for 2-3 hours tomarinate.
3. Preheat your Sous Vide machine to 174°F.
4. Put the lamb in the bag together with themarinade
5. Seal the bag and set the timer for 6hours.
6. 30 minutes before the time is up, preheat the oven to 428 degreesF.
7. Cook the ribs in the preheated oven for 5 minutes untilcrispy.
8. Serve on a plate with any preferred Sous Videsauce.

Nutritional Value Per Serving:

Calories 334, Carbohydrates 17 g, Fats 14 g, Protein 35 g

Glazed Lamb Leg

Prep time: 10 minutes, Cook time: 24 hours, Serves: 4

Ingredients:

- 1 lamb leg
- 2 tbsp tomato paste
- 2 cups balsamic vinegar
- 4 garlic cloves
- 4 thyme sprigs
- Salt and pepper to taste

Instructions:

1. Preheat your Sous Vide machine to 167°F.
2. Combine the vinegar and tomato paste in a medium pan and reduce the mixture until thick over the medium heat.
3. Rub salt and pepper into the leg, pour the sauce over it.
4. Put the leg into the vacuum bag.
5. Add thyme and garlic cloves
6. Seal the bag and set the timer for 24 hours.
7. When the time is up, carefully open the bag, remove the leg and pour the cooking juices into a pan.
8. Reduce the liquid over medium heat until thick, mixing it carefully with a spoon and making sure it does not burn.
9. Pour the sauce over the leg and serve.

Nutritional Value Per Serving:

Calories 315, Carbohydrates 10 g, Fats 23 g, Protein 17 g

Amazing Prime Rib

Prep time: 45 minutes, Cook time: 6 hours, Serves: 12

Ingredients:

- 3-pound, bone-in beef Ribeye roast
- Kosher salt
- 1 tablespoon, black peppercorn coarsely ground
- 1 tablespoon, green peppercorn coarsely ground
- 1 tablespoon, pink peppercorn coarsely ground 1
- tablespoon, dried celery seeds
- 2 tablespoon, dried garlicpowder
- 4 sprigs, rosemary
- 1 quart, beef stock
- 2 egg whites

Instructions:

1. Season the beef with kosher salt and chill for 12hours
2. Prepare the Sous Vide water bath by dipping the immersion cooker and waitinguntil the temperature has been raised to 132°F
3. Transfer beef to zip bag and seal using immersionmethod
4. Cook for 6 hours
5. Preheat your oven to 425°F and remove the beef, pat itdry
6. Take a bowl and whisk together peppercorn, celery seeds, garlic powder androsemary
7. Brush the top of your cooked roast with egg white and season with the mixture andsalt
8. Place the roast on a baking rack and roast for 10-15 minutes. Allow it to rest10-15 minutes and carve
9. Take a large saucepan and add the cooking liquid from the bag, bring to a boiland simmer until half.
10. Carve the roast and serve with thejuice

Nutritional Value Per Serving:

Calories 532, Carbohydrates 10 g, Fats 40 g, Protein 33 g

Beef Willy Cheesesteak

Prep time: 5 minutes, Cook time: 1 hour and 2 minutes, Serves: 4

Ingredients:

- 1 thinly sliced bell pepper
- 1 thinly sliced yellow bell pepper
- ½, white onion thinly sliced up
- 2 tablespoon, extra virgin oliveoil
- Kosher salt asneeded
- Black pepper as needed
- 1 pound, thinly sliced cooked beef skirt steak
- 4 soft hoagie rolls
- 8 slices, Provolone cheese

Instructions:

1. Prepare the Sous Vide water bath by dipping the immersion cooker and waitinguntil the temperature has been raised to 185°F
2. Take a heavy-duty zip bag and add yellow pepper, onion, olive oil, red pepperand season the mixture with salt andpepper
3. Seal using immersion method and cook for 1 hour
4. Take another bag and add steak, seal using immersion method, submerge and cookfor 5 minutes
5. Pre-heat your oven to 400°F
6. Slice the rolls in half and top them up withcheese
7. Transfer them to your oven and bake for 2minutes
8. Add pepper, steak, and onion
9. Serve

Nutritional Value Per Serving:

Calories 543, Carbohydrates 32 g, Fats 27 g, Protein 43 g

Mesmerizing Beef Burgers

Prep time: 15 minutes, Cook time: 1 hour + 1-minute sear time, Serves: 4

Ingredients:

- 10-ounce, ground beef
- 2 hamburger buns
- 2 slices, American cheese
- Salt
- Pepper
- Condiments, topping
- Butter, toasting

Instructions:

1. Prepare the Sous Vide water bath by dipping the immersion cooker and waitinguntil the temperature has been raised to 137ºF
2. Shape the beef into patties and season them with salt andpepper
3. Transfer to zip bag and seal using immersion method, cook for 1hour
4. Toast the buns in butter warm cast ironpan
5. Once the burgers are cooked, transfer them to the pan and sear for 30 seconds perside
6. Place cheese on top and allow tomelt
7. Assemble burger with topping andcondiments
8. Serve!

Nutritional Value Per Serving:

Calories 288, Carbohydrates 34 g, Fats 12 g, Protein 11 g

Authentic Italian Sausage

Prep time: 15 minutes, Cook time: 1 hour + 3 minutes , Serves: 4

Ingredients:

- 2 and a ½ cups, seedless red grapes with their stems removed 1
- tablespoon, chopped fresh rosemary
- 2 tablespoons, butter
- 4 sweet Italian sausage
- 2 tablespoons, balsamic vinegar
- Salt
- Ground black pepper

Instructions:

1. Prepare your Sous Vide water bath by dipping your immersion circulator andraising the temperature to 160°F
2. Take a heavy-duty zip bag and add butter, grapes, rosemary, sausages in a singlelayer
3. Seal using immersion method and cook for 1 hourunderwater
4. Remove the sausages and transfer toplate
5. Take a small sized saucepan and add grapes alongside theliquid
6. Add balsamic vinegar and simmer for about 3 minutes over medium-highheat
7. Sear the sausages in the same saucepan for 3 minutes and serve with thegrapes
8. Enjoy!

Nutritional Value Per Serving:

Calories 995, Carbohydrates 10 g, Fats 51 g, Protein 33 g

Party Beef Hot Dogs

Prep time: 5 minutes, Cook time: 1 hour, Serves: 4

Ingredients:

- 8 hot dogs
- 8 hot dog buns
- Mustard
- Ketchup

Instructions:

1. Prepare the Sous Vide water bath by dipping the immersion cooker and waitinguntil the temperature has been raised to 140°F
2. Add the hot dogs to your zip bag and seal using immersionmethod
3. Submerge and cook for 60 minutes
4. Serve by adding the hot dogs in the bun and dressing with a bit of mustard andketchup
5. Enjoy!

Nutritional Value Per Serving:

Calories 150, Carbohydrates 9 g, Fats 10 g, Protein 6 g

Original Soy Garlic Tri-Tip

Prep time: 5 minutes, Cook time: 2 hours 2 minutes, Serves: 4

Ingredients:

- 2 pounds, Tri-Tip Steak Roast
- Salt
- Pepper
- 2 tablespoon of soy sauce
- 6 cloves of pre-roasted garlic, crushed

Instructions:

1. Prepare your Sous Vide water bath and increase the temperature to 129°F
2. Season the tri-tip well with pepper and salt
3. Add the meat to your zip bag alongside soy sauce and crushed garlic cloves
4. Seal the bag using immersion method
5. Submerge and cook for 10 minutes
6. Take a cast iron skillet and place it over medium heat
7. Sear the meat for 1 minute per side until browned
8. Slice and serve!

Nutritional Value Per Serving:

Calories 371, Carbohydrates 10 g, Fats 23 g, Protein 31 g

Rolled Beef

Prep time: 30 minutes, Cook time: 37 hours, Serves: 8

Ingredients:

Filli ng:

- 4oz. peas
- 1 sprigthyme
- 1 pinch sugar
- 4oz. carrots, chopped
- 8 teaspoon Dijon mustard
- 16 slices bacon

Beef:

- 8 4oz. sliced beef
- Salt and pepper, to taste
- ¼ cup vegetable oil, to fry

Instructions:

1. Preheat Sous Vide cooker to 176°F.
2. Place the peas in a Sous Vide bag. Add the carrots, a pinch of sugar and salt totaste.
3. Vacuum seal the bag and place in a water bath. Cook the veggies 30minutes.
4. Remove from the bag.
5. Cover the beef slices with parchment paper. Pound with a meat tenderizer to make the beef this.
6. Spread the mustard over meat, and top each slice with two pieces bacon. Roll the meat into roulade and
7. Roll the meat over veggies and secure the roulades with a kitchen twine. Season with salt and pepper.
8. Heat the oil in a skillet and sear the roulades on all sides. Cool the roulades and transfer in a Sous Vide bag.
9. Vacuum seal the beef and cook 37 hours at 153°F.
10. Remove the meat from the cooker. Allow cooling completely before removing fromthe bag. Remove the kitchen twine and slice beforeserving.

Nutritional Value Per Serving:

Calories 324, Carbohydrates 14 g, Fats 23 g, Protein 15.2 g

Simple Spiced Ribs

Prep time: 10 minutes, Cook time: 24 hours, Serves: 4

Ingredients:

- 1.5 lb. baby back ribs
- 1 tablespoon fine salt
- 1 tablespoon brown sugar
- 1 tablespoon smoked paprika
- ½ tablespoon ground cumin
- ½ tablespoon ground coriander
- ½ tablespoon black pepper
- ¼ tablespoon dried garlic
- 1 tablespoon dried parsley
- ½ cup BBQ sauce

Instructions:

1. Preheat Sous-vide cooker to 155°F.
2. Combine all the spices and parsley in abowl.
3. Rub the ribs with this drymixture.
4. Place the ribs in a Sous Vide bag (one or two) and submerge inwater.
5. Cook the ribs 24 hours.
6. Remove the ribs from thebag.
7. Preheat your grill.
8. Cook the ribs 7-8 minutes, basting with BBQ sauce all theway.
9. Serve while hot with fresh salad.

Nutritional Value Per Serving:

Calories 435, Carbohydrates 15.6 g, Fats 21.3 g, Protein 45.3 g

Spiced Beef Brisket

Prep time: 20 minutes, Cook time: 32 hours, Serves: 4

Ingredients:

- 2lb. beef brisket
- Salt and pepper, to taste
- 2 tablespoons olive oil
- ½ tablespoon tomato paste
- 4 cloves garlic, minced
- 1 tablespoon smoked paprika
- ½ tablespoon beef demi-glace
- 1 teaspoon chopped thyme
- 1 cup beef stock
- ½ cup red wine
- 2 tablespoons honey
- ¾ lb. carrots, peeled, cut into matchsticks

Instructions:

1. Preheat your Sous Vide cooker to 155°F.
2. Season the brisket with salt and pepper.
3. Place the brisket into Sous Vide cooking bag. Place aside.
4. Heat ½ tablespoon olive oil in a saucepan.
5. Add tomato paste, garlic, smoked paprika, demi-glace, thyme, stock, and wine.
6. Simmer 5 minutes. Stir in the honey and season to taste. Simmer 1 minute.
7. Pour the mixture into the bag with beef and vacuum seal the bag.
8. Carefully place the bag into the cooker and cook 32 hours.
9. 25 minutes before the beef is done, toss the carrots with 1 tablespoon olive oil.
10. Roast the carrots 20-25 minutes at 450°F.
11. Remove the bag from cooker and open carefully. Strain the sauce into a small saucepot. Simmer 3 minutes over medium heat.
12. Heat the remaining olive oil in a large skillet.
13. Sear the beef 3 minutes per side.
14. Serve the beef with roasted carrots and prepared sauce.

Nutritional Value Per Serving:

Calories 294, Carbohydrates 20.4 g, Fats 15.4 g, Protein 18.3 g

Beef Goulash

Prep time: 20 minutes, Cook time: 12 hours, Serves: 8

Ingredients:

- 2lb. stew meat
- ½ teaspoon garlic powder
- ½ teaspoon smoked paprika
- 1 onion, chopped
- 4 cloves garlic, chopped
- 2 tablespoons smoked paprika
- 28oz. can crushed tomatoes
- 1 cup beef stock
- 1 tablespoon all-purpose flour
- 4 tablespoons water
- ½ cup chopped parsley
- Salt and pepper, to taste

Instructions:

1. Preheat Sous Vide cooker to 131°F.
2. Cut the stew meat into cubes and season with garlic powder andpaprika.
3. Place into Sous Vide bag and vacuum seal thebag.
4. Submerge in water and cook 24 hours.
5. 3 hours before the cooking cycle is done, combine all the remaining ingredients(except the flour and water) into Sous Videbag.
6. Vacuum seal the bag and submerge in water. Cook 3hours.
7. Remove both bags from the Sus Vide cooker and transfer into a largepot.
8. Bring to a simmer over medium-highheat.
9. Dissolve flour in cold water and stir the flour mixture into thestew.
10. Simmer untilthickened.
11. Season to taste and stir in the parsley. Servewarm.

Nutritional Value Per Serving:

Calories 349.8, Carbohydrates 16.5 g, Fats 15 g, Protein 37.2 g

Thyme Garlic Lamb Chops

Prep time: 10 minutes, Cook time: 2 hours, Serves: 4

Ingredients:

- 8 lamb chops
- 2 tablespoons minced garlic
- 4 sprigs fresh thyme
- 4 tablespoons olive oil
- ½ tablespoon lemon zest
- Salt and pepper, to taste

Instructions:

1. Preheat Sous Vide cooker to 140°F.
2. Generously season lamb chops with salt andpepper.
3. Place the lamb chops in a cooking bags, along with garlic, thyme, olive oil, andlemon zest.
4. Vacuum seal the bags and submerge inwater.
5. Cook the lamb chops 2 hours.
6. Remove the bag from acooker.
7. Pat dry and place aside.
8. Heat some oil in a skillet. Sear the chops 2 minutes per side, or use a torch to create a beautiful crust.
9. Servewarm.

Nutritional Value PerServing:

Calories 521, Carbohydrates 22.2 g, Fats 26.6 g, Protein 48.1 g

Herbed Rack of Lamb

Prep time: 20 minutes, Cook time: 2 ½ hours, Serves: 4

Ingredients:

- 2 racks of lamb, Frenched*
- 2 teaspoons Herbs de Provence
- Salt and pepper to taste

Sauce:

- 2 tablespoons butter
- 1 clove garlic,minced
- 1 teaspoon mincedthyme
- 2 teaspoons freshmint
- ½ teaspoon onion powder

Instructions:

1. Fill the Sous Vide cooker with water and heat to134°F.
2. Season the rack generously with salt andpepper.
3. Sprinkle with Herbs de Provence and place the racks into Sous Vide cookingbags.
4. Vacuum seal the racks and submerge inwater.
5. Cook the lamb 2 ½ hours.
6. Remove the racks from the bag. Place aside and patdry.
7. Melt butter in a saucepan over mediumheat.
8. Stir in garlic, thyme, mint, and onionpowder.
9. Brush the lamb with butter and sear in a heated skillet over medium-highheat.
10. Serve warm, but before serving slice intoracks.

Nutritional Value Per Serving:

Calories 500, Carbohydrates 20.8 g, Fats 25.8 g, Protein 46.2 g

Lamb Leg Steak with

Prep time: 15 minutes, Cook time: 6 hours, Serves: 4

Ingredients:

- 4 5oz. lamb leg steaks 4
- tablespoons butter Salt
- and pepper, totaste

Chimichurri:

- 1 bunch fresh parsley, chopped
- ½ bunch fresh mint, chopped
- 1 bunch fresh basil, chopped
- 2 cloves garlic, chopped
- 1 teaspoon salt
- 1-inch minced ginger
- 2 red chili peppers, seeded, chopped
- ¾ cup olive oil
- ¼ cup vinegar
- ¼ cup water
- 1 lime,juiced
- 1 splash soy sauce

Instructions:

1. Preheat Sous Vide cooker to 140°F.
2. Season lamb steaks with salt and pepper. Place the lamb steaks and butter into Sous Vide bags. Vacuum seal.
3. Cook the lamb 6 hours.
4. Make the chimichurri; in a bowl, combine all the chimichurri ingredients. Stirwell.
5. Remove the lamb from the bag and patdry.
6. Sear in a very hot skillet until browned on allsides.
7. Serve warm with chimichurri.

Nutritional Value Per Serving:

Calories 740, Carbohydrates 33.2 g, Fats 53.9 g, Protein 30.6 g

Lamb Shoulder with

Prep time: 10 minutes, Cook time: 14 hours, Serves: 4

Ingredients:

- 3lb. lamb shoulder
- 1 cup beef stock
- 4 tablespoons olive oil
- 2 sprigs thyme

Vegetables:

- 1 zucchini, trimmed, sliced
- 2 red bell peppers, seeded,quartered
- 3 sprigs parsley
- 1 tablespoon oliveoil
- 1 clove garlic
- Salt and pepper, to taste
- 1 tablespoon butter

Instructions:

1. Preheat Sous Vide cooker to 155°F.
2. Remove any fat from the lamb and season generously with salt andpepper.
3. Heat some oil in askillet.
4. Sear the lamb shoulder in a large skillet and transfer into Sous Vide cookingbag.
5. Add the beef stock, remaining olive oil, and thyme. Vacuum seal the lamband submerge in water.
6. Cook the lamb 14 hours.
7. Make the vegetables; melt butter in askillet.
8. Add garlic and cook 30 seconds. Add the bell peppers and cook 3minutes.
9. Toss in the remaining ingredients and cook 3 minutes. Placeaside.
10. Remove the lamb from the cooking bag. Using a torch create a brown crust on thelamb.
11. Serve lamb with prepared veggies.

Nutritional Value Per Serving:

Calories 569, Carbohydrates 26.8 g, Fats 37.8 g, Protein 30.3 g

Teriyaki Beef Cubes

Prep time: 10 minutes, Cook time: 1 hour, Serves: 2

Ingredients

- 2 fillet mignon steaks
- ½ cup teriyaki sauce, extra 6 tablespoons
- 2 tablespoons soy sauce
- 2 teaspoons fresh chilis, chopped
- 1½ tablespoons sesame seeds, toasted
- Rice noodles
- 2 tablespoons sesame oil
- 1 tablespoon scallion for garnishing, finely chopped

Instructions:

1. Prepare the Sous Vide water bath using your immersion circulator and raisethe temperature to 134°F
2. Slice the steaks into small portions and put them in a zipperbag
3. Add ½ a cup of teriyaki sauce to the bag. Seal using the immersion method,submerge and cook for 1 hour.
4. Add the soy sauce and chopped chilis in a smallbowl
5. Add the sesame seeds in anotherbowl
6. After 50 minutes of cooking, start cooking the rice noodles according to thepackage's instructions
7. Once done, drain the noodles and put them on a servingplatter
8. Take the bag out from the water and remove the beef. Discard themarinade
9. Take a large skillet and put it over a high heat. Add your sesame oil and allow the oil to heat up.
10. Add the beef and 6 tablespoons of teriyaki sauce, and cook for 5seconds
11. Transfer the cooked beef to your serving platter and garnish with toasted sesame seeds and scallions
12. Serve with the prepped chili-soy dip

Nutritional Value Per Serving:

Calories 446, Carbohydrates 15 g, Fats 26 g, Protein 38 g

Willy Cheesesteak

Prep time: 1 minutes, Cook time: 1 hour, Serves: 4

Ingredients

- 1 red bell pepper, thinly sliced
- 1 yellow bell pepper, thinly sliced
- ½ white onion, thinly sliced
- 2 tablespoons extra-virgin olive oil
- Kosher salt and black pepper as needed
- 1 lb. cooked skirt steak, thinlysliced
- 4 soft hoagie rolls
- 8 slices of Provolone cheese

Instructions:

1. Prepare the Sous Vide water bath using your immersion circulator and raisethe temperature to 185°F
2. Add the bell peppers, onion and olive oil in a heavy-duty zipbag
3. Season the mixture with salt andpepper
4. Seal the bag using the immersion method and submerge and cook for 1hour.
5. At the 55-minute mark, put the cooked steak in another zip bag and submergeit
6. Allow both to cook for 5-minutes more and take themout
7. Preheat your oven to400°F
8. Slice the hoagie rolls in half and top them withcheese
9. Place them in the oven and bake for 2minutes
10. Add the pepper, steak and onions, thenserve!

Nutritional Value Per Serving:

Calories 295, Carbohydrates 18 g, Fats 19 g, Protein 13 g

Fried Spinach & Tri Tip

Prep time: 5 minutes, Cook time: 2 hours, Serves: 2

Ingredients

- 1-piece tri tip roast
- Kosher salt and black pepper
- 2 teaspoons garlic powder
- 2 teaspoons canolaoil
- 1 pack baby spinach

Instructions:

1. Prepare the Sous Vide water bath using your immersion circulator and raisethe temperature to 134°F
2. Season the steak with pepper, garlic powder andsalt
3. Add the steak in a heavy-duty resealable bag and submerge. Allow it to cook forabout 2 hours
4. Once cooked, remove the bag from the waterbath.
5. Take a cast-iron skillet and place it over medium-highheat
6. After 2 minutes, put 1 teaspoon of canola oil in theskillet
7. Add the spinach and toss well
8. Pour the bag juices into the skillet and toss well. Keep cooking for 30seconds
9. Transfer to a serving platter and slice the steak against the grain, into ¼ inchpieces
10. Transfer it to the platter with the spinach andserve!

Nutritional Value Per Serving:

Calories 446, Carbohydrates 15 g, Fats 26 g, Protein 38 g

Prime Rib

Prep time: 45 minutes, Cook time: 6 hours, Serves: 12

Ingredients

- 3 lbs. bone-in beef ribeyeroast
- Kosher salt
- 1 tablespoon black peppercorn, coarsely ground
- 1 tablespoon green peppercorn, coarsely ground
- 1 tablespoon pink peppercorn, coarsely ground 1
- tablespoon dried celery seeds
- 2 tablespoons dried garlicpowder
- 4 sprigs rosemary
- 1-quart beef stock
- 2 egg whites

Instructions:

1. Season the beef with kosher salt and chill for 12hours
2. Prepare the Sous Vide water bath using your immersion circulator and raisethe temperature to 132°F
3. Add the beef in a zip bag and seal using the immersion method. Cook for 6hours
4. Pre-heat the oven to 425°F and remove the beef. Pat itdry
5. Mix the peppercorns, celery seeds, garlic powder and rosemary together in abowl
6. Brush the top of your cooked roast with egg white and season with the mixture andsalt
7. Put the roast on a baking rack and roast for 10-15 minutes. Allow it to rest for10-15 minutes and carve
8. Pour the cooking liquid from the bag in a large saucepan, bring to a boil andsimmer until the amount hashalved.
9. Carve the roast and serve with thestock.

Nutritional Value Per Serving:

Calories 588, Carbohydrates 24 g, Fats 40 g, Protein 33 g

New York Strip Steak

Prep time: 5 minutes, Cook time: 1 hour, Serves: 1

Ingredients

- New York Strip Steak
- Salt and pepper as needed
- Olive oil
- Steak seasoning as you prefer
- Rosemary and thyme

Instructions:

1. Prepare the Sous Vide water bath using your immersion circulator and raisethe temperature to 129°F
2. Season the steak with pepper and salt and place the herbs ontop
3. Add it in a zip bag and seal using the immersion method. Cook for 1hour
4. Once done, remove from the bag and patdry
5. Drizzle olive oil over andseason
6. Grill for 1 minute (each side) at400°F
7. Slice and serve!

Nutritional Value Per Serving:

Calories 776, Carbohydrates 10 g, Fats 56 g, Protein 58 g

Veal Marsala

Prep time: 15 minutes, Cook time: 1 hour 30 minutes, Serves: 4

Ingredients

- 1 lb. veal cutlets
- 2 teaspoons garlic salt
- 2 cups thinly sliced Cremini mushrooms
- ½ cup heavy cream
- 1 shallot, thinly sliced
- 3 tablespoonsMarsala
- 2 tablespoons unsalted butter
- 1 teaspoon freshly ground blackpepper
- 2 sprigs fresh thyme
- 2 tablespoons chives for garnishing, finely

Instructions:

1. Prepare the Sous Vide water bath using your immersion circulator and raisethe temperature to 140°F. Season the veal with garlicsalt
2. Add the mushrooms, cream, marsala, pepper, shallot, butter, and thyme along with the seasoned veal, in a heavy-duty resealable zip bag and seal using the immersionmethod
3. Submerge underwater and cook for 90minutes
4. Once cooked, remove it from the water bath and place the cutlets on a servingplate
5. Discard the thyme and remove the cookingliquid
6. Pour the mixture into a non-stick skillet and bring to a simmer over medium-highheat
7. Keep simmering for about 5 minutes
8. Lower down the heat to low and add the veal to your sauce. Cookwell
9. Put the veal back on the serving plate and serve withrice
10. Garnish with chives and serve!

Nutritional Value Per Serving:

Calories 442, Carbohydrates 13 g, Fats 26 g, Protein 39 g

Italian Sausage

Prep time: 15 minutes, Cook time: 1 hour, Serves: 4

Ingredients

- 2½ cups seedless red grapes, stems removed
- 1 tablespoon fresh rosemary, chopped
- 2 tablespoons butter
- 4 sweet Italian sausages
- 2 tablespoons balsamic vinegar
- Salt and ground black pepper

Instructions:

1. Prepare the Sous Vide water bath using your immersion circulator and raisethe temperature to 165°F
2. Add the butter, grapes, salt, pepper, rosemary and sausages in a resealable zip bag and whisk well
3. Seal using the immersion method and submerge underwater. Cook for 1hour.
4. Once done, remove the sausage and transfer them to your servingplatter
5. Place the grapes and any remaining liquid in a small-sizedsaucepan
6. Add the balsamic vinegar and simmer for 3 minutes over medium-highheat
7. Serve the sausages with the grapes

Nutritional Value Per Serving:

Calories 304, Carbohydrates 10 g, Fats 24 g, Protein 12 g

Sirloin Steak with Smashed Yukon

Prep time: 20 minutes, Cook time: 60 minutes, Serves: 4

Ingredients

- 4 sirloin steaks
- 2 lbs. baby Yukon potatoes, cubed
- ¼ cup steak seasoning
- Salt and pepper as needed
- 4 tablespoon butter
- Canola oil for searing

Instructions:

1. Prepare the Sous Vide water bath using your immersion circulator and raisethe temperature to 129°F
2. Season the steaks. Seal the steaks in a zip bag using the immersion method and cookfor 1 hour
3. Take the potatoes and cook them in boiling water for 15minutes
4. Strain the potatoes into a large mixing bowl and add the butter. Mash using the backof your spoon until mixed well
5. Season with salt and pepper
6. Once cooked, take the steak out from the bag and pat it dry using a kitchentowel
7. Heat a heavy bottomed pan over medium-heat and add the oil. Sear the steak for1 minute
8. Serve with the smashed potatoes

Nutritional Value Per Serving:

Calories 491, Carbohydrates 32 g, Fats 27 g, Protein 30 g

Beef Wellington

Prep time: 1 hour, Cook time: 2 hours, Serves: 4

Ingredients

- 1 lb. beef tenderloinfillet
- Salt and pepper
- 2 tablespoons Dijonmustard
- 1 sheet puff pastry, thawed 8
- oz. creminimushrooms
- 1 shallot, diced
- 3 cloves garlic,chopped
- 1 tablespoon unsaltedbutter
- 6 slices prosciutto

Instructions:

1. Prepare the Sous Vide water bath using your immersion circulator and raisethe temperature to 124°F
2. Take the beef tenderloin and generously season it with pepper andsalt
3. Place in a zip bag and seal using the immersion method. Cook for 2hours
4. Chop the mushrooms in a food processor, put the shallots and garlic in a hotpan
5. Cook until tender, add the chopped mushrooms and cook until water hasevaporated
6. Add 1 tablespoon of butter andcook
7. Once done, remove the beef from the bag and patdry
8. Heat the oil in a cast iron pan until shimmering. Sear the beef on all sides for 30 seconds
9. Spread the Dijon mustard all over thetenderloin
10. Lay a plastic wrap on a surface and arrange your prosciutto slices horizontally. Spread the Duxelles thinly over the prosciutto and place the tenderloin ontop
11. Roll the tender loin in the plastic wrap tightly and chill for 20minutes
12. Roll out your thawed pastry and brush with egg wash. Unwrap the tender loin andplace in the pastry puff
13. Bake for 10 minutes in your oven at 475°F, slice andserve!

Nutritional Value Per Serving:

Calories 342, Carbohydrates 11 g, Fats 22 g, Protein 25 g

Short Rib Tacos

Prep time: 15 minutes, Cook time: 2 hours, Serves: 4

Ingredients

- 2 lbs. short rib, thinly sliced
- ½ cup soy sauce
- 3 green onion stalks, sliced
- 1 tablespoon Sambal chilipaste
- 6 cloves garlic, chopped
- 2 tablespoons brown sugar
- 1-inch ginger, peeled and grated
- 1 tablespoon sesame oil
- ½ a teaspoon red pepper powder
- 8 corn tortillas
- Kimchi for topping
- Sliced avocado

Instructions:

1. Preparethe Sous Videwater bathusingyour immersion circulator and increase the temperature to 138°F
2. Add the soy sauce, green onion, garlic, chili paste, brown sugar, ginger, redpepper powder and sesame oil in a saucepan and simmer until the sugar hasdissolved
3. Allow to chill and put in a zipper bag, seal using the immersion method and cook for2 hours
4. Add the marinade from the bag in a saucepan and reduce over medium heatuntil syrupy
5. Take the short ribs and transfer them to a baking sheet, place them under your broiland broil for 10minutes
6. Dice the short ribs into ¼ inchcubes
7. Assemble the tacos with avocado, tortilla, and Kimchi and finish withsauce

Nutritional Value Per Serving:

Calories 453, Carbohydrates 60 g, Fats 13 g, Protein 24 g

Hot Dogs

Prep time: 5 minutes, Cook time: 1 hour, Serves: 4

Ingredients

- 8 hot dogs
- 8 hot dog buns
- Mustard
- Ketchup

Instructions:

1. Prepare the Sous Vide water bath using your immersion circulator and raisethe temperature to 140°F
2. Seal the hot dogs in a zip bag using the immersionmethod
3. Submerge underwater and cook for 1 hour
4. Serve by placing the hot dogs in the buns and dressing them with mustard andketchup

Nutritional Value Per Serving:

Calories 206, Carbohydrates 13 g, Fats 10 g, Protein 16 g

Italian Sausage Sandwich

Prep time: 15 minutes, Cook time: 3 hours, Serves: 4

Ingredients

- 1 lb. Italian sausage
- 1 red bell pepper, seeded, cored
- 1 yellow bell pepper, seeded cored
- 1 large onion, thinly sliced
- 1 garlic clove, minced
- 1 cup chopped tomatoes, with juice
- 1 teaspoon dried oregano
- 1 teaspoon dried basil
- 1 teaspoon oil
- Salt and pepper
- 4 pieces' bread loaves

Instructions:

1. Prepare the Sous Vide water bath using your immersion circulator and raisethe temperature to 140°F
2. Take 2 separate resealable zip bags and divide your sausage intothem
3. Do the same with garlic, basil, onion, peppers, tomato andoregano
4. Seal both bags, using the immersion method, and submerge underwater. Cook for3 hours
5. Add the oil in a skillet and add in the sausage and fry for 1 minute perside
6. Push the sausages to one side and add the remaining contents of the bags to theskillet. Season with pepper and salt
7. Cook until the water hasevaporated
8. Serve by making a sandwich of the sausage with bread loaves and the othercontents

Nutritional Value Per Serving:

Calories 234, Carbohydrates 15 g, Fats 14 g, Protein 12 g

Crispy Noodle & Beef

Prep time: 10 minutes, Cook time: 2 hours, Serves: 2

Ingredients

- 2 rib eye steaks
- 1 nest noodles, boiled,drained
- 2 cups cooking oil
- 2 cups broccoli, boiled,drained
- 1 onion, sliced
- 2 cups warm chicken stock
- 2 tablespoons cornstarch
- 1 tablespoon fish sauce
- Salt and pepper

Instructions:

1. Prepare the Sous Vide water bath using your immersion circulator and raisethe temperature to 134°F
2. Place the steak in a zip bag and seal using the immersion method. Submerge andcook for 1-2 hours
3. Add the chicken stock, cornstarch and fish sauce in abowl
4. Heat the oil and deep fry the noodles for about 5 minutes (half at atime)
5. Place them to one side
6. Fry the onion and add the broccoli, chicken stock, cornstarch and fishsauce
7. Cook for a few minutes until itthickens
8. Take the cooked steaks and pat them dry using a kitchen towel. Sear them for 1minute using the same pan used to fry thenoodles
9. Serve by assembling the noodles on the bottom, vegetables above, and steak overthe whole dish
10. Season with extra pepper and salt

Nutritional Value Per Serving:

Calories 511, Carbohydrates 28 g, Fats 7 g, Protein 84 g

Lamb Chops

Prep time: 15 minutes, Cook time: 2 hours, Serves: 2

Ingredients

- 2 lamb loin chops
- Salt and pepper
- 1 teaspoon spice blend
- 4 prunes
- 1 tablespoon honey
- 1 teaspoon extra-virgin olive oil

Instructions:

1. Prepare the Sous Vide water bath using your immersion circulator and increase the temperature to 134°F
2. Take the lamb chops and season them thoroughly with salt and pepper. Rub thelamb chops with the spice blend
3. Place the chops in a zip bag, add the prunes and honey, and seal using theimmersion method
4. Submerge it underwater and cook for 2hours
5. Once done, remove the lamb chops and save prunes and cookingliquid
6. Take out the cooked lamb chops and pat them dry using a kitchentowel
7. Place an iron skillet over medium heat for about 5minutes
8. Add the olive oil and the lamb chops and sear for 30 seconds perside
9. Put on a serving plate and let it stay for 5minutes
10. Drizzle some of the cooking liquid from the bag over the chops and serve withthe prunes

Nutritional Value Per Serving:

Calories 441, Carbohydrates 56 g, Fats 13 g, Protein 25 g

Teriyaki Skewered Lamb

Prep time: 10 minutes, Cook time: 3 hours, Serves: 2

Ingredients

- 2 lamb backstop loin steaks, cut into 2-inchcubes
- 1 tablespoon soy sauce
- 1 tablespoon mirin
- 2 tablespoons sesame oil

Instructions:

1. Prepare the Sous Vide water bath using your immersion circulator and raisethe temperature to 140°F
2. Add the lamb, soy and mirin in a zipper bag and seal using the immersionmethod
3. Cook for 3 hours
4. Once cooked, take the bag out from the water bath and take out the cooked lamb,pat them dry using kitchen towel
5. Thread onto skewers and discard the cooking liquid
6. Take a skillet and place it over medium-high heat, add the oil. Sear both sidesand serve!

Nutritional Value Per Serving:

Calories 413, Carbohydrates 26 g, Fats 17 g, Protein 39 g

Lamb Rack with Dijon

Prep time: 5 minutes, Cook time: 60 minutes, Serves: 4

Ingredients

- 1 rack of lamb,trimmed
- 3 tablespoons honey
- 2 tablespoons Dijonmustard
- 1 teaspoon sherry vinegar
- ¼ teaspoon salt
- 2 tablespoons avocado oil
- Mustard seeds and chopped green onion for garnishing

Instructions:

1. Prepare the Sous Vide water bath using your immersion circulator and raisethe temperature to 135°F
2. Take a small-sized bowl and add all the listed ingredients (exceptlamb)
3. Mix well and place the trimmed lamb meat into a zip bag. Pour the sauce in and seal using the immersion method. Cook for 1 hour
4. Once done, take the bag out from the water bath and transfer the lamb to aserving plate, keep the juice on the side
5. Place a frying pan over medium-high heat, add 2 tablespoon of oil and allow it toheat up, and when it shimmers, add in the lamb and sear for 2 minutes perside
6. Slice it and drizzle the bag sauceover
7. Garnish with the mustard seeds and greenonions
8. Enjoy!

Nutritional Value Per Serving:

Calories 305, Carbohydrates 25 g, Fats 17 g, Protein 13 g

Quail Breast

Prep time: 15 minutes, Cook time: 2 hours, Serves: 4

Ingredients

- 8 quail breasts, bone-in, skin-on
- Kosher salt, freshly ground black pepper
- 1 tablespoon extra-virgin olive oil

Instructions:

1. Prepare the Sous Vide water bath using your immersion circulator and increase the temperature to 134°F
2. Season the quail and place in a zip bag. Seal using the immersionmethod
3. Cook for 2 hours
4. Once done, remove the bag and take out the quail, pat itdry
5. Rub the cooked quail with oil
6. Take one cast iron skillet and heat it. Sear the breast for 1 minute perside
7. Transfer to a platter and serve

Nutritional Value Per Serving:

Calories 179, Carbohydrates 28 g, Fats 3 g, Protein 10 g

Beef Bone Marrow

Prep time: 15 minutes, Cook time: 1 hour, Serves: 4

Ingredients

- 2 pieces' large beef bone marrow, split lengthwise
- Kosher salt
- Ground black pepper

Instructions:

1. Prepare the Sous Vide water bath using your immersion circulator and increase the temperature to 155°F
2. Add the bones in a zip bag and seal using the immersion method
3. Submerge underwater and cook for 1 hour
4. Once done, remove the cooked bone marrow from the bag and transfer it to a baking sheet (make sure to keep the marrow side facing up)
5. Season with salt and pepper
6. Broil the bones for about 2 minutes until the marrow is golden brown
7. Serve!

Nutritional Value Per Serving:

Calories 772, Carbohydrates 18 g, Fats 48 g, Protein 67 g

Dry Aged Steak

Prep time: 20 minutes, Cook time: 1 hour, Serves: 1

Ingredients

- 1 dry-aged ribeye steak,boneless
- Salt and pepper as needed
- Lavender Greek seasoning
- 2 tablespoons chopped freshparsley
- 2 tablespoons extra-virgin oliveoil
- ½ teaspoon garlic, minced
- 1 lemon
- 1 tablespoon unsaltedbutter
- 1 cup mashed potatoes

Instructions:

1. Prepare the Sous Vide water bath using your immersion circulator and raisethe temperature to 137°F
2. Season the steak with salt, pepper and lavender Greekseasoning
3. Place in a zip bag and seal using the immersion method. Submerge underwaterand cook for 1 hour
4. After 55 minutes, prepare your Gremolata* by combining the parsley, garlic andolive oil in a small bowl
5. Add the juice of ½ the lemon and stirwell
6. Season with pepper and salt
7. Once the meat is cooked, remove the steak and patdry
8. Heat a cast iron skillet over medium high heat for 5 minutes. Add the butter and allow to melt
9. Transfer the steaks and sear both sides for 30seconds
10. Transfer the steak to a platter and rest for 5minutes
11. Serve with mashed potatoes and Gremolata

Nutritional Value Per Serving:

Calories 531, Carbohydrates 44 g, Fats 27 g, Protein 28 g

Chapter 5: Pork

BBQ Pork

Prep time: 5 minutes, Cook time: 3 hours 10 minutes, Serves: 4

Ingredients:

- 1-pound pork tenderloin
- 2 garlic cloves, coarselychopped
- 2 tbsp garlic powder
- 2 tbsp ground paprika
- Salt and pepper to taste
- 1 tbsp dried oregano
- ½ tsp liquid smoke
- ¼ cup BBQ sauce

Instructions:

1. Preheat the water bath to 150°F.
2. Mix salt, pepper, garlic powder, paprika and oregano in abowl.
3. Rub the pork with the spice mixture and put it into the vacuumbag.
4. Add 1 garlic clove to thebag.
5. Seal the bag and cook in the preheated water bath for 3hours.
6. When the time is up, carefully removing the pork from the bag and sear it on bothsides over the high heat in 1 tbsp olive oil until lightbrown.
7. Slice the pork and serve with the BBQsauce.

Nutritional Value Per Serving:

Calories 246, Carbohydrates 11 g, Fats 14 g, Protein 19 g

Chili Pork Chops

Prep time: 5 minutes, Cook time: 1 hour 10 minutes, Serves: 2

Ingredients:

- 2 pork rib chops
- 1 small onion, chopped
- 2 garlic cloves
- 2 tbsp Worcestershire sauce
- ½ tsp chili powder
- Salt and pepper to taste
- 1 tbsp unsalted butter
- 1 tbsp vegetable oil

Instructions:

1. In a small bowl, mix salt, pepper and chili powder.
2. Rub the pork chops and put them into the vacuum bag.
3. Preheat your sous vide machine to 144°F.
4. Add the garlic cloves, chopped onion, Worcestershire sauce and olive oil to the bag and seal it.
5. Set the cooking time for 1 hour.
6. When the time is up, carefully dry the chops with the paper towels.
7. Sear the chops in 1 tbsp butter on both sides for about 40 seconds (until light brown).

Nutritional Value Per Serving:

Calories 289, Carbohydrates 15 g, Fats 13 g, Protein 28 g

Sherry Braised Pork Ribs

Prep time: 10 minutes, Cook time: 18 hours 10 minutes, Serves: 4

Ingredients:

- 2 pounds pork ribs, chopped into bone sections
- 1 tbsp ginger root, sliced
- ½ tsp ground nutmeg
- 2 tbsp soy sauce
- 1 tsp salt
- 1 tsp white sugar
- 1 anise star pod
- ¼ cup dry sherry
- 1 tbsp butter

Instructions:

1. In a small bowl, combine salt, sugar and ground nutmeg, and rub the pork ribs withthis mixture.
2. Put the ribs into the vacuum bag, add sliced ginger root, soy sauce, anise star andsherry wine.
3. Preheat your sous vide machine to 176°F.
4. Set the cooking time for 18hours.
5. When the time is up, carefully dry the ribs with the papertowels.
6. Sear the ribs in 1 tbsp butter on both sides for about 40 seconds untilcrusty.

Nutritional Value Per Serving:

Calories 284, Carbohydrates 32 g, Fats 12 g, Protein 12 g

Beer Braised Pork Ribs

Prep time: 10 minutes, Cook time: 18 hours 10 minutes, Serves: 4

Ingredients:

- 2 pounds pork ribs, chopped into bone sections
- 1 big onion, finely chopped
- 12 ounce can light beer Salt
- and pepper to taste
- 1 tbsp butter

Instructions:

1. Rub the pork ribs with salt and pepper.
2. Put the ribs into the vacuum bag, add chopped onion and beer.
3. Preheat your sous vide machine to 176°F.
4. Set the cooking time for 18 hours.
5. When the time is up, carefully dry the ribs with the paper towels.
6. Sear the ribs in 1 tbsp butter on both sides for about 40 seconds until crusty.
7. Serve with mashed potatoes, cole slaw or white rice.

Nutritional Value Per Serving:

Calories 283, Carbohydrates 17 g, Fats 15 g, Protein 20 g

Pork Medallions

Prep time: 10 minutes, Cook time: 1 hour, Serves: 4

Ingredients:

- 1 tablespoon olive oil
- 1 pinch salt
- 1 pinch black pepper
- 1 teaspoon ground cumin
- ¼ cup chopped fresh parsley
- 1 ¾ lb. pork tenderloin

Instructions:

1. Preheat the Sous Vide cooker to 145°F.
2. Cut the pork tenderloin in medallions.
3. Season with salt, pepper, and cumin.
4. Place the seasoned pork into Sous Vide bag and add parsley.
5. Vacuum seals the bag and submerge in water.
6. Cook the medallions 1 hour.
7. Heat olive oil in a large skillet.
8. Remove the medallions from the cooker.
9. Sear on both sides.
10. Serve warm.

Nutritional Value Per Serving:

Calories 322, Carbohydrates 4.5 g, Fats 10.6 g, Protein 52.1 g

Indian Style Pork

Prep time: 15 minutes, Cook time: 2 hours, Serves: 4

Ingredients:

- 1.5lb. pork tenderloin, sliced
- 2 cups yogurt
- 1 cup sour cream
- 2 tablespoons tandooripaste
- 1 tablespoon currypaste
- 1-inch ginger, minced
- 2 cloves garlic, minced
- Salt and pepper, to taste

Instructions:

1. In a large bowl, combine yogurt, sour cream, tandoori paste, curry paste, garlic,and ginger.
2. Add sliced pork. Cover and marinate 20 minutes in afridge.
3. Preheat your Sous Vide cookcr to 135°F.
4. Remove the pork from marinade and place into Sous Vide bag. Vacuum seal thebag.
5. Submerge pork in the water bath and cook 2hours.
6. Remove the bag from water and opencarefully.
7. Heat 1 tablespoon olive oil in a largeskillet.
8. Sear the pork 3 minutes perside.
9. Servewarm.

Nutritional Value PerServing:

Calories 350, Carbohydrates 13.1 g, Fats 19.5 g, Protein 30.4 g

Pork Knuckles

Prep Time: 20 minutes, Cook time: 24 hours, Serves: 4

Ingredients:

- 2 10oz. pork knuckles
- Salt and pepper, to taste
- 4 cloves garlic, chopped
- ½ cup mustard
- ½ cup raw apple cider vinegar
- 2 ¾ cups apple juice
- ½ cup brown sugar
- 4 sprigs thyme
- 1 bay leaf

Instructions:

1. Preheat Sous Vide cooker to 158°F.
2. Generously season pork knuckles with salt and pepper.
3. Heat some oil in a large skillet. Sear pork 2 minutes per side. Remove from the skillet.
4. Toss the remaining ingredients into a skillet, and cook until reduced by half. Place aside to cool.
5. Place the pork knuckles in Sous Vide bag along with the prepared sauce.
6. Vacuum seal the bag. Submerge bag in a water bath.
7. Cook 24 hours.
8. Remove shanks from the bag and place aside.
9. Strain cooking juices into a saucepan.
10. Simmer over medium heat until thickened.
11. Pour the sauce over shanks and serve.

Nutritional Value Per Serving:

Calories 357.8, Carbohydrates 45.2 g, Fats 8.6 g, Protein 24.9 g

Pulled Pork

Prep time: 10 minutes, Cook time: 24 hours, Serves: 6

Ingredients:

- 2lb. pork shoulder, trimmed
- 1 tablespoon ketchup
- 4 tablespoons Dijon mustard
- 2 tablespoons maple syrup
- 2 tablespoons soy sauce

Instructions:

1. Preheat your Sous Vide cooker to 158°F.
2. In a bowl, combine ketchup, mustard, maple syrup, and soy sauce.
3. Place the pork with prepared sauce into Sous Vide bag.
4. Vacuum seal the bag and submerge in water.
5. Cook the pork 24 hours.
6. Open the bag and remove pork.
7. Strain cooking juices into a saucepan. Torch the pork to create a crust.
8. Simmer the cooking juices in a saucepan until thickened.
9. Pull pork before serving.
10. Serve with thickened sauce.

Nutritional Value Per Serving:

Calories 504, Carbohydrates 16.1 g, Fats 32.8 g, Protein 36 g

Pork Cheeks

Prep time: 30 minutes, Cook time: 5 hours, Serves: 4

Ingredients

- 1 lb. skinless pork cheeks
- Kosher salt, and black pepper
- 1 cup beef stock
- ½ cup tomato sauce
- 1 stalk celery, cut up into 1-inch dice
- 1 quartered shallot
- 3 sprigs fresh thyme
- 1 oz. whiskey
- Mashed potatoes

Instructions:

1. Prepare the Sous Vide water bath using your immersion circulator and increase the temperature to 180°F.
2. Take the cheeks and season it with salt and pepper and transfer them to aheavy-duty resealable zip bag.
3. Add in the stock, tomato sauce, shallot, whiskey, celery, and thyme to thebag.
4. Seal up the bag using the immersion method and submerge it underwater. Cook for5 hours.
5. Once cooked, remove the bag and transfer it to aplate.
6. Strain the cooking liquid through a fine mesh strainer into a large saucepan. Discard any solid remains.
7. Bring the mixture to a simmer by placing it over medium-highheat.
8. Reduce the heat to medium-low and keep simmering for 20minutes.
9. Lower down the heat to low levels and transfer thecheeks.
10. Simmer for 2-3 minutes.
11. Serve with the mashed potatoes.

Nutritional Value Per Serving:

Calories 358, Carbohydrates 8 g, Fats 18 g, Protein 41 g

Pork Bacon – The Secret Canadian

Prep time: 7 minutes, Cook time: 6 hours, Serves: 4

Ingredients

- 8 slices Canadian bacon
- 1 teaspoon vegetable oil
- Salt and pepper

Instructions:

1. Prepare the Sous Vide water bath using your immersion circulator and raisethe temperature to 145°F.
2. Take a resealable plastic zip bag and add the bacon in thebag.
3. Seal using the immersionmethod.
4. Submerge it underwater and cook for 6hours.
5. Sprinkle with salt and pepper andserve!

Nutritional Value Per Serving:

Calories 384, Carbohydrates 53 g, Fats 12 g, Protein 16 g

Bacon Strips & Eggs

Prep time: 10 minutes, Cook time: 1 hour, Serves: 2

Ingredients

- 4 egg yolks
- 2 slices British-style bacon rashers cut up into ½ inch by 3-inch slices 4
- slices crisp toasted bread

Instructions:

1. Prepare the Sous Vide water bath using your immersion circulator and raisethe temperature to 143°F.
2. Gently place each of your egg yolks in the resealable zipper bag and seal it usingthe immersion method.
3. Submerge it underwater and cook for about 1 hour.
4. In the meantime, fry your bacon slices until they arecrisp.
5. Drain them on a kitchentowel.
6. Once the eggs are cooked, serve by carefully removing the yolks from the zip bagand placing it on top of thetoast.
7. Top with the slices of bacon andserve!

Nutritional Value Per Serving:

Calories 404, Carbohydrates 49 g, Fats 16 g, Protein 16 g

Pork Hoagies

Prep time: 15 minutes, Cook time: 12 hours, Serves: 4

Ingredients

- 1 lb. boneless pork shoulder chops
- 1 tablespoon dry rub + additional teaspoon for later use
- ¼ cup BBQ sauce
- 4 hoagie rolls
- 1 cup prepped fried pickles for topping

Instructions:

1. Prepare the Sous Vide water bath using your immersion circulator and increase the temperature to 187°F.
2. Slice up the pork into bite-sized portions and season with 1 tablespoon of dryrub.
3. Transfer the chops to a large resealable zipper bag and seal using the immersion method.
4. Cook for 12 hours.
5. Once cooked, remove the pork from the bag and shredit.
6. Season using the dry rub
7. Serve by topping the hoagie rolls with soft fried pickles and a drizzle of BBQsauce.

Nutritional Value Per Serving:

Calories 273, Carbohydrates 11 g, Fats 9 g, Protein 37 g

Bacon Potato Mix

Prep time: 30 minutes, Cook time: 1 hour 30 minutes, Serves: 6

Ingredients

- 1 ½ lb. Yukon potatoes, sliced up into ¾ inch pieces
- ½ cup chicken stock
- Salt and pepper, as needed
- 4 oz. thick bacon cut up into ¼ inch thick strips
- ½ cup onion, chopped
- 1/3 cup apple cider vinegar
- 4 thinly sliced scallions

Instructions:

1. Prepare the Sous Vide water bath using your immersion circulator and increase the temperature to 185°F.
2. Take a heavy-duty resealable bag and add the potatoes alongsidestock.
3. Season with some salt and seal it using the immersion method. Submerge and cookfor about 1 and a ½ hour.
4. Place a large-sized skillet over medium-highheat.
5. Add the bacon and cook for 5-7 minutes.
6. Transfer it to a kitchen towel and dry it. Reserve thefat.
7. Return the heat to the skillet and add the onions. Cook for 1minute.
8. Take a skillet and place it over medium heat, remove the bag from the water bath and pour the stock and potatoes from the bag into theskillet.
9. Add the cooked bacon and vinegar.
10. Bring the mixture to a simmer.
11. Add the scallions and season with a bit of pepper andsalt.

Nutritional Value Per Serving:

Calories 423, Carbohydrates 28 g, Fats 27 g, Protein 17 g

Molasses Pork Loin

Prep time: 15 minutes, Cook time: 240 minutes, Serves: 6

Ingredients

- 2 lbs. pork loin roast
- 1-piece bay leaf
- 3 oz. molasses
- ½ oz. soy sauce
- ½ oz. honey
- Juice of 2 lemons
- 2 strips lemon peel
- 4 chopped scallions
- ½ teaspoon garlic powder
- ¼ teaspoon Dijon mustard
- ¼ teaspoon ground ginger
- 1 oz. crushed corn chips
- Green onion for serving, sliced

Instructions:

1. Prepare the Sous Vide water bath using your immersion circulator and raisethe temperature to 142°F.
2. Transfer the pork loin and bay leaf into a resealable zipbag.
3. Take a small bowl and mix the molasses, soy, lemon peel, honey, bay leaf,scallions, garlic powder, mustard, and ginger.
4. Ladle 1/3 of the mixture over the porkloin.
5. Seal using the immersion method. Cook for 4 hours.
6. Once cooked, take the pork out from the water bath and add the remaining glaze toa saucepan.
7. Boil all over high heat and cook until reduced to glaze.
8. Pour glaze over pork loin and toss crushed corn chips overall.
9. Serve with the sliced green onion

Nutritional Value Per Serving:

Calories 264, Carbohydrates 29 g, Fats 12 g, Protein 10 g

Japanese Pork Cutlet

Prep time: 15 minutes, Cook time: 1 hour, Serves: 3

Ingredients

- 3 pork loin chops
- Salt andpepper
- 1 cup flour
- 2 whole eggs
- Panko crumbs as needed to coat the chops

Instructions:

1. Prepare the Sous Vide water bath using your immersion circulator and raisethe temperature to 140°F.
2. Make tiny slits on the loin body and trim any excess fat. Season with salt andpepper.
3. Transfertoaresealablezip bag and seal using theimmersion method. Submergeand cook for 1 hour.
4. Once cooked, remove the loin chops from the bag and pat themdry.
5. Dredge the loin in flour, egg and finally pankocrumbs.
6. Heat up the oil to 450°F and fry chops for 1minute.
7. Put on a cooling rack and slice.
8. Serve on top of the steamed rice withvegetables.

Nutritional Value Per Serving:

Calories 275, Carbohydrates 45 g, Fats 7 g, Protein 8 g

Apple Butter Pork Tenderloin

Prep time: 10 minutes, Cook time: 3 hours, Serves: 3

Ingredients

- 1 pork tenderloin
- 1 jar apple butter
- Fresh rosemary sprigs
- Salt and pepper

Instructions:

1. Prepare the Sous Vide water bath using your immersion circulator and raisethe temperature to 145°F.
2. Season the pork with salt and pepper.
3. Spread apple butter on pork.
4. Transfer to a resealable zip bag and add the rosemary sprigs.
5. Seal using the immersion method and cook for 2 hours.
6. Once done, remove the pork from the bag and patdry.
7. Season with salt and pepper and apply apple butter generously.
8. Sear on hot grill.
9. Slice and serve!

Nutritional Value Per Serving:

Calories 636, Carbohydrates 84 g, Fats 28 g, Protein 12 g

Pork Chop with Corn

Prep time: 15 minutes, Cook time: 1 hour, Serves: 3

Ingredients

- 4 pieces' pork chop
- 1 small red bell pepper, diced
- 1 small yellow onion, diced 3
- ears corn kernels
- ¼ cup cilantro, chopped
- Salt and pepper
- Vegetable oil

Instructions:

1. Prepare the Sous Vide water bath using your immersion circulator and raisethe temperature to 140°F.
2. Season the pork chop with salt.
3. Transfer to a resealable zip bag and seal using the immersion method. Cook for 1hour.
4. Take a pan and put it over medium heat, add the oil and allow the oil to heatup
5. Add the onion, corn, and bell pepper.
6. Sauté for a while until barely browned.
7. Finish the corn mix with cilantro and set itaside.
8. Wipe the pan clean and place the pan over mediumheat.
9. Add the oil and sear the pork chop for 1 minute perside.
10. Slice and serve with the salad.

Nutritional Value Per Serving:

Calories 356, Carbohydrates 12g, Fats 16 g, Protein 41 g

Mango Salsa & Pork

Prep time: 45 minutes, Cook time: 2 hours, Serves: 4

Ingredients

- ¼ cup light broth sugar
- 1 tablespoon ground allspice
- ½ teaspoon cayenne pepper
- ¼ teaspoon ground cinnamon
- ¼ teaspoon ground cloves
- Kosher salt and black pepper
- 2 lbs. pork tenderloin
- 2 tablespoons canola oil
- 2 pitted and peeled mangoes, finely diced
- ¼ cup fresh cilantro, chopped
- 1 red bell pepper, stemmed, seeded, finelydiced
- 3 tablespoons red onion, finelydiced
- 2 tablespoons freshly squeezed limejuice
- 1 small jalapeno seeded and finelydiced

Instructions:

1. Prepare the Sous Vide water bath using your immersion circulator and raisethe temperature to 135°F.
2. Take a medium bowl and mix the sugar, allspice, cinnamon, cayenne, cloves,2 teaspoons of salt, and 1 teaspoon ofpepper.
3. Rub the mixture over thetenderloins.
4. Take a large-sized skillet and put it over medium heat, add the oil and once theoil simmers, transfer the pork and sear for 5 minutes, browning allsides.
5. Transfer to a plate and rest for 10minutes.
6. Transferthepork chopto a resealable zipperbag and seal using the immersion method. Cook for 2 hours.
7. Once cooked, take the bag out and allow it to rest for a while, take the chop outand slice it.
8. Prepare the salsa by mixing the mango, cilantro, bell pepper, onion, lime juice,and jalapeno in a mixing bowl.
9. Serve the sliced pork with salsa with a seasoning salt andpepper.

Nutritional Value Per Serving:

Calories 216, Carbohydrates 11 g, Fats 8 g, Protein 25 g

Lemongrass Pork Chops

Prep time: 30 minutes, Cook time: 2 hours, Serves: 2

Ingredients

- 2 tablespoons coconut oil
- 1 stalk sliced lemon grass
- 1 tablespoon minced shallot
- 1 tablespoon soy sauce
- 1 tablespoon mirin
- 1 tablespoon rice wine vinegar
- 1 tablespoon light brown sugar
- 1 teaspoon minced fresh ginger
- 1 teaspoon fish sauce
- 1 teaspoon kosher salt
- 2 (10-ounce) bone-in pork rib chops
- 1 teaspoon minced garlic

Instructions:

1. Prepare the Sous Vide water bath using your immersion circulator and raisethe temperature to 140°F.
2. Take a food processor and add 1 tablespoon of coconut oil, lemon grass, soysauce, shallot, vinegar, mirin, brown sugar, garlic, fish sauce, ginger, andsalt.
3. Process for 1 minute.
4. Place the pork chops into a resealable zip bag alongside soy-lemon grass mixtureand seal using the immersion method. Cook for 2hours.
5. Once cooked, remove the bag and take the pork chops out, pat themdry.
6. Heat a grill to high heat and sear the chops until wellbrowned.
7. Allow it to rest for 2-3minutes.
8. Serve!

Nutritional Value Per Serving:

Calories 260, Carbohydrates 12 g, Fats 12 g, Protein 26 g

Pork & Zucchini Ribbons

Prep time: 20 minutes, Cook time: 3 hours, Serves: 2

Ingredients

- 2 (6-ounce) bone-in pork loinchops
- Salt and black pepper
- 3 tablespoons extra-virgin olive oil
- 1 tablespoon freshly squeezed lemonjuice
- 2 teaspoons red winevinegar
- 2 teaspoons honey
- 2 tablespoons rice bran oil
- 2 medium zucchinis, sliced into ribbons
- 2 tablespoons pine nuts, toasted up

Instructions:

1. Prepare the Sous Vide water bath using your immersion circulator and raisethe temperature to 140°F.
2. Take the pork chops and season it with salt and pepper, transfer to a heavy-duty zipbag and add 1 tablespoon of oil.
3. Seal using the immersion method and cook for 3hours.
4. Prepare the dressing by whisking lemon juice, honey, vinegar, 2 tablespoons ofolive oil and season with salt andpepper.
5. Once cooked, remove the bag from the water bath and discard theliquid.
6. Heat up rice bran oil in a large skillet over high heat and add the pork chops, searuntil browned (1 minute per side)
7. Once done, transfer it to a cutting board and allow to rest for 5minutes.
8. Take a medium bowl and add the zucchini ribbons withdressing
9. Thinly slice the pork chops and discard thebone.
10. Place the pork on top of thezucchini.
11. Top with pine nuts and serve!

NutritionalValuePerServing:

Calories 173, Carbohydrates 4 g, Fats 9 g, Protein 19 g

Herbed Pork Loin

Prep time: 20 minutes, Cook time: 2 hours, Serves: 4

Ingredients

- 1 (1 lb.) pork tenderloin, trimmed
- Salt and fresh ground pepper
- 1 tablespoon chopped fresh basil
- 1 tablespoon chopped fresh parsley
- 1 tablespoon chopped fresh rosemary
- 2 tablespoons unsalted butter

Instructions:

1. Prepare the Sous Vide water bath using your immersion circulator and raisethe temperature to 134°F. Season the tenderloin with pepper andsalt
2. Rub herbs (amixture of basil, parsley and rosemary) all over the tenderloin and transfer to a resalable zip bag
3. Add 1 tablespoon of butter
4. Seal using the immersion method. Submerge underwater and cook for 2hours
5. Once cooked, remove the bag and remove the pork from thebag
6. Place a large-sized skillet over medium–highheat
7. Add the remaining butter and herb mixture and allow the butter to heatup
8. Add the pork and sear it well for 1-2 minutes each side, making sure to keepscooping the butter over thepork
9. Remove the heat and transfer the pork to a cuttingboard
10. Allow it to rest for 5 minutes and slice intomedallions
11. Serve with extra herbs and a sprinkle ofsalt

Nutritional Value Per Serving:

Calories 441, Carbohydrates 3 g, Fats 33 g, Protein 33 g

Red Pepper Salad & Pork

Prep time: 15 minutes, Cook time: 1 hour, Serves: 4

Ingredients

- 4 pork chops
- 1 small red bell pepper,diced
- 1 small yellow onion, diced 2
- cups frozen cornkernels
- ¼ cup cilantro, chopped
- Salt and pepper
- Vegetable oil

Instructions:

1. Prepare the Sous Vide water bath using your immersion circulator and raisethe temperature to 140°F.
2. Season the pork carefully with salt
3. Transfer the pork to a resealable zip bag and seal using the immersionmethod. Submerge underwater and cook for 1 hour
4. Take a pan and put it over medium heat and add the oil, allow it to heatup
5. Add the onion, red pepper, corn and sauté for a while until they are slightlybrowned
6. Season with salt and pepper
7. Finish the corn mix with a garnish of chopped cilantro, keep itaside
8. Remove the pan from heat and wipe theoil
9. Place it back to medium-high heat
10. Put the oil and allow it to heatup
11. Transfer the cooked pork chops to the pan and sear each side for 1minute
12. Serve the pork chops with thesalad!

Nutritional Value Per Serving:

Calories 674, Carbohydrates 49 g, Fats 41 g, Protein 25 g

Fragrant Nonya Pork Belly

Prep time: 10 minutes, Cook time: 7 hours, Serves: 7

Ingredients

- 1 lb. pork belly
- ¼ cup chopped shallots
- 3 sliced garlic cloves
- ½ tablespoon coriander seeds
- 2-star anise
- 4 large dried shiitake mushrooms
- 2 tablespoons coconut aminos
- 2 teaspoons brown sugar
- ½ teaspoon salt
- ¼ teaspoon ground white pepper

Instructions:

1. Prepare the Sous Vide water bath using your immersion circulator and raisethe temperature to 176°F.
2. Chop up the pork belly into 1-inch cubes and transfer to abowl.
3. Add the remaining ingredients and whisk themwell.
4. Transfer to a resealable zip bag and seal using the immersionmethod.
5. Cook for 7 hours and remove thebag.
6. Transfer the solids to serving dish and discard the staranise.
7. Tip the cooking liquid to a small pan and reduce it over mediumheat.
8. Pour the sauce over pork belly andserve!

Nutritional Value Per Serving:

Calories 306, Carbohydrates 5 g, Fats 30 g, Protein 4 g

Italian Sausage & Autumn

Prep time: 15 minutes, Cook time: 1 hour, Serves: 4

Ingredients

- 2 ½ cups seedless purple grapes with stem removed
- 1 tablespoon chopped fresh rosemary
- 2 tablespoons butter
- 4 whole sweet Italian sausages
- 2 tablespoons balsamic vinegar
- Salt and ground black pepper

Instructions:

1. Prepare the Sous Vide water bath using your immersion circulator and raisethe temperature to 160°F.
2. Take a plastic bag and add the grapes, rosemary, butter, and sausage in onelayer.
3. Seal using the immersion method. Cook for 1 hour.
4. Remove the sausage to serving platter and pour the grapes and liquid in asaucepan.
5. Add the balsamic vinegar and simmer for 3 minutes over medium-high heat andseason the mixture with salt and pepper.
6. Grill the sausage on medium-high heat for 3-4 minutes and serve with thegrapes.

Nutritional Value Per Serving:

Calories 345, Carbohydrates 11 g, Fats 21 g, Protein 28 g

Mushroom Mixed Pork

Prep time: 5 minutes, Cook time: 55 minutes, Serves: 2

Ingredients

- 2 thick-cut bone-in pork chops
- Salt and fresh groundpepper
- 2 tablespoons unsalted butter,cold
- 4 oz. mixed wildmushrooms
- ¼ cup sherry
- ½ cup beef stock
- 1 tablespoon steakmarinade
- Chopped garlic forgarnish

Instructions:

1. Prepare the Sous Vide water bath using your immersion circulator and raisethe temperature to 140°F.
2. Take the pork chop and season it thoroughly with salt and pepper and transfer toa resealable zip bag, seal using the immersion method and cook for 55minutes.
3. Remove the pork chop and pat dry, discard cookingliquid.
4. Take a large skillet and put it over medium-high heat, add 1 tablespoon of butterand allow the butter to melt.
5. Add the pork chops and sear 1 minute per side and transfer to aplatter.
6. Heat up the skillet once more and add the mushrooms, cook for 2-3minutes.
7. Add the sherry and bring the mixture to a nice simmer, add the stock, andsteak marinade and simmer until you have a thicksauce.
8. Remove the heat and swirl the remaining butter, season with salt and pepper andpour over the pork chops.
9. Garnish with chopped garlic and serve!

Nutritional Value Per Serving:

Calories 385, Carbohydrates 20 g, Fats 17 g, Protein 38 g

Pork Cheek Tacos

Prep time: 20 minutes, Cook time: 12 hours, Serves: 8

Ingredients

- 2 lbs. skinless pork cheeks
- 1 tablespoon ancho chili powder
- 1 tablespoon kosher salt
- 1 tablespoon light brown sugar
- 2 teaspoons ground cumin
- 2 teaspoons garlic powder
- 1 teaspoon cayenne pepper
- 1 teaspoon freshly ground black pepper
- Corn tortillas
- Pickled red onion and fresh cilantro for serving

Instructions:

1. Prepare the Sous Vide water bath using your immersion circulator and raise the temperature to 180°F.
2. Add the pork cheeks, chili powder, salt, brown sugar, garlic powder, cumin, cayenne, and black pepper to a resealable zipper bag and seal using the immersion method.
3. Cook for 12 hours.
4. Once cooked, remove the bag and take the pork out, reserve the cooking liquid.
5. Take the pork and shred the pork into 1-inch pieces and transfer to a large bowl.
6. Stir in the cooking liquid and serve on tortillas with a topping of pickled red onion and fresh cilantro.

Nutritional Value Per Serving:

Calories 490, Carbohydrates 20 g, Fats 26 g, Protein 44 g

Honey Mustard Pork

Prep time: 20 minutes, Cook time: 3 hours, Serves: 2

Ingredients

- 3 tablespoons extra-virgin olive oil
- 1 tablespoon + 2 teaspoons whole grainmustard
- 1 tablespoon + 1 teaspoonhoney
- Salt and ground black pepper
- 2 pieces' bone-in pork loin chops
- 1 tablespoon freshly squeezed lemonjuice
- 2 teaspoons red winevinegar
- 2 tablespoons rice branoil
- 2 cups mixed babylettuce
- 2 tablespoons thinly sliced sundried tomatoes
- 2 teaspoons pine nuts, toasted

Instructions:

1. Preparethe Sous Vide waterbath using the immersion circulator and raise the temperature to 140°F.
2. Take a small bowl and mix in 1 tablespoon olive oil, 1 tablespoon mustard, 1 tablespoon honey, and season with salt andpepper
3. Transfer to a resealable zip bag alongside the pork chop and toss well to coatit.
4. Seal using the immersion method and cook for 3hours.
5. To prepare the dressing, add the lemon juice, vinegar, 2 tablespoons of olive oil, 2 teaspoons of mustard and the remaining honey in a bowl. Season with salt andpepper.
6. Remove the bag and remove the pork chop, discard theliquid.
7. Take a large skillet over high heat and add bran oil, heat it up and wait until it starts to smoke. Add the pork chops and sear for 30 seconds perside.
8. Rest for 5 minutes.
9. Take a medium bowl and add the lettuce, sun-dried tomatoes and pine nuts, tosswell with 3 quarter of thedressing.
10. Take the pork chops and transfer them to your serving plate and top with the saladand dressing.
11. Serve!

Nutritional Value Per Serving:

Calories 348, Carbohydrates 22 g, Fats 8 g, Protein 47 g

Pork Cheek Ragout

Prep time: 30 minutes, Cook time: 10 hours, Serves: 8

Ingredients

- 2 lbs. skinless pork cheeks
- 2 finely diced carrots
- ½ white onion, finely diced
- 1 cup canned tomato sauce
- 1 cup canned diced tomatoes
- 3 sprigs oregano
- 3 garlic cloves, crushed
- 1 teaspoon granulated sugar
- 2 pieces' bay leaves
- Kosher salt and black pepper
- Cooked pasta and fresh parsley for serving

Instructions:

1. Prepare the Sous Vide water bath using your immersion circulator and raisethe temperature to 180°F.
2. Add the pork cheeks, carrots, onion, tomato sauce, diced tomatoes, garlic, oregano, sugar, bay leaves, 1 teaspoon of pepper, 1 tablespoon of salt to a heavy-dutyre-sealable zip bag.
3. Seal using the immersion method. Cook for 10hours.
4. Once done, remove the bag and then the pork, make sure to reserve the cookingliquid.
5. Shred using 2 forks into 1-inch pieces, transfer to large bowl and set it to theside.
6. Remove and discard the oregano from the cooking liquid, pour the contents to afood processor and pulse until the ingredients are uniformlychopped.
7. Take the sauce and season it well with pepper and salt, pour it over the pork tossto combine.
8. Toss the pasta with the mixture and serve withparsley!

Nutritional Value Per Serving:

Calories 444, Carbohydrates 40 g, Fats 20 g, Protein 26 g

Pork Slices with Noodle Salad

Prep time: 20 minutes, Cook time: 12 hours, Serves: 2

Ingredients

- ½ pound boneless pork leg
- 1 tablespoon extra-virgin olive oil
- 1 tablespoon freshly squeezed lime juice
- 1 tablespoon fish sauce
- 1 tablespoon soy sauce
- 1 tablespoon rice vinegar
- 1 tablespoon palm sugar
- 2 vermicelli noodle nests
- ½ thinly sliced scallion
- 2 tablespoons roasted peanuts chopped up
- 2 tablespoons chopped fresh cilantro
- 2 tablespoons chopped fresh mint

Instructions:

1. Prepare the Sous Vide water bath using your immersion circulator and raise the temperature to 176°F.
2. Add the pork leg to a resealable zip bag alongside the olive oil.
3. Seal using the immersion method and cook for 12 hours.
4. Prepare your dressing by mixing the lime juice, soy sauce, fish sauce, rice vinegar, and palm sugar in a small-sized bowl, give the whole mixture a nice stir.
5. Once cooked, take the pork out from the water bath and allow it to cool.
6. Shred using forks into bite-sized pieces.
7. Bring a large pot of water and bring it to a boil over high heat, add the vermicelli noodle and cook for 2-3 minutes.
8. Transfer to a bowl and add the scallions, mint, cilantro, peanuts, dressing, and pork to the noodle and toss well.
9. Serve!

Nutritional Value Per Serving:

Calories 439, Carbohydrates 62 g, Fats 11 g, Protein 23 g

Pork Chili Verde

Prep time: 40 minutes, Cook time: 24 hours, Serves: 8

Ingredients

- 2 lbs. boneless pork shoulder cut up into 1-inch pieces
- 1 tablespoon kosher salt
- 1 tablespoon ground cumin
- 1 teaspoon fresh ground black pepper
- 1 tablespoon extra-virgin olive oil
- 1 lb. tomatillos
- 3 poblano pepper, finely seeded, diced
- ½ white onion finely diced
- 1 jalapeno seeded, diced
- 3 garlic cloves, crushed
- 1 bunch roughly chopped cilantro
- 1 cup chicken broth
- ½ cup fresh squeezed lime juice
- 1 tablespoon Mexican oregano

Instructions:

1. Prepare the Sous Vide water bath using your immersion circulator and raisethe temperature to 150°F.
2. Season the pork with salt, cumin, and pepper.
3. Take a large skillet and place it over medium-high heat, add the oil and allow it to heat up.
4. Add the pork and sear for 5-7 minutes.
5. Increase the heat back to medium-high and add the tomatillos, poblano pepper, onion, jalapeno, and garlic. Cook for 5 minutes until slightly charred.
6. Transfer the whole prepared mixture to a food processor and add the cilantro, lime juice, chicken broth, oregano, and process for 1 minute.
7. Transfer the sauce to a resealable zip bag alongside the pork and seal usingthe immersion method. Submerge it underwater and cook for 24hours.
8. Once cooked, remove the bag and transfer the contents to a serving bowl. Sprinkle some salt and pepper and serve overrice.

Nutritional Value Per Serving:

Calories 338, Carbohydrates 29 g, Fats 18 g, Protein 15 g

Garlic & Ginger Pork Kebobs

Prep time: 30 minutes, Cook time: 4 hours, Serves: 4

Ingredients

- 1 lb. boneless pork shoulder cut up into 1-inch pieces
- 1 tablespoon kosher salt
- 1 tablespoon minced salt
- 1 tablespoon minced fresh ginger
- 1 tablespoon garlic, minced
- 1 teaspoon cumin
- 1 teaspoon coriander
- 1 teaspoon garlic powder
- 1 teaspoon brown sugar
- 1 teaspoon fresh ground black pepper

Instructions:

1. Prepare the Sous Vide water bath using your immersion circulator and raisethe temperature to 150°F.
2. Rub the pork with salt, garlic, ginger, cumin, coriander, garlic powder, pepper,and brown sugar, and transfer to a resealablebag.
3. Seal using the immersion method and cook for 4hours.
4. Heat up the grill to medium-high heat and remove the pork from the bag oncecooking is done, pierce it into skewers.
5. Grill for 3 minutes until browned allaround
6. Serve!

Nutritional Value Per Serving:

Calories 243, Carbohydrates 14 g, Fats 15 g, Protein 13 g

Cream-Poached Pork Loin

Prep time: 30 minutes, Cook time: 4 hours, Serves: 4

Ingredients

- 1 – 3 lbs. boneless pork loinroast
- Kosher salt andpepper
- 2 thinly sliced onion
- ¼ cup cognac
- 1 cup whole milk 1
- cup heavycream

Instructions:

1. Prepare the Sous Vide water bath using your immersion circulator and raisethe temperature to 145°F.
2. Season the pork withpepper and salt, take a large iron skilletand place it overmedium- heat for 5 minutes.
3. Add the pork and sear for 15 minutes until all sides arebrowned.
4. Transferto aplatter, add the onion to the rendered fat (in the skillet) and cook for 5 minutes.
5. Add the cognac and bring to a simmer. Allow it to cool for 10minutes.
6. Add the pork, onion, milk, and cream to a resealable zipper bag and seal usingthe immersion method. Submerge underwater and cook for 4hours.
7. Once cooked, remove the bag from the water and take the pork out, transfer the porkto cutting board and cover it to keep itwarm.
8. Pourthe bag contents to askillet and bring the mixture to a simmer over medium heat, keep cooking for 10 minutes and season with salt andpepper.
9. Slice the pork and serve with the creamsauce.

Nutritional Value Per Serving:

Calories 688, Carbohydrates 23 g, Fats 40 g, Protein 59 g

Hoisin Glazed Pork Tenderloin

Prep time: 20 minutes, Cook time: 3 hours, Serves: 3

Ingredients

- 1-piece pork tenderloin, trimmed
- 1 teaspoon kosher salt
- ½ teaspoon freshly ground black pepper
- 3 tablespoons hoisin sauce

Instructions:

1. Prepare the Sous Vide water bath using your immersion circulator and raisethe temperature to 145°F.
2. Takethe tenderloins and season it with pepper and saltand transfer to aresealable zip bag.
3. Seal using the immersion method and cook for 3 hours.
4. Remove the bag and then the pork, brush with hoisinsauce.
5. Heat up your grill to high grill and add the tenderloin, sear for 5 minutes until all sides are caramelized.
6. Allow it to rest and slice the tenderloin into medallions,serve!

Nutritional Value Per Serving:

Calories 283, Carbohydrates 13 g, Fats 11 g, Protein 33 g

Smoked Sausage & Cabbage

Ingredients

- ½ head green cabbage, cored, thinly sliced
- 1 Granny smith apple, peeled and cored, cut up into small dices
- 24 oz. red potatoes cut up into quarters and into ¼ inch thick wedges 1
- small onion thinly sliced
- ¼ teaspoon celery salt
- 2 tablespoons cider vinegar
- 2 tablespoons packed brown sugar
- Salt and black pepper, as needed
- 1-pound precooked smoked pork sausage sliced up into 4 portions with eachportion sliced into half lengthwise
- ½ cup chicken broth
- 2 tablespoons unsalted butter

Instructions:

1. Prepare the Sous Vide water bath using your immersion circulator and raisethe temperature to 185°F.
2. Take a large bowl and add the cabbage, potatoes, onion, apple, cider vinegar,brown sugar, and celery salt. Season with salt andpepper
3. Divide the mixture and sausage among 2 resealable zip bags and add ¼ cup ofchicken broth to each bag.
4. Seal using the immersion method and cook for 2hours.
5. Take a skillet and place it over medium-high heat and add 1 tablespoon of butter, heatit up and add the bag contents to theskillet.
6. Bring it to a boil and reduce the heat, cook until the liquid evaporates. It shouldtake about 5-6 minutes for the onion, potatoes, cabbage to bebrowned.
7. Transferto a serving platter and repeat the process with the remaining cabbage-sausage mix.
8. Serve!

Nutritional Value Per Serving:

Calories 516, Carbohydrates 39 g, Fats 32 g, Protein 18 g

Boneless Pork Ribs

Prep time: 30 minutes, Cook time: 8 hours, Serves: 4

Ingredients

- 1/3 cup unsweetened coconut milk
- 2 tablespoons peanut butter
- 2 tablespoons soy sauce
- 2 tablespoons light brown sugar
- 2 tablespoons dry white wine
- 2-inch fresh lemongrass
- 1 tablespoon Srirachasauce
- 1-inch peeled fresh ginger 2
- garlic cloves
- 2 teaspoons sesame oil
- 12 oz. boneless country style pork ribs
- Chopped up fresh cilantro and steamed basmati rice for serving

Instructions:

1. Preparethe Sous Videwater bath usingyour immersion circulatorand increase the temperature to 134°F.
2. Add the coconut milk, peanut butter, soy sauce, brown sugar, wine, lemongrass,ginger, Sriracha sauce, sesame oil and garlic to a blender, blend untilsmooth.
3. Add the ribs to aresealable zip bag alongside the sauce and seal using theimmersion method. Cook for 8 hours.
4. Once done, remove the bag and take the ribs out from the bag, transfer toplate.
5. Pour the bag contents to a large skillet and place it over medium-high heat, bring toa boil and lower heat to medium-low. Simmer for 10-15minutes.
6. Then, add the ribs to the sauce and turn well to coatit.
7. Simmer for 5minutes.
8. Garnish with fresh cilantro and serve with therice!

Nutritional Value Per Serving:

Calories 839, Carbohydrates 24 g, Fats 59 g, Protein 53 g

Coffee-Chili Pork Porterhouse

Prep time: 20 minutes, Cook time: 2 hours 30 minutes, Serves: 4

Ingredients

- 2 pieces bone-in pork porterhouse
- 1 tablespoon ancho chilis powder
- 1 tablespoon ground coffee
- 1 tablespoon light brown sugar
- 1 tablespoon garlic salt
- 1 tablespoon extra-virgin olive oil

Instructions:

1. Prepare your Sous Vide water bath using your immersion circulator and increase the temperature to 145°F.
2. Add the pork to a resealable bag and seal using the immersion method. Cook for 2½ hours.
3. Make your seasoning mixture by adding the chili powder, coffee, brown sugar,and garlic salt to a small bowl.
4. Remove the bag. Then take the pork out from the bag, pat it dry using kitchentowel.
5. Rub the chop with seasoning.
6. Take a cast iron skillet and put it over high heat and add the olive oil and sear theport for 1-2 minutes per side.
7. Once done, transfer the pork to a cutting board and allow it to rest for 5 minutes, slice and serve!

Nutritional Value Per Serving:

Calories 807, Carbohydrates 4 g, Fats 63 g, Protein 56 g

Balsamic Glazed Pork Rib Chop

Prep time: 20 minutes, Cook time: 3 hours, Serves: 2

Ingredients

- 1-piece bone-in pork chop
- Kosher salt and black pepper
- 1 tablespoon extra-virgin olive oil
- 4 tablespoons aged balsamic vinegar

Instructions:

1. Prepare your Sous Vide water bath using your immersion circulator and increase the temperature to 145°F.
2. Take the pork and carefully season it with pepper and salt, transfer to a resealable zipper bag and seal using the immersion method.
3. Cook for 3 hours and remove the bag from the water bath and then the pork and patit dry.
4. Take a sauté pan and place it over high heat for 5 minutes, add the olive oil andthe pork chops.
5. Sear until browned on both sides.
6. Add 3 tablespoons of balsamic vinegar to the skillet and bring to a rapid simmer,keep simmer while spooning the vinegar over the chop. Keep repeating for 1minute.
7. Once done, transfer the dish to your serving plate and serve it with the rest ofthe balsamic.

Nutritional Value Per Serving:

Calories 533, Carbohydrates 45 g, Fats 29 g, Protein 23 g

Siu-Style Chinese Baby Back Ribs

Prep time: 30 minutes, Cook time: 4 hours, Serves: 6

Ingredients

- 1/3 cup hoisin sauce
- 1/3 cup dark soy sauce
- 1/3 cup granulated sugar
- 3 tablespoons honey
- 3 tablespoons sherry vinegar
- 1 tablespoon fermented beanpaste
- 2 teaspoons sesame oil
- 2 crushed garlic cloves
- 1-inch piece fresh grated ginger
- 1 ½ teaspoon five spice powder
- ½ teaspoon salt
- ½ teaspoon white pepper
- ½ teaspoon fresh ground black pepper
- 3 lbs. baby back ribs with the membraneremoved
- Cilantro leaves forgarnishing

Instructions:

1. Prepare the Sous Vide water bath using your immersion circulator and raisethe temperature to 167°F.
2. Take a large bowl and add the hoisin sauce, dark soy sauce, sugar, sherry vinegar, honey, bean paste, sesame oil, garlic, five spice powder, salt, ginger, white pepper,and black pepper.
3. Take a small-sized bowl and add 1/3 cup of the marinade, chill for lateruse.
4. Add the ribs to the remaining marinade and mix well to coat theribs.
5. Divide the mixture among 3 large resealable bags and seal using theimmersion method. Cook for 4 hours.
6. Heatup the grill to 400°F and transfer the ribs to the grill, brush with the reserved marinade and cook for 3 minutes.
7. Flip them up and brush with more marinade, cook for another 3minutes.
8. Transferthe dish to the cutting board and allow it to rest for 5 minutes, slice the rack into ribs and garnish with cilantro leaves. Serve!

Nutritional Value Per Serving:

Calories 1033, Carbohydrates 33 g, Fats 77 g, Protein 52 g

Sous Vide Pork Shoulder

Prep time: 10 minutes, Cook time: 12 hours, Serves: 6

Ingredients:

- 1 pork shoulder, around 2 ½ pounds.
- 1 tbsp, brown sugar
- 1 tsp, garlicpowder
- 1 tbsp, paprika
- 2 pieces, star anise
- 2 tablespoons olive oil
- 2 pinches cumin
- 2 pinches salt

Instructions:

1. Prepareyour Sous Vide waterbath by placing the immersion circulatorand setting the temperature to 160°F.
2. Season the pork shoulder with all the dry seasonings and salt and place with theolive oil in the bag.
3. Submergeinto the water bath and let cook for 12 hours (if water evaporates, replace with new water).
4. Take the pork shoulder and shred/tear it apart with the help of a big fork and aknife.
5. Keep the pork shoulder for sandwiches, tacos, or any other combo you wish for up to3 days (in the fridge).

Nutritional Value Per Serving:

Calories 246, Carbohydrates 5.2 g, Fats 6. 4 g, Protein 41. 8 g

Mediterranean Style Pork

Prep time: 5 minutes, Cook time: 6 hours, Serves: 5

Ingredients:

- 1 pork loin, cut into cubes
- ½ cup, white wine
- 1 medium tomato, cubed
- 1 carrot, sliced
- 1 red onion, thickly chopped
- 2 tablespoons olive oil
- 2 sprigs, fresh rosemary
- 1 can, cooked white beans, drained
- Salt/Pepper

Instructions:

1. Prepare your Sous Vide water bath by attaching immersion circulator and setting the temperature to 140°F.
2. In a deep-frying pan, heat the olive oil and sauté the pork cubes with the carrots, onion, and garlic for 3-4 minutes. Season with salt and pepper.
3. Place the pork cubes with all the ingredients (except for the cooked white beans) in the bag. Seal using a vacuum sealer or the water displacement method.
4. Let cook in the bath of water for 6 hours.
5. Remove everything from the bag and serve over the cooked white beans with a bit of olive oil and parsley (optionally) on the top.

Nutritional Value Per Serving:

Calories 380, Carbohydrates 6. 8 g, Fats 17 g, Protein 50.1 g

Chapter 6: Fish & Seafood

Garlic & Herbs Cod

Prep time: 10 minutes, Cook time: 30 minutes, Serves: 2

Ingredients:

- 2 medium cod fillets
- 2 garlic cloves, minced
- 1 tbsp fresh rosemary, chopped
- 1 tbsp fresh thyme, chopped
- 2 tbsp unsalted butter
- 1 tbsp olive oil
- Juice of 1 lemon
- Salt and pepper to taste

Instructions:

1. Preheat the water bath to 135°F.
2. Rub the cod fillets with salt and pepper, and put them into the vacuum bag adding rosemary, thyme, butter, minced garlic and lemon juice.
3. Seal the bag and set the timer for 30 minutes.
4. When the time is up, sear the fish in a cast iron skillet in 1 tbsp olive oil on both sides and serve over white rice.

Nutritional Value Per Serving:

Calories 200, Carbohydrates 18 g, Fats 8 g, Protein 22 g

Coconut Cream Sea Bass

Prep time: 10 minutes, Cook time: 30 minutes, Serves: 2

Ingredients:

For the fish

- 2 medium cod fillets
- 2 tbsp coconut milk
- Salt and pepper to taste

For the sauce

- ½ cup coconut milk
- ½ cup chicken broth
- ½ tsp white sugar
- 1 tsp lime juice
- 2 slices ginger root
- Chopped cilantro for serving

Instructions:

1. Preheat the water bath to 135°F.
2. Rub the sea bass fillets with salt, pepper, and coconut milk and put them intothe vacuum bag.
3. Seal the bag and set the timer for 30minutes.
4. While the fish is cooking, make thesauce.
5. Combine the chicken broth and coconut milk in a pan, and simmer for about 10minutes over the medium heat.
6. Add the lime juice, sugar and ginger root, mix well and take the sauce off theheat. Close the pan with the lid and set aside for a couple ofminutes.
7. Put the fish in bowls, pour the sauce over and serve topped with the freshlychopped cilantro.

Nutritional Value Per Serving:

Calories 339, Carbohydrates 28g, Fats 15 g, Protein 23 g

Thai Tom Yum Fish

Prep time: 10 minutes, Cook time: 30 minutes, Serves: 2

Ingredients:

- 2 medium fish fillets
- 2 tbsp Tom Yum paste
- Fresh cilantro for serving
- 1 tbsp lime juice for serving

Instructions:

1. Preheat the water bath to 135°F.
2. Rub the fillets with the Tom Yum paste, and put them into the vacuumbag.
3. Seal the bag and set the timer for 30minutes.
4. Serve over white rice sprinkled with lime juice and topped with freshlychopped cilantro.

Nutritional Value Per Serving:

Calories 181, Carbohydrates 14 g, Fats 5 g, Protein 20 g

Butter Shrimps

Prep time: 10 minutes, Cook time: 25 minutes, Serves: 4

Ingredients:

- 16 shrimps, peeled and deveined
- 1 shallot, minced
- 1 tbsp unsalted butter, melted
- 2 tsp thyme
- 1 tsp lemon zest, grated

Instructions:

1. Preheat your cooking machine to 125°F.
2. Put all ingredients in the vacuum bag.
3. Seal the bag, put it into the water bath and set the timer for 25 minutes.
4. Serve immediately as an appetizer or tossed with penne pasta.

Nutritional Value Per Serving:

Calories 257, Carbohydrates 23 g, Fats 5 g, Protein 30 g

Garlic Shrimps

Prep time: 10 minutes, Cook time: 25 minutes, Serves: 4

Ingredients:

- 16 shrimps, peeled and deveined
- 1 shallot, minced
- 1 tbsp unsalted butter, melted
- 2 garlic cloves, minced

Instructions:

1. Preheat your cooking machine to 125°F.
2. Put all ingredients in the vacuum bag.
3. Seal the bag, put it into the water bath and set the timer for 25minutes.
4. Serve immediately as an appetizer or tossed with penne pasta.

Nutritional Value Per Serving:

Calories 153, Carbohydrates 9 g, Fats 1 g, Protein 27 g

Shrimps Cajun

Prep time: 10 minutes, Cook time: 25 minutes, Serves: 4

Ingredients:

- 16 shrimps, peeled and deveined
- 1 shallot, minced
- 1 tbsp unsalted butter, melted
- 1 tbsp Cajun seasoning
- 2 garlic cloves, minced
- 1 tbsp lemon juice
- Freshly ground black pepper to taste
- 4 tbsp freshly chopped parsley

Instructions:

1. Preheat your cooking machine to 125°F.
2. Put all ingredients except parsley into the vacuumbag.
3. Seal the bag, put it into the water bath and set the timer for 25minutes.
4. Serve immediately as an appetizer garnished with the choppedparsley.

Nutritional Value Per Serving:

Calories 167, Carbohydrates 8 g, Fats 7 g, Protein 18 g

Oriental Shrimp Salad

Prep time: 10 minutes, Cook time: 25 minutes, Serves: 4

Ingredients:

For the shrimps

- 16 shrimps, peeled and deveined
- 1 tbsp coconut oil
- 2 garlic cloves, minced
- Salt and pepper to taste

For the salad

- ½ cup sliced shallot
- ½ cup chopped parsley
- For the dressing
- ½ cup mayo
- 4 tbsp lime juice
- 1 tsp ginger powder
- 1 tsp curry powder

Instructions:

1. Preheat your cooking machine to 125°F.
2. Put shrimp ingredients into the vacuum bag.
3. Seal the bag, put it into the water bath and set the timer for 25minutes.
4. In the meantime, cook the dressing. Whisk the dressing ingredients together in abowl.
5. When the shrimps are ready, let them cool down and mix in the dressing,chopped parsley and sliced shallot.

Nutritional Value Per Serving:

Calories 357, Carbohydrates 37 g, Fats 13 g, Protein 23 g

Butter Scallops

Prep time: 10 minutes, Cook time: 30 minutes, Serves: 4

Ingredients:

- 16 scallops
- Salt and pepper to taste
- 1 tbsp olive oil
- 1 tbsp butter
- Sous Vide Hollandaise sauce

Instructions:

1. Preheat your cooking machine to 125°F.
2. Remove the muscles from scallops and sprinkle them with salt andpepper.
3. Put the scallops into the vacuum bag, add oliveoil.
4. Seal the bag, put it into the water bath and set the timer for 30minutes.
5. When the scallops are ready, dry them with a paper towel and sear in 1 tbsp butter until golden on both sides.
6. Serve with hollandaise sauce.

Nutritional Value Per Serving:

Calories 213, Carbohydrates 26 g, Fats 9 g, Protein 7 g

Shrimp Penne

Prep time: 10 minutes, Cook time: 25 minutes, Serves: 4

Ingredients:

- 16 shrimps, peeled and deveined
- 1 tbsp lemon zest
- 3 tbsp lemon juice
- Salt and pepper to taste
- 2 tbsp butter
- Cooked penne pasta for 4 persons

Instructions:

1. Preheat your cooking machine to 125°F.
2. Put the shrimps into the vacuum bag, add butter and salt and pepper totaste.
3. Seal the bag, put it into the water bath and set the timer for 25minutes.
4. Carefully pour the cooked shrimps together with all cooking liquid into a mediumpot.
5. Add the lemon juice, lemon zest and 2 cups dry white wine to thepot.
6. Simmer the mixture until it thickens, pour the sauce over the cooked penne andserve.

Nutritional Value Per Serving:

Calories 449, Carbohydrates 55 g, Fats 17 g, Protein 19 g

Lobster Provencal

Prep time: 10 minutes, Cook time: 1 hour, Serves: 4

Ingredients:

- 4 lobster tails
- 10 tbsp butter
- 2 tbsp Provencal herbs
- Salt and pepper to taste
- 4 tbsp lemon juice for serving

Instructions:

1. Preheat your cooking machine to 135°F.
2. Remove the shell from the lobster tails; sprinkle them with salt and pepper, season evenly with herbs.
3. Put the tails into the vacuum bag, add butter and seal thebag.
4. Set the timer for 1 hour.
5. Drizzle the cooked lobster tails with the cooking liquid, sprinkle each with 1 tbsp lemon juice and serve.

Nutritional Value Per Serving:

Calories 260, Carbohydrates 8 g, Fats 16 g, Protein 21 g

Blue Cheese Lobster Tails

Prep time: 10 minutes, Cook time: 1 hour, Serves: 4

Ingredients:

- 4 lobster tails, shells removed
- 10 tbsp butter
- Salt and pepper to taste
- Sous Vide Blue Cheese sauce for serving

Instructions:

1. Preheat your cooking machine to 135°F.
2. Sprinkle the lobster tails with salt and pepper.
3. Put the tails into the vacuum bag and add the butter.
4. Seal the bag and set the timer for 1 hour.
5. Drizzle the cooked lobster tails with the cooking liquid and serve with Sous Vide Blue Cheese sauce.

Nutritional Value Per Serving:

Calories 240, Carbohydrates 10 g, Fats 12 g, Protein 23 g

Lobster Roll

Prep time: 10 minutes, Cook time: 1 hour, Serves: 4

Ingredients:

- 2 lobster tails, shells removed
- 2 tbsp butter
- Salt and pepper to taste
- 4 tbsp mayo
- 1 tbsp lemon juice
- 4 big salad leaves
- 4 hot dog buns

Instructions:

1. Preheat your cooking machine to 135°F.
2. Sprinkle the lobster tails with salt and pepper.
3. Put the tails into the vacuum bag and add the butter.
4. Seal the bag and set the timer for 1 hour.
5. When the time is up, carefully removing the cooked lobster tails, let them cool down a bit and chop them into bite-size pieces.
6. Mix the lobster pieces with mayo, sprinkle with lemon juice.
7. Put 1 big salad leave into each hot dog bun, lay the lobster mayo mixture on each leave and serve.

Nutritional Value Per Serving:

Calories 196, Carbohydrates 6 g, Fats 8 g, Protein 25 g

Lobster Cajun Spaghetti

Prep time: 10 minutes, Cook time: 25 minutes, Serves: 4

Ingredients:

- 2 lobster tails, shellremoved
- 1 shallot, minced
- 1 tbsp unsalted butter,melted
- 1 tbsp Cajun seasoning
- 2 garlic cloves, minced
- 4 tbsp lemon juice
- 1 tbsp lemon zest
- Salt and pepper to taste
- 2 cups dry white wine
- 4 tbsp freshly chopped parsley
- Cooked spaghetti

Instructions:

1. Preheat your cooking machine to 135°F.
2. Season the lobster tails with Cajun, salt and pepper, and put into the vacuum bag.Add shallots and butter.
3. Seal the bag, put it into the water bath and set the timer for 1hour.
4. Carefully chop the cooked lobster tails into bite-size pieces and pour them together with all cooking liquid into a medium pot.
5. Add the lemon juice, lemon zest and 2 cups dry white wine to thepot.
6. Simmer the mixture until it thickens, pour the sauce over the cooked penne andserve with chopped fresh parsley.

Nutritional Value Per Serving:

Calories 449, Carbohydrates 55 g, Fats 17 g, Protein 19 g

Aromatic Shrimps

Prep time: 10 minutes, Cook time: 30 minutes, Serves: 2

Ingredients:

- 1-pound large shrimps, peeled and deveined
- 1 tsp olive oil
- Any aromatics of your choice
- Salt to taste
- 2 tbsp lemon juice

Instructions:

1. Preheat your cooking machine to 125°F.
2. Season the shrimps with salt and put into the vacuumbag.
3. Add 1 tsp olive oil and aromatics.
4. Seal the bag, put it into the water bath and set the timer for 30minutes.
5. Serve with any sauce of your choice or sprinkled with lemonjuice.

Nutritional Value Per Serving:

Calories 153, Carbohydrates 9 g, Fats 1 g, Protein 27 g

Drunken Mussels

Prep time: 10 minutes, Cook time: 15 minutes, Serves: 2

Ingredients:

- 2 pounds mussels in their shells
- 1 cup dry white wine
- 2 garlic cloves, chopped
- 4 tbsp butter
- Salt to taste

Instructions:

1. Preheat your cooking machine to 194°F.
2. Season the mussels with salt and put into the vacuumbag.
3. Reduce the air in the bag to 30% (70% of vacuum) otherwise the shell won'topen.
4. Add dry white wine, garlic cloves andbutter
5. Seal the bag, put it into the water bath and set the timer for 15minutes.
6. Serve sprinkled with lemon juice.

Nutritional Value Per Serving:

Calories 369, Carbohydrates 18 g, Fats 25 g, Protein 18 g

Garlic Squid

Prep time: 10 minutes, Cook time: 2 hours, Serves: 4

Ingredients:

- 4 small clean squids
- 2 garlic cloves, chopped
- 2 tbsp olive oil
- Salt and pepper to taste

Instructions:

1. Preheat your cooking machine to 140°F.
2. Season the squid with salt and put into the vacuumbag.
3. Add olive oil and chopped garlic
4. Seal the bag, put it into the water bath and cook for 2hours.
5. Serve sprinkled with lemon juice.

Nutritional Value Per Serving:

Calories 171, Carbohydrates 8 g, Fats 7 g, Protein 19 g

Hong Kong Style Squid with Teriyaki Sauce

Prep time: 10 minutes, Cook time: 2 hours, Serves: 4

Ingredients:

- 4 small clean squids
- 2 garlic cloves, chopped
- 4 tbsp olive oil
- 4 tbsp Teriyaki sauce
- 1 tbsp sesame seeds
- Salt and pepper to taste

Instructions:

1. Preheat your cooking machine to 140°F.
2. Season the squid with salt and put into the vacuum bag.
3. Add 2 tbsp olive oil and chopped garlic
4. Seal the bag, put it into the water bath and cook for 2 hours.
5. Preheat 2 tbsp olive oil in the skillet, pour the Teriyaki sauce and sear the squids on medium to high heat from both sides until brown.
6. Serve sprinkled with sesame seeds.

Nutritional Value Per Serving:

Calories 171, Carbohydrates 8 g, Fats 7 g, Protein 19 g

Seafood Mix with Tomato, Wine and Parsley

Prep time: 10 minutes, Cook time: 2 hours, Serves: 4

Ingredients:

- 2 pounds seafood mix, thawed
- 1 cup tomatoes in own juice, diced
- ½ cup dry white wine
- 1 bay leaf
- 1 tsp dried oregano
- 2 garlic cloves, minced
- 2 tbsp olive oil
- Salt and pepper to taste
- Lemon juice for sprinkling
- Chopped parsley for sprinkling

Instructions:

1. Preheat your cooking machine to 140°F.
2. Sprinkle the thawed seafood mix with salt and pepper and put it into the vacuumbag adding tomatoes, bay leaf, dried oregano, garlic, olive oil and whitewine.
3. Seal the bag, put it into the water bath and cook for 2hours.
4. Serve over rice sprinkled with freshly chopped parsley and lemonjuice.

Nutritional Value Per Serving:

Calories 369, Carbohydrates 18 g, Fats 25 g, Protein 18 g

Poached Halibut

Prep time: 10 minutes, Cook time: 30 minutes, Serves: 2

Ingredients:

- 2 5oz. halibut fillets
- 1/3 cup sea salt
- 1/3 cup sugar
- ¼ cup Vin Jaune

Sauce:

- ½ cup Vin Jaune
- ¾ cup chicken stock
- 1 cup unsalted butter
- 2 tablespoon chopped chives
- Salt, to taste

Instructions:

1. Preheat Sous Vide cooker to 132ºF.
2. Sprinkle the fish fillets with salt and sugar. Place asideminutes.
3. Place the halibut fillets into separate Sous Vide bags. Add VinJaune.
4. Vacuum seal the bags and submerge in water.
5. Cook the fish 30 minutes.
6. Make the sauce; simmer Vin Jaune and chicken stock in a saucepan until reducedby half.
7. Add the butter and whisk until sauce-like consistency. Season totaste.
8. Remove the fish from the bags and arrange on aplate.
9. Drizzle with sauce and sprinkle withchives.
10. Serve.

Nutritional Value Per Serving:

Calories 684, Carbohydrates 33.8 g, Fats 47.5 g, Protein 30.2 g

Asian Style Salmon

Prep time: 10 minutes, Cook time: 30 minutes, Serves: 4

Ingredients:

- 4 5oz. salmon fillets
- 2 tablespoons rice wine
- 2 tablespoons sweet rice wine
- 2 tablespoons miso paste
- 1 tablespoon Sriracha
- 2 tablespoon unsaltedbutter
- 1 tablespoon vegetableoil
- 2 spring onions, chopped
- 1 tablespoon toasted sesame seeds

Instructions:

1. Preheat Sous Vide cooker to 105°F.
2. Combine rice wine, sweet rice wine, miso paste, Sriracha, and butter in abowl.
3. Spread the miso paste oversalmon.
4. Place the salmon into Souse Vide bags and vacuumseal.
5. Submerge in water and cook 30minutes.
6. Remove the salmon frombag.
7. Heat vegetable oil in a largeskillet.
8. Sear salmon on both sides, 1 minute perside.
9. Serve on a plate. Top with chopped spring onion and sesameseeds.

Nutritional Value Per Serving:

Calories 396, Carbohydrates 9.2 g, Fats 29.1 g, Protein 24.4 g

Perfect Scallops in Citrus Sauce

Prep time: 15 minutes, Cook time: 30 minutes, Serves: 4

Ingredients:

- 2lb. scallops, cleaned
- 2 lemons, 1 quartered, 1 zested and juiced
- 2 tablespoons ghee
- 2 shallots, chopped
- ¼ cup pink grapefruit juice
- ¼ cup orange juice
- 2 tablespoons acacia honey
- Salt and pepper, to taste

Instructions:

1. Preheat Souse Vide cooker to 122°F.
2. Rinse scallops and drain.
3. Season scallops with salt and pepper. Divide scallops between two Sous Videbags.
4. Place 2 quarters lemon in each bag and vacuum seal.
5. Cook the scallops 30 minutes.
6. Make the sauce; heat ghee in asaucepan.
7. Add the chopped shallots and cook until tender 4minutes.
8. Remove the scallops from the bag and sear on both sides in a lightly greasedskillet.
9. Remove the scallops from the skillet.
10. Deglaze the pan with orange juice. Pour in pink grapefruit juice and lemonjuice.
11. Add shallots and lemon zest. Simmer until half reduces the sauce. Stir in honey and simmer until thickened.
12. Serve scallops with sauce.

Nutritional Value Per Serving:

Calories 275, Carbohydrates 11.7 g, Fats 8.2 g, Protein 38.7 g

Haddock on Vegetable

Prep time: 10 minutes, Cook time: 1 hour 10 minutes, Serves: 4

Ingredients:

- 4 6oz. haddock fillets

Marinade:

- 1 pinch curry
- 1 pinch brown sugar
- 1 pinch fine sea salt
- 5 tablespoons olive oil
- 1 sprig thyme, chopped
- 1 teaspoon lemon juice

Vegetables:

- 1 pinch chili powder
- 1 cucumber
- 3 carrots
- 1 leek, chopped
- 1 tablespoon olive oil
- 3 bell peppers, red, yellow, andgreen
- 1 sweet potato
- Salt, and pepper, to taste

Instructions:

1. Preheat Sous Vide cooker to 130°F.
2. In a Sous Vide bag combine marinadeingredients.
3. Add haddock fillets and shake to coat thefish.
4. Vacuum seal the bag and cook 30minutes.
5. In a separate Sous Vide bag, combine all vegetables, with seasonings, and oliveoil. Vacuum seal the bag and cook the veggies in Sous Vide at 185F40
6. minutes.
7. Open the bagscarefully.
8. Heat some olive oil in a large skillet. Cook the fish fillets 2 minutes perside.
9. Serve fish with vegetables.

Nutritional Value Per Serving:

Calories 359, Carbohydrates 23.2 g, Fats 19 g, Protein 23.7 g

Teriyaki Salmon

Prep time: 10 minutes, Cook time: 15 minutes, Serves: 2

Ingredients:

- ½ cup plus 1 teaspoon teriyaki sauce
- 2 skinless salmon fillets
- 4 oz. Chinese egg noodles
- 1 tablespoon sesame oil
- 2 teaspoons soy sauce
- 2 teaspoons thinly sliced scallions, plus 4 pieces scallion greens, for serving
- 1-inch fresh ginger, peeled and sliced into thin strips
- 4 oz. lettuce, chopped
- 1/8 small red onion, thinly sliced
- 1 tablespoon Japanese roasted sesamedressing
- 1 tablespoon sesame seeds, toasted

Instructions:

1. Divide ½ cup teriyaki sauce between 2 zip-lock bags.
2. Place 1 salmon fillet in each bag and seal bags using water immersionmethod.
3. Do not place salmon fillets, but place aside to marinate at room temperature for 15 minutes.
4. Meanwhile, set the Sous Vide precision cooker to 131°F.
5. Place the bags in a water bath and cook for 15minutes.
6. While salmon is cooking, prepare egg noodles according to packageinstructions.
7. Drain well, return to cooking pot and stir in sesame oil and soy sauce, reservingone teaspoon
8. Divide pasta between serving plates.
9. Prepare the dipping sauce; combine scallions, ginger, remaining teriyaki sauce and one teaspoon soy sauce.
10. Also, prepare the salad by combining lettuce and onion with one tablespoonroasted sesame dressing.
11. When the timer goes off, remove salmon from the water bath, reserving cookingliquid.
12. Top the pasta with salmon fillets and drizzle all with reserved cookingliquid.
13. Garnish salmon with sesame seeds and serve with prepared salad and dippingsauce.

Nutritional Value Per Serving:

Calories 294, Carbohydrates 15.2 g, Fats 11.2 g, Protein 33 g

Sole Fish with Bacon

Prep time: 10 minutes, Cook time: 25 minutes, Serves: 2

Ingredients:

- 2 5oz. sole fish fillets
- 2 tablespoons olive oil
- 2 slices bacon
- ½ tablespoon lemon juice
- Salt and pepper, to taste

Instructions:

1. Preheat Sous Vide cooker to 132°F.
2. Cook the bacon in a non-stick skillet and cook bacon untilcrispy.
3. Remove the bacon and placeaside.
4. Season fish fillets with salt, pepper, and lemon juice. Brush the fish with oliveoil.
5. Place the fish in a Sous Vide bag. Top the fish with the bacon. Vacuum seal thebag.
6. Submerge in a water bath and cook 25 minutes.
7. Remove the fish from thebag.
8. Serve while warm.

Nutritional Value Per Serving:

Calories 297, Carbohydrates 0.4 g, Fats 22.9 g, Protein 22.4 g

Crusted Tuna Fish

Prep time: 10 minutes, Cook time: 25 minutes, Serves: 4

Ingredients:

- 3 tablespoons all-purposeflour
- 3 tablespoons groundalmonds
- ½ tablespoon butter
- 4 5oz. tuna fillets

Marinade:

- 1 pinch chili powder
- 1 pinch salt
- 1 pinch black pepper
- 5 tablespoons vegetable oil
- 2 teaspoons lemon juice

Instructions:

1. Preheat Sous Vide cooker to132°F.
2. Combine the marinade ingredients in a Sous Videbag.
3. Add the tuna and vacuumseal.
4. Submerge in a water bath and cook 25minutes.
5. Remove the fish from Sous vide bag. Pat dry thefish.
6. In a bowl, combine all-purpose flour and almonds. Sprinkle with a pinch ofsalt.
7. Heat the butter in a largeskillet.
8. Coat the tuna with the flour-nut mixture and fry in butter until goldenbrown.
9. Servewarm.

NutritionalValuePerServing:

Calories 182, Carbohydrates 5.4 g, Fats 15.2 g, Protein 5.9 g

Crab Zucchini Roulade with Mousse

Prep time: 30 minutes, Cook time: 10 minutes, Serves: 4

Ingredients:

- 3lb. crab legs and claws
- 2 tablespoons olive oil
- 1 medium zucchini
- Salt and pepper, to taste

Mousse:

- 1 avocado, peeled, pitted
- 1 tablespoon Worcestershiresauce
- 2 tablespoons crèmeFraiche
- 2 tablespoons fresh limejuice
- Salt, to taste

Instructions:

1. Preheat Sous vide cooker to185°F.
2. Place the claws and legs in a Sous Vide bag and vacuumseal.
3. Submerge the bag with content in a water bath. Cook the crab 10minutes.
4. Slice the zucchini with a vegetable peeler. This way you will have some skinnystrips.
5. Remove the crab from the water bath and crack theshell.
6. Flake the meat and transfer into a bowl. Add olive oil, salt, and pepper, and stir tobind gently.
7. Make the mousse; in a food blender, blend the avocado and crème Fraicheuntil smooth.
8. Stir in the remaining ingredients and spoon the mixture into pipingbag.
9. Arrange the zucchini slices on aluminum foil and fill with the crabmeat.
10. Roll up the zucchinis and crab into a log and refrigerate 30minutes.
11. To serve; cut the roulade into four pieces. Serve onto a plate with someavocado mousse.
12. Enjoy.

Nutritional Value Per Serving:

Calories 322, Carbohydrates 1.6 g, Fats 13.1 g, Protein 49.3 g

Herbed Prawns

Prep time: 20 minutes, Cook time: 25 minutes, Serves: 4

Ingredients:

Prawns:

- 12 large prawns, cleaned
- 3 tablespoons olive oil
- 1 cup basil, chopped
- ½ cup parsley, chopped
- ½ cup dill, chopped
- 1 large organic lemon, sliced
- 2 chili peppers, seeded, chopped

Pasta:

- 1 cup pine nuts
- ¾ cup basil
- ¾ cup parsley
- ¼ cup dill
- ½ cup olive oil
- 2 cloves garlic
- Salt and pepper, to taste
- 1lb. spaghetti, cooked

Instructions:

1. Preheat Sous Vide cooker to 134°F.
2. In a bowl, combine all ingredients. Toss to coat the prawns with olive oil andherbs.
3. Transfer the coated prawns into Sous Vide cooking bag, and top with lemonslices. Vacuum seal thebag.
4. Submerge the prawns into a water bath and cook the prawns 25minutes.
5. While the prawns are cooking, make the pesto. In a food blender, blend pine nuts,basil, parsley, dill, and garlic until just smooth. Set the blender to run on low and stream in the oil. Mix 2 minutes.
6. Toss the spaghetti withpesto.
7. Open the bag and spread the prawns over thespaghetti.
8. Serve.

Nutritional Value Per Serving:

Calories 201, Carbohydrates 6.5 g, Fats 12 g, Protein 16.8 g

Coriander-Garlic Squids

Prep time: 20 minutes, Cook time: 2 hours, Serves: 4

Ingredients:

- 4 4oz. squids, cleaned
- ¼ cup olive oil
- ¼ cup chopped coriander
- 4 cloves garlic,minced
- 2 chili pepper,chopped
- 2 teaspoons minced ginger
- ¼ cup vegetable oil
- 1 lemon, cut into wedges
- Salt and pepper, to taste

Instructions:

1. Set the Sous vide cooker to 136°F.
2. Place the squids and 2 tablespoons olive oil in a Sous Vide bags. Season to tasteand vacuum seal thebag.
3. Submerge in water and cook 2 hours.
4. Heat remaining olive oil in a skillet. Add garlic, chili pepper, and ginger and cook1 minute. Add half the coriander and stir well. Remove from theheat.
5. Remove the squids from thebag.
6. Heat vegetable oil in a skillet, until sizzling hot. Add the squid and cook 30 secondsper side.
7. Transferthe squidsonto aplate. Top with garlic-coriandermixtureand sprinkle with the remaining coriander.
8. Serve with lemon.

Nutritional Value Per Serving:

Calories 351, Carbohydrates 6.7 g, Fats 27.9 g, Protein 18.2 g

Slow Cooker Shellfish

Prep time: 30 minutes, Cook time: 1 hour, Serves: 2

Ingredients

- 4 oz. canned snails
- ¼ cup dry white wine
- 1 diced celery stalk
- 1 diced carrot
- 1 quartered shallot
- 1 bay leaf
- 1 tablespoon black peppercorn
- 1 tablespoon extra-virgin oliveoil
- 8 tablespoons unsalted butter, roomtemperature 1
- tablespoon minced fresh parsley
- 2 garlic cloves, minced
- 2 teaspoons kosher salt
- ¼ cup panko breadcrumbs
- Sliced up baguette

Instructions:

1. Prepare your Sous-vide water bath to a temperature of154°F
2. Take a large-sized, heavy-duty resealable bag and add in the snails, shallots, celery, carrots, wine, peppercorns, olive oil, and bay leaf
3. Seal the bag using the immersion method, submerge it underwater and cook forabout 60 minutes
4. Take a stand mixer and add the butterin
5. Add the parsley, salt, garlic, and ground pepper and mix gently until all theingredients are finely mixed
6. Put the mixture to a plastic wrap and roll it into a smalllog
7. Compress the log, using the plastic wrap, and let it chill in thefridge
8. Once the snails are done, remove them from the bag and discard any cookingliquid alongside the vegetables
9. Set your broiler to highheat
10. Arrange your snails in a large-sized ramekin and slice the butter into thinrounds
11. Place the butter on top of yoursnails
12. Sprinkle some breadcrumbs over the butter and broil for about 3 minutes untilthe crumbs are done
13. Serve with some warmed baguetteslices!

Nutritional Value Per Serving:

Calories 256, Carbohydrates 2 g, Fats 24 g, Protein 8 g

Shrimp Salad

Prep time: 10 minutes, Cook time: 24 minutes, Serves: 4

Ingredients

- 1 chopped red onion
- Juice, 2 limes
- 1 teaspoon extra-virgin olive oil
- ¼ teaspoon sea salt
- ⅛ teaspoon white pepper
- 1 lb. raw shrimp, peeled, de-veined
- 1 diced tomato
- 1 diced avocado
- 1 jalapeno, seeded, diced
- 1 tablespoon chopped cilantro

Instructions:

1. Prepare your Sous-vide water bath to a temperature of148°F
2. Add the lime juice, red onion, sea salt, white pepper, extra virgin olive oil, white pepper and shrimp into your heavy-duty plastic bag
3. Seal the bag using the immersion method
4. Submerge the bag underwater and cook for 24minutes
5. Remove and chill the plastic bag in an ice bath for about 10minutes
6. Take a large-sized bowl and add the tomato, avocado, jalapeno and cilantro
7. Remove it from the bag and top it up with the salad.
8. Serve!

Nutritional Value Per Serving:

Calories 142, Carbohydrates 7 g, Fats 2 g, Protein 24 g

Moroccan Red Snapper

Prep time: 10 minutes, Cook time: 30 minutes, Serves: 4

Ingredients

- 4 pieces cleaned red snapper
- 2 tablespoons butter
- Salt and pepper as needed

For Citrus Sauce

- 1 lemon
- 1 grapefruit
- 1 lime
- 3 oranges
- 2 tablespoons canola oil
- 1 yellow onion
- 1 diced zucchini
- 1 teaspoon saffron threads
- 1 teaspoon diced chili pepper
- 1 tablespoon sugar
- 3 cups fish stock
- 3 tablespoons chopped cilantro

Instructions:

1. Prepare your Sous-vide water bath to a temperature of132°F
2. Season the snapper fillets with salt and pepper and transfer them to aheavy-duty Sous Vide zip bag.
3. Divide the butter equally between the bags if more than one bag is used. If not, addthe whole amount of butter to the singlebag
4. Seal using the immersion method and submerge underwater, cook for 30minutes
5. While the fish is being cooked, start preparing your sauce by peeling the fruitsand dicing up the flesh (make sure to remove thepith)
6. Take a large-sized pan and place it over medium-heat, add the oil and allow it to heat up
7. Add in the onion and zucchini and sauté for 2-3minutes
8. Add the saffron, fruits, diced pepper and sugar and cook for 1 moreminute
9. Add the fish stock and bring the mix to a boil, lower down the heat to low andsimmer for 10 minutes
10. Remove the heat and stir in cilantro, keep it on theside
11. Take the fish out from the bag and transfer them to your servingplatter
12. Spoon the fruity-saffron sauce over the top andserve

Nutritional Value Per Serving:

Calories 257, Carbohydrates 21 g, Fats 5 g, Protein 32 g

Shrimp & Leek

Prep time: 20 minutes, Cook time: 1 hour, Serves: 4

Ingredients

- 6 leeks
- 5 tablespoons extra-virgin olive oil
- Kosher salt
- Freshly ground black pepper
- 1 small-sized shallot, minced
- 1 tablespoon champagne vinegar
- 1 teaspoon Dijon mustard
- 1/3 lb. cooked bay shrimp
- Chopped fresh parsley for garnishing

Instructions:

1. Prepare your Sous-vide water bath to a temperature of 183°F
2. Cut off the top of your leeks and discard them
3. Trim the root ends of each leek and wash them in cold water
4. Brush the leek with 1 tablespoon of olive oil
5. Season with salt and put the leeks in a large-sized zipper bag and seal it using the immersion method
6. Submerge the bag underwater and cook for about 1 hour
7. To make the vinaigrette, take a small-sized bowl and whisk the shallot, Dijon mustard, vinegar and ¼ cup of olive oil all together. Season with some salt and pepper.
8. Once cooked, remove the bag from the water bath and transfer it to an ice bath. Chill the leeks
9. Divide the leeks between four plates and season them with salt
10. Top the leeks with the bay shrimp and spoon on some vinaigrette
11. Sprinkle with fresh parsley and serve!

Nutritional Value Per Serving:

Calories 142, Carbohydrates 7 g, Fats 2 g, Protein 24 g

Pumpkin Shrimp

Prep time: 10 minutes, Cook time: 35 minutes, Serves: 6

Ingredients

- 8 large raw shrimps, peeled, de-veined
- 1 tablespoon butter
- Salt and pepper
- For Soup
- 1 lb. pumpkin
- 4 tablespoons lime juice 2
- yellow onions,chopped
- 1-2 small red chilies, finely chopped
- 1 stem of lemon grass, white part only, chopped
- 1 teaspoon shrimp paste
- 1 teaspoon sugar
- 1½ cups coconut milk
- 1 teaspoon tamarind paste
- 1 cup water
- ½ cup coconut cream
- 1 tablespoon fish sauce
- 2 tablespoons fresh Thai basil, chopped

Instructions:

1. Prepare your Sous-vide water bath to a temperature of122°F
2. Add the shrimps into your Sous Vide bag with thebutter
3. Sprinkle salt and pepper in and seal the bag using the immersion method and cookfor 15-35 minutes
4. Peel the pumpkin and remove the seeds. Cut the flesh into 1-inchchunks
5. Add the onion, lemon grass, chili, shrimp paste, sugar and ½ the coconut milk intoa food processor. Mix them well
6. Add the onion puree, remaining coconut milk, tamarind paste and water into aseparate pot
7. Put the pumpkin to this pot and bring to aboil
8. Once the boiling point is reached, lower down the heat and simmer for 10minutes
9. Remove the shrimps from the bag and add them to thesoup
10. Add in the coconut cream, fish sauce, lime juice and basil, stir themwell.
11. Serve!

Nutritional Value Per Serving:

Calories 238, Carbohydrates 11 g, Fats 14 g, Protein 17 g

Miso Butter Cod

Prep time: 15 minutes, Cook time: 30 minutes, Serves: 2

Ingredients

- 1 large Atlantic Codfillet
- 2 tablespoons misopaste
- 1½ tablespoons brown sugar
- 2 tablespoons soy sauce
- 2 tablespoons mirin
- 2 tablespoons butter
- Sesame seeds forgarnishing

Instructions:

1. Prepare your Sous-vide water bath to a temperature of131°F
2. Marinate the cod with the brown sugar, miso paste, mirin and soy saucemixture
3. Transfer the fish to a heavy-duty sous vide zip bag and seal it using theimmersion method
4. Cook for 30 minutes
5. Place a pan over the medium heat. Add in 1 tablespoon ofbutter
6. Sear the cod for 1 minute and pour the juices from the bag into thepan
7. Reduce until it thickened and add 1 tablespoon of butter on top andstir
8. Drizzle the sauce onto the cod and garnish with some sesameseeds
9. Serve over steamedrice!

Nutritional Value Per Serving:

Calories 315, Carbohydrates 7 g, Fats 15 g, Protein 38 g

Dijon Cream Sauce with Salmon

Prep time: 15 minutes, Cook time: 45 minutes, Serves: 2

Ingredients

- 4 skinless salmon fillets
- 1 bunch, spinach
- ½ cup Dijon mustard
- 1 cup heavy cream
- 1 tablespoon lemon juice
- Salt and pepper

Instructions:

1. Prepare your Sous-vide water bath to a temperature of115°F
2. Season the salmon with salt
3. Transfer to a resealable bag and seal using the immersion method. Cook for 45minutes
4. Take a pan and place it on a medium heat and add the spinach and cook untilwilted
5. Add the lemon juice, pepper and salt, and keep cooking over a lowheat
6. Take another saucepan and place it over mediumheat
7. Add the heavy cream and Dijon mustard. Let it all boil a bit and then lower downthe heat
8. Mix them well and season with salt andpepper
9. Take out the cooked salmon, drizzle the sauce on top, assemble the spinach on theside, and serve!

Nutritional Value Per Serving:

Calories 212, Carbohydrates 7 g, Fats 8 g, Protein 28 g

Lobster Rolls

Prep time: 15 minutes, Cook time: 25 minutes, Serves: 2

Ingredients

- 1 lobster tails
- 1 tablespoon butter
- 2 green onions, chopped 3
- tablespoons mayonnaise
- A pinch of salt
- A pinch of black pepper 2
- teaspoons lemon juice
- Buttered Buns forserving

Instructions:

1. Prepare your Sous-vide water bath to a temperature of140°F
2. Pour the water into a small pot and bring to aboil
3. Cut the lobster tails down the center from the top of theshell
4. Once the water has reached boiling point, submerge the lobsters and cook for90 seconds
5. Remove them and soak in cold water for 5minutes
6. Crack the shells and remove the tails from theshell
7. Add the shells in a bag and add the butter. Seal the bag using the immersionmethod, and cook for 25 minutes
8. Remove the tails from the water bath and pat them dry. Place them in a small bowl and chill for 30 minutes
9. Chop up the tail and mix with the mayonnaise, green onions, salt, pepper, andlime juice.
10. Serve with some toasted, buttered buns

Nutritional Value Per Serving:

Calories 597, Carbohydrates 23 g, Fats 21 g, Protein 79 g

Dover Sole

Prep time: 5 minutes, Cook time: 30 minutes, Serves: 2

Ingredients

- 2 sole fillets
- Kosher salt
- Freshly ground black pepper
- 1 garlic clove, minced
- 4 tablespoons unsalted butter
- 4 tablespoons dry white wine
- The zest of 1 lemon
- 2 tablespoons fresh lemon juice
- Fresh parsley for garnishing, chopped

Instructions:

1. Prepare your Sous-vide water bath to a temperature of134°F
2. Season the sole with some pepper andsalt
3. Divide the soles into their own medium-sized zip bags and divide the butter,lemon zest, wine, garlic and lemon juice between thebags
4. Seal the bags using the immersion method and cook for 30minutes
5. Once done, remove the bags from the water and arrange them on a servingplate
6. Spoon some of your cooking liquid over the fish and garnish with parsley.Serve!

Nutritional Value Per Serving:

Calories 572, Carbohydrates 27 g, Fats 28 g, Protein 53 g

Shrimp Cocktail Slider

Prep time: 30 minutes, Cook time: 15 minutes, Serves: 2

Ingredients

- 10 small-sized shrimps, peeled, de-veined
- Kosher salt and pepper
- 4 tablespoons fresh dill, chopped
- 1 tablespoon unsalted butter
- 4 tablespoons mayonnaise
- 2 tablespoons red onions, minced
- 2 teaspoons freshly squeezed lemon juice
- 2 teaspoons ketchup
- Tabasco sauce
- 4 small-sized, oblong dinner rolls 8
- small-sized leaves, butter lettuce
- ½ lemon, sliced into wedges

Instructions:

1. Prepare your Sous-vide water bath to a temperature of149°F
2. Take a bowl and add the mayonnaise, red onion, lemon juice, ketchup andTabasco sauce in it. Whisk them well to create theseasoning
3. Take the mixture and season it well with pepper and salt and divide the mixtureand shrimps equally between two heavy-duty, resealable plasticbags
4. Add 1 tablespoon of dill and ½ tablespoon of butter to each of thebags
5. Seal the bags using the immersion method, submerge and cook for 15minutes
6. Preheat your oven to 400°F and warm the rolls for about 10minutes
7. Remove them and slice in halflengthwise
8. Once done, remove the contents of the bag and strain over a mediumbowl
9. Transfer the shrimps to the bowl with the dressing. Give it a nicetoss
10. Take 2 lettuce leaves and place the shrimp mixture on top of the lettucerolls
11. Serve with lemon

Nutritional Value Per Serving:

Calories 380, Carbohydrates 15 g, Fats 28 g, Protein 17 g

Poached Salmon

Prep time: 20 minutes, Cook time: 25 minutes, Serves: 2

Ingredients

- 2 skinless, center-cut salmon fillets
- Kosher salt and black pepper
- ¾ cup extra virgin olive oil
- 1 large-sized shallot, sliced into thin rings
- 12 whole Thai basil leaves, lightly bruised
- 1 teaspoon ginger, minced
- 3 Oz mixed greens
- 1 lemon

Instructions:

1. Prepare your Sous-vide water bath to a temperature of128°F
2. Season the salmon with salt and pepper and add the fillets in a heavy-duty zipperbag. Add in the shallot slices, olive oil, ginger, mixed greens and basilleaves
3. Whisk well and seal the bag using the immersionmethod
4. Submerge the bag underwater and cook for about 25minutes
5. Once done, transfer the greens from the bag to a servingplatter
6. Take the salmon fillets and put them on top of your servingplatter
7. Pass the rest of the mixture through a metal mesh and into a medium-sizedbowl
8. Add some lemon juice to your oliveoil
9. Mix well and drizzle the mixture on top of yoursalmon
10. Serve!

Nutritional Value Per Serving:

Calories 270, Carbohydrates 0 g, Fats 18 g, Protein 27 g

Pan Tomate Espelette Shrimp

Prep time: 15 minutes, Cook time: 25 minutes, Serves: 4

Ingredients

- 1 lb. shrimps, peeled, de-veined
- 1 tablespoon extra-virgin olive oil
- ¾ teaspoon Piment d'Espelette
- Kosher salt as needed
- ½ high-quality loaf of bread cut up into 1½ inch slices 1
- garlic clove, halved
- 2 beefsteak tomatoes, 1 sliced horizontally, the other sliced into wedges
- Flaky sea salt

Instructions:

1. Prepare your Sous-vide water bath to a temperature of 122°F
2. Take a large-sized bowl and put the shrimps in it along with the olive oil, a pinch of kosher salt and the Piment d'Espelette
3. Whisk it well and transfer the mixture to a large-sized heavy-duty zip bag. Seal the bag using the immersion method
4. Submerge the bag underwater and cook for 25 minutes
5. Place a grill pan over a medium-high heat for 5 minutes before the shrimps are done
6. Carefully arrange the bread slices in a single layer in your pan and toast them on both sides
7. Once toasted, remove the bread and rub one side of the slices with the garlic clove
8. Rub the tomato halves over your toast as well and divide them between your serving plates
9. Once cooked, remove the bag and drain the liquid
10. Return the grill pan to a medium-high heat and add the shrimp a single layer
11. Sear for 10 seconds and divide the shrimps among the tomato bread
12. Drizzle the olive oil over your shrimps
13. Sprinkle some salt over and serve with the tomato wedges!

Nutritional Value Per Serving:

Calories 238, Carbohydrates 25 g, Fats 6 g, Protein 21 g

Chapter 7: Vegan

Germany's Potato Salad

Prep time: 30 minutes, Cook time: 1 ½ hours, Serves: 6

Ingredients:

- 1 ½ pound, Yukon potatoes, sliced up into ¾ inch pieces
- ½ a cup of chicken stock
- Salt
- Pepper
- 4-ounce, thick bacon cut up into ¼ inch thick strips
- ½ a cup, chopped onion
- 1/3 cup, apple cider vinegar
- 4 thinly sliced scallions

Instructions:

1. Prepare your Sous Vide water bath by dipping your immersion cooker and raisingthe temperature to 185°F
2. Take a heavy-duty re-sealable bag and add potatoes alongside thestock
3. Season with some salt and seal up the bag using immersionmethod
4. Submerge the bag underwater and let it cook for 1 and a ½hours
5. Take a large sized non-stick skillet and place it over medium-highheat
6. Add bacon and cook for about 5-7minutes
7. Transfer it to a paper towel-lined plate using a slottedspoon
8. Make sure to keep reserved fat
9. Return the skillet to medium-high heat and addonions
10. Cook them for a 1 minute
11. Once the cooking is done, remove the bag from the water and return the skilletto medium heat again
12. Add the bacon and add vinegar
13. Bring it to a simmer
14. Add the contents of the bag to the skillet and stir well to combine and allow the liquid to come to a simmer
15. Add scallions and toss well
16. Season with some pepper and salt
17. Servewarm!

Nutritional Value PerServing:

Calories 75, Carbohydrates 5 g, Fats 3 g, Protein 7 g

Momofuku Brussels

Prep time: 20 minutes , Cook time: 40 minutes , Serves: 2

Ingredients:

- 2 pounds of Brussels sprouts with stems trimmed and slice up inhalf 2
- ¼ tablespoon, extra virgin olive oil
- ¼ teaspoon of kosher salt
- ¼ cup, fish sauce
- 2 tablespoons, water
- 1 and a ½ tablespoon, granulated sugar
- 1 tablespoon, rice vinegar
- 1 and a ½ teaspoon, lime juice
- 12 pieces, thinly sliced Thai chills
- 1 small sized minced garlic clove
- Chopped up fresh mint
- Chopped up fresh cilantro

Instructions:

1. Prepare your Sous Vide water bath by dipping your immersion cooker and raisingthe temperature to 183°F
2. Take a heavy-duty re-sealable bag and add Brussels sprouts, salt, and oliveoil
3. Seal it up using immersion method and cook underwater for 40minutes
4. Take a small sized bowl and add fish sauce, sugar, water, rice vinegar, lime juice, garlic and chills to prepare the vinaigrette
5. Once the cooking is done, transfer the Brussels to an aluminum foil lined bakingsheet
6. Heat up your broiler to high
7. Broil the Brussels in your broiler for about 5 minutes until they are just slightlycharred
8. Transfer them to a medium-sized bowl and add thevinaigrette
9. Toss well
10. Sprinkle a bit of cilantro and mint
11. Serve!

Nutritional Value Per Serving:

Calories 126, Carbohydrates 6 g, Fats 10 g, Protein 3 g

Long Green Beans in Tomato

Ingredients:

- 1 pound, trimmed green beans
- 1 can, whole crushed tomatoes
- 1 thinly sliced onion
- 3 peeled and thinly sliced garlic clove
- Kosher salt as needed
- Extra virgin olive oil

Instructions:

1. Prepare your Sous Vide water bath by dipping your immersion cooker and raisingthe temperature to 183°F
2. Take a heavy-duty zip bag and add tomatoes, green bean, garlic, andonion
3. Submerge underwater and cook for 3 hours
4. Remove the bag and transfer content to a large sizedbowl
5. Season with salt and drizzle a bit of oliveoil
6. Serve and enjoy!

Nutritional Value Per Serving:

Calories 54, Carbohydrates 5 g, Fats 2 g, Protein 4 g

Hearty White Beans

Prep time: 15 minutes , Cook time: 3 hours , Serves: 8

Ingredients:

- 1 cup, dried and soaked navy beans
- 1 cup, water
- ½ a cup, extra virgin olive oil
- 1 peeled carrot cut up into 1-inch dices
- 1 stalk, celery cut up into 1-inch dices 1
- quartered shallot
- 4 cloves, crushed garlic
- 2 sprigs, fresh rosemary
- 2 pieces, bay leaves
- Kosher salt
- Freshly ground black pepper

Instructions:

1. Prepare your Sous Vide water bath by dipping your immersion cooker and raisingthe temperature to 190°F
2. Carefully drain and rinse your beans and add them to a heavy-duty zipperbag
3. Seal it up using immersion method and submerge itunderwater
4. Let it cook for about 3 hours
5. Once done, taste the beans
6. If they are firm, then cook for another 1 hour, or cook for another hour and servethem on a bowl
7. Serve!

Nutritional Value Per Serving:

Calories 119, Carbohydrates 9 g, Fats 3 g, Protein 14 g

Delicious Cardamom and

Prep time: 15 minutes , Cook time: 1 hour , Serves: 4

Ingredients:

- 1 pint, mall and halved apricots
- 1 tablespoon, unsalted butter
- 1 teaspoon, cardamom seeds freshly ground
- ½ a teaspoon, ground ginger
- Just a pinch, smoked sea salt
- Chopped up fresh basil

Instructions:

1. Prepare your Sous Vide water bath by increasing the temperature to a 180°F usingan immersion cooker
2. Take a large sized heavy-duty plastic bag and add butter, apricots, ginger,cardamom, salt and mix the whole mixturewell
3. Seal up the bag using water displacement method and submerge itunderwater
4. Let it cook for 1 hour and remove the bag oncedone
5. Take serving bowls and add the apricots to thebowl
6. Garnish with a bit of basil andserve!

Nutritional Value Per Serving:

Calories 28, Carbohydrates 6 g, Fats 0 g, Protein 1 g

Gnocchi Pillows and Caramelized Peas with Parmesan

Prep time: 20 minutes , Cook time: 30 minutes , Serves: 2

Ingredients:

- 1 pack, store-bought gnocchi
- 1 tablespoon, unsalted butter
- ½, thinly sliced sweet onion
- Salt
- Fresh ground black pepper
- ½ cup, frozen peas
- ¼ cup, heavy cream
- ½ cup, grated Parmesan

Instructions:

1. Prepare your Sous Vide water bath by dipping your immersion cooker and raisingthe temperature to 183°F
2. Take a large zip bag and add gnocchi to thebag
3. Seal using immersion method and cook for 1 and a ½hours
4. Take a cast iron skillet and place it over mediumheat
5. Add butter and allow the butter tomelt
6. Add onion and season with salt and Sauté for 3minutes
7. Add frozen peas, cream and simmer
8. Stir in gnocchi and stir well to coat with thesauce
9. Season with pepper and salt
10. Transfer to a platter andserve!

Nutritional Value Per Serving:

Calories 260, Carbohydrates 5 g, Fats 20 g, Protein 15 g

Balsamic Braised Cabbage

Ingredients:

- 1 and ½ pound, red cabbage
- ¼ cup, currants
- 1 thinly sliced shallot
- 3 thinly sliced garlic clove
- 1 tablespoon, balsamic vinegar
- 1 tablespoon, unsalted butter
- ½ teaspoon, kosher salt

Instructions:

1. Prepare your Sous Vide water bath by dipping your immersion cooker and raisingthe temperature to 185°F
2. Slice up your cabbage into quarters and remove thecore
3. Chop up the cabbage into 1 and ½ inch pieces
4. Take 2 large sized heavy-duty zip bag and divide the cabbages between thebags
5. Divide the dry ingredients between the bags aswell
6. Seal up the bags using immersionmethod
7. Submerge the bag underwater and let them cook for 2hours
8. Once the cooking is done, remove the bag from the water and transfer it to aserving bowl
9. Add the juices
10. Season with some salt and vinegar andserve!

Nutritional Value Per Serving:

Calories 204, Carbohydrates 9 g, Fats 16 g, Protein 6 g

Cabbage Wedges

Prep time: 15 minutes , Cook time: 4 hours , Serves: 2

Ingredients:

- 1 medium-sized savoy cabbage cut up into wedges
- 2 tablespoons, unsalted butter
- ½ teaspoon, kosher salt

Instructions:

1. Prepare your Sous Vide water bath by dipping your immersion cooker and raisingthe temperature to 183°F
2. Take a large sized zip bag and add 1 tablespoon of butter, salt, andcabbages
3. Mix well and seal using immersionmethod
4. Cook for 4 hours and remove the cabbage, pat dry using kitchentowel
5. Take a tablespoon of butter and add to a medium-sized skillet over mediumheat
6. Allow the butter to melt and addcabbages
7. Sear for 5-7 minutes until golden
8. Serve and enjoy!

Nutritional Value Per Serving:

Calories 42, Carbohydrates 4 g, Fats 2 g, Protein 2 g

Perfect Curried Squash

Prep time: 20 minutes , Cook time: 1 ½ hours, Serves: 6

Ingredients:

- 1 medium-sized winter squash
- 2 tablespoons, unsalted butter
- 1 to 2 tablespoon, Thai curry paste
- ½ teaspoon, kosher salt
- Fresh cilantro
- Limewedges

Instructions:

1. Prepare your Sous Vide water bath by dipping your immersion cooker and raisingthe temperature to 185°F
2. Slice the squash into half lengthwise and scoop out the seeds alongside innermembrane
3. Keep the seeds for lateruse
4. Slice the squash into wedges of 1 and ½ inchthickness
5. Take a large sized zip bag and add squash wedges, curry paste, butter, salt andseal using immersion method
6. Submerge and cook for 1 and ½ hours
7. Remove the bag and slight squeezeit
8. If soft then take out, otherwise cook for 40 minutesmore
9. Transfer to serving platter and drizzle a bit of curry buttersauce
10. Top with cilantro and enjoy!

Nutritional Value Per Serving:

Calories 152, Carbohydrates 5 g, Fats 12 g, Protein 6 g

Cauliflower Puree and Whipped

Prep time: 10 minutes , Cook time: 2 hours , Serves: 4

Ingredients:

- 1-pound, trimmed cauliflower
- ½ teaspoon, garlic powder
- 1 teaspoon, kosher salt
- 1 tablespoon, butter
- 1 tablespoon, heavy whipping cream

Instructions:

1. Prepare the Sous Vide water bath by dipping the cooker and increasing thetemperature to 183°F
2. Add cauliflower, salt, garlic powder, heavy whip cream to a large-sized re-sealablebag
3. Seal using immersion method
4. Cook for about 2 hours
5. Pour the contents into a blender andpuree
6. Season and serve!

Nutritional Value Per Serving:

Calories 308, Carbohydrates 7 g, Fats 28 g, Protein 7 g

Vegan Steel Cut Oats

Prep time: 5 minutes, Cook time: 3 hours, Serves: 2

Ingredients

- 2 cups water
- ½ cup steel cut oats
- ½ teaspoon salt
- Cinnamon and maple syrup for topping

Instructions:

1. Prepare the Sous Vide water bath by using your immersion circulator and raisethe temperature to 180°F.
2. Take a heavy-duty resealable zipper bag and add all the listed ingredients except the cinnamon and maple syrup
3. Seal the bag using the immersion method and submergeunderwater.
4. Cook for about 3 hours.
5. Once cooked, remove it and transfer the oats to your servingbowl.
6. Serve with a sprinkle of cinnamon and some maplesyrup.

Nutritional Value Per Serving:

Calories 150, Carbohydrates 19 g, Fats 6 g, Protein 5 g

Honey Drizzled Carrots

Prep time: 5 minutes, Cook time: 1 hour 15 minutes, Serves: 4

Ingredients

- 1-pound baby carrots
- 4 tablespoons vegan butter
- 1 tablespoon agave nectar
- 3 tablespoons honey
- ¼ teaspoon kosher salt
- ¼ teaspoon ground cardamom

Instructions:

1. Prepare the Sous-vide water bath using your immersion circulator and increase the temperature to 185°F
2. Add the carrots, honey, whole butter, kosher salt, and cardamom to a resealablebag
3. Seal using the immersion method. Cook for 75 minutes and once done, remove itfrom the water bath.
4. Strain the glaze by passing through a fine mesh.
5. Set it aside.
6. Take the carrots out from the bag and pour any excess glaze over them. Serve witha little bit of seasonings.

Nutritional Value Per Serving:

Calories 185, Carbohydrates 42 g, Fats 1 g, Protein 2 g

Pickled Fennel

Prep time: 30 minutes, Cook time: 30 minutes, Serves: 5

Ingredients

- 1 cup white wine vinegar
- 2 tablespoons beetsugar
- Juice and zest from 1 lemon
- 1 teaspoon kosher salt
- 2 medium bulb fennels, trimmed up and cut into ¼ inch thickslices

Instructions:

1. Prepare the Sous Vide water bath using your immersion circulator and raisethe temperature to 180°F.
2. Take a large bowl and add the vinegar, sugar, lemon juice, salt, lemon zest, andwhisk them well.
3. Transfer the mixture to your resealable zipbag.
4. Add the fennel and seal using the immersionmethod.
5. Submerge underwater and cook for 30minutes.
6. Transfer to an ice bath and allow the mixture to reach the roomtemperature.
7. Serve!

Nutritional Value Per Serving:

Calories 161, Carbohydrates 33 g, Fats 1 g, Protein 5 g

Lemon & Garlic Artichokes

Prep time: 30 minutes, Cook time: 90 minutes, Serves: 4

Ingredients

- 4 tablespoons freshly squeezed lemon juice
- 12 pieces' baby artichokes
- 4 tablespoons veganbutter
- 2 fresh garlic cloves, minced
- 1 teaspoon fresh lemon zest
- Kosher salt, and black pepper, to taste
- Chopped up fresh parsley for garnishing

Instructions:

1. Prepare the Sous Vide water bath using your immersion circulator and raisethe temperature to 180°F.
2. Take a large bowl and add the cold water and 2 tablespoons of lemonjuice.
3. Peel and discard the outer tough layer of your artichoke and cut them intoquarters.
4. Transfer to a cold-water bath and let it sit for awhile.
5. Take a large skillet and put it over medium highheat.
6. Add in the butter to the skillet and allow the butter tomelt.
7. Add the garlic alongside 2 tablespoons of lemon juice and thezest.
8. Remove from heat and season with a bit of pepper andsalt.
9. Allow it to cool for about 5minutes.
10. Then, drain the artichokes from the cold waterand place them in a largeresealable bag. Add in the butter mixture aswell.
11. Seal it up using the immersion method and submerge underwater for about 1 and a½ hour.
12. Once cooked, transfer the artichokes to a bowl and serve with a garnish ofparsley.

Nutritional Value Per Serving:

Calories 424, Carbohydrates 49 g, Fats 20 g, Protein 12 g

Truffle Sunchokes

Prep time: 15 minutes, Cook time: 90 minutes, Serves: 4

Ingredients

- 8 ounces peeled Sunchokes, sliced into ¼ inch thick pieces
- 3 tablespoons unsalted vegan butter
- 2 tablespoons agave nectar
- 1 teaspoon truffle oil
- Kosher salt, and black pepper, to taste

Instructions:

1. Prepare the Sous Vide water bath using your immersion circulator and raisethe temperature to 180°F.
2. Take a heavy-duty resealable zip bag and add the butter, nectar, sunchokes, truffleoil and mix them well.
3. Sprinkle some salt and pepper, and then seal using the immersionmethod.
4. Submerge it underwater and cook for 1 ½hour.
5. Once cooked, transfer the contents to askillet.
6. Put the skillet over medium-high heat and cook for 5 minutes more until the liquidhas evaporated.
7. Season with pepper and salt to adjust the flavor ifneeded
8. Serve!

Nutritional Value Per Serving:

Calories 270, Carbohydrates 40 g, Fats 10 g, Protein 5 g

Spicy Giardiniera

Prep time: 30 minutes, Cook time: 1 hours, Serves: 8

Ingredients

- 2 cups white winevinegar
- 1 cup water
- ½ cup beet sugar
- 3 tablespoons kosher salt
- 1 tablespoon whole black peppercorns
- 1 cup cauliflower, cut up into ½-inch pieces
- 1 stemmed and seeded bell pepper, cut up into ½-inchpieces 1
- cup carrots, cut up into ½-inchpieces
- ½ thinly sliced white onion
- 2 seeded and stemmed Serrano peppers, cut up into ½-inchpieces

Instructions:

1. Prepare the Sous-vide water bath using your immersion circulator and raisethe temperature to 180°F.
2. Take a large bowl and mix in vinegar, sugar, salt, water, andpeppercorns.
3. Transferthemixturetoalargeresealablezipperbagandaddthecauliflower, onion, serrano peppers, vinegar mixture, bell pepper, andcarrots.
4. Seal it up using the immersion method and submerge underwater, cook for about1 hour.
5. Once cooked, take it out from the bag andserve

Nutritional Value Per Serving:

Calories 247, Carbohydrates 42 g, Fats 7 g, Protein 4 g

Vegan Alfredo

Prep time: 15 minutes, Cook time: 1-hour 3o minutes, Serves: 6

Ingredients

- 4 cups chopped cauliflower
- 2 cups water
- 2/3 cup cashews
- 2 garlic cloves
- ½ teaspoon dried oregano
- ½ teaspoon dried basil
- ½ teaspoon dried rosemary
- 4 tablespoons nutritional yeast
- Salt, and pepper to taste

Instructions:

1. Prepare the Sous-vide water bath using your immersion circulator and increase the temperature to 170°F.
2. Take a heavy-duty resealable zip bag and add the cashews, cauliflower, oregano, water, garlic, rosemary, and basil.
3. Seal using the immersion method. Submerge underwater and cook for 90minutes.
4. Transfer the cooked contents to a blender and puree.
5. Use the Alfredo over your favorite pasta.

Nutritional Value Per Serving:

Calories 171, Carbohydrates 10 g, Fats 11 g, Protein 8 g

White Cannellini Beans

Prep time: 15 minutes, Cook time: 3 hours, Serves: 5

Ingredients

- 1 cup cannellini beans (dried) soaked overnight in salty cold water 1
- cup water
- ½ cup extra-virgin olive oil
- 1 peeled carrot, cut up into 1-inch dice
- 1 celery stalk, cut up into 1-inch dice 1
- quartered shallot
- 4 crushed garlic cloves
- 2 fresh rosemary sprigs
- 2 bay leaves
- Kosher salt, and pepper to taste

Instructions:

1. Prepare the Sous Vide water bath using your Sous-vide immersion circulator and raise the temperature to 190°F.
2. Drain the soaked beans and rinse them.
3. Transfer to a heavy-duty resealable zip bag and add the olive oil, celery, water, carrot, shallot, garlic, rosemary, and bay leaves.
4. Season with pepper and salt.
5. Seal using the immersion method and cook for 3 hours.
6. Once cooked, remove the beans and check for seasoning.
7. Discard the rosemary and serve!

Nutritional Value Per Serving:

Calories 594, Carbohydrates 77 g, Fats 18 g, Protein 31 g

Tofu Delight

Prep time: 20 minutes, Cook time: 1 hour, Serves: 8

Ingredients

- 1 cup vegetable broth
- 2 tablespoons tomato paste
- 1 tablespoon grated ginger
- 1 tablespoon rice wine
- 1 tablespoon rice winevinegar
- 1 tablespoon agave nectar
- 2 teaspoons Srirachasauce
- 3 minced garlic cloves
- 2 boxes cubed tofu

Instructions:

1. Prepare your Sous Vide water bath using your immersion circulator and raisethe temperature to 185°F.
2. Take a medium bowl and add all the listed ingredients except thetofu.
3. Mix well.
4. Transfer the mixture to a heavy-duty resealable zipper bag and top with thetofu.
5. Seal it up using the immersion method. Cook for 1 hour.
6. Pour the contents into a serving bowl
7. Serve!

Nutritional Value Per Serving:

Calories 206, Carbohydrates 28 g, Fats 6 g, Protein 10 g

White Beans

Prep time: 15 minutes, Cook time: 3-4 hours, Serves: 8

Ingredients

- 1 cup dried and soaked navy beans
- 1 cup water
- ½ cup extra-virgin olive oil
- 1 peeled carrot, cut up into 1-inch dices
- 1 stalk celery, cut up into 1-inch dices 1
- quartered shallot
- 4 cloves crushed garlic
- 2 sprigs fresh rosemary
- 2 pieces' bay leaves
- Kosher salt, to taste
- Freshly ground black pepper, to taste

Instructions:

1. Prepare your Sous-vide water bath using your immersion circulator and raisethe temperature to 190°F.
2. Carefully drain and rinse your beans and add them alongside the rest of theingredients to a heavy-duty zip bag.
3. Seal using the immersion method and submerge it underwater. Cook for about 3hours.
4. Once cooked, taste the beans.
5. If they are firm, then cook for another 1 hour and pour them in a servingbowl.
6. Serve!

Nutritional Value Per Serving:

Calories 218, Carbohydrates 36 g, Fats 2 g, Protein 14 g

Radishes with "Vegan"

Prep time: 5 minutes, Cook time: 45 minutes, Serves: 4

Ingredients

- 1-pound radishes, cut up in half lengthwise
- 3 tablespoons vegan butter
- ½ teaspoon sea salt

Instructions:

1. Prepare your Sous Vide water bath using your immersion circulator and raisethe temperature to 190°F.
2. Add your radish halves, butter, and salt in a resealable zipper bag and seal it upusing the immersion method.
3. Submerge underwater and cook for 45minutes.
4. Once cooked, strain the liquid anddiscard.
5. Serve the radishes in abowl!

Nutritional Value Per Serving:

Calories 205, Carbohydrates 30 g, Fats 9 g, Protein 1 g

Sous-vide Rhubarb

Prep time: 15 minutes, Cook time: 40 minutes, Serves: 4

Ingredients

- 2 cups rhubarb
- 1 tablespoon Grand Marnier
- 1 teaspoon beet sugar
- ½ teaspoon kosher salt
- ½ a teaspoon freshly ground black pepper

Instructions:

1. Prepare the Sous-vide water bath to a temperature of 140°F using yourimmersion circulator.
2. Takealargeheavy-dutyresealablezipbagandaddallthelistedingredients. Whisk everything well.
3. Seal the bag using the immersion method/water displacementmethod.
4. Place it under your preheated water and cook for about 40minutes.
5. Once cooked, take the bag out from the water bath, take the contents out and place iton a serving plate.
6. Servewarm!

NutritionalValuePerServing:

Calories 112, Carbohydrates 27 g, Fats 0 g, Protein 1 g

Chipotle & Black Beans

Prep time: 25 minutes, Cook time: 6 hours, Serves: 6

Ingredients

- 1 cup dry black beans
- 2 2/3 cup water
- 1/3 cup freshly squeezed orange juice
- 2 tablespoons orange zest
- 1 teaspoon salt
- 1 teaspoon cumin
- ½ teaspoon chipotle chili powder

Instructions:

1. Prepare the Sous-vide water bath using your immersion circulator and raisethe temperature to 193°F.
2. Take a heavy-duty resealable plastic bag and add the listed ingredients into thebag.
3. Submerge it underwater and cook for 6hours.
4. Once cooked, take the bag out from the waterbath.
5. Pour the contents into a nice sauté pan and place it over mediumheat.
6. Simmer until the amount has beenreduced.
7. Once your desired texture is achieved, remove from the heat andserve!

Nutritional Value Per Serving:

Calories 473, Carbohydrates 15 g, Fats 37 g, Protein 20 g

Pickled Mixed Veggies

Prep time: 10 minutes, Cook time: 40 minutes, Serves: 4

Ingredients

- 12 oz. beets, cut up into ½-inch slices
- ½ Serrano pepper, seeds removed
- 1 garlic clove, diced
- 2/3 cup white vinegar
- 2/3 cup filtered water
- 2 tablespoons pickling spice

Instructions:

1. Prepare the Sous-vide water bath using your immersion circulator and raisethe temperature to 190°F.
2. Take 4-6 ounces' mason jar and add the Serrano pepper, beets, and garliccloves
3. Take a medium stock pot and add the pickling spice, filtered water, whitevinegar, and bring the mixture to a boil
4. Remove the stock and strain the mix over the beets in thejar.
5. Fill them up.
6. Seal it loosely and submerge it underwater. Cook for 40minutes.
7. Allow the jars to cool and serve!

Nutritional Value Per Serving:

Calories 170, Carbohydrates 34 g, Fats 2 g, Protein 4 g

Root Vegetables Mix

Prep time: 15 minutes, Cook time: 3 hours, Serves: 4

Ingredients

- 1 peeled turnip, cut up into 1-inch pieces
- 1 peeled rutabaga, cut up into 1-inch pieces
- 8 pieces petite carrots peeled up and cut into 1-inch pieces 1
- peeled parsnip, cut up into 1-inch pieces
- ½ red onion, cut up into 1-inch pieces and peeled
- 4 pieces' garlic, crushed
- 4 sprigs fresh rosemary
- 2 tablespoons extra-virgin olive oil
- Kosher salt, and black pepper to taste
- 2 tablespoons unsalted vegan butter

Instructions:

1. Prepare the Sous-vide water bath using your immersion circulator and raisethe temperature to 185°F.
2. Take two large heavy-duty resealable zipper bags and divide the vegetables andthe rosemary between the bags.
3. Add 1 tablespoon of oil to the bag and season with some salt andpepper.
4. Seal the bags using the immersion method. Submerge underwater and cook for 3hours
5. Take a skillet and place it over high heat and add in theoil.
6. Once done, add the contents of your bag to the skillet. Cook the mixture for about5-6 minutes until the liquid comes to a syrupyconsistency.
7. Add the butter to your veggies and toss themwell.
8. Keep cooking for another 5 minutes until they are nicelybrowned.
9. Serve!

Nutritional Value Per Serving:

Calories 286, Carbohydrates 43 g, Fats 10 g, Protein 6 g

Pickled Carrots

Prep time: 30 minutes, Cook time: 1 hour 30 minutes, Serves: 1

Ingredients

- 1 cup white wine vinegar
- ½ cup beet sugar
- 3 tablespoons kosher salt
- 1 teaspoon black peppercorns
- 1/3 cup ice cold water
- 10-12 pieces' petite carrots, peeled with the stems trimmed
- 4 sprigs fresh thyme
- 2 peeled garlic cloves

Instructions:

1. Prepare the Sous-vide water bath using your immersion circulator and raisethe temperature to 190°F.
2. Take a medium-sized saucepan and add the vinegar, salt, sugar, and peppercornsand place it over mediumheat.
3. Then, let the mixture reach the boiling point and keep stirring until the sugarhas dissolved alongside the salt
4. Remove the heat and add the coldwater.
5. Allow the mixture to cool down to roomtemperature.
6. Take a resealable bag and add the thyme, carrots, and garlic alongside thebrine solution and seal it up using the immersionmethod.
7. Submerge underwater and cook for 90minutes.
8. Once cooked, remove the bag from the water bath and place into an icebath.
9. Carefully take the carrots out from the bag andserve!

Nutritional Value Per Serving:

Calories 113, Carbohydrates 24 g, Fats 1 g, Protein 2 g

Sous Vide Garlic Tomatoes

Prep time: 10 minutes, Cook time: 45 minutes, Serves: 4

Ingredients

- 4 pieces cored and diced tomatoes 2
- tablespoons extra-virgin olive oil 3
- minced garlic cloves
- 1 teaspoon dried oregano
- 1 teaspoon fine sea salt

Instructions:

1. Prepare the Sous-vide water bath using your immersion circulator and raisethe temperature to 145°F.
2. Add all the listed ingredients to the resealable bag and seal using the immersion method.
3. Submerge underwater and let it cook for 45minutes.
4. Once cooked, transfer the tomatoes to a servingplate.
5. Serve with some vegan French bread slices.

Nutritional Value Per Serving:

Calories 292, Carbohydrates 44 g, Fats 8 g, Protein 11 g

Sweet Curried Winter Squash

Prep time: 20 minutes, Cook time: 1 hour 30 minutes, Serves: 6

Ingredients

- 1 medium winter squash
- 2 tablespoons unsalted veganbutter
- 1 to 2 tablespoons Thai currypaste
- ½ teaspoon kosher salt
- Fresh cilantro for serving
- Lime wedges for serving

Instructions:

1. Prepare the Sous-vide water bath using your immersion circulator and raisethe temperature to 185°F.
2. Slice up the squash into half lengthwise and scoop out the seeds alongside theinner membrane. Keep the seeds for lateruse.
3. Slice the squash into wedges of about 1 ½-inchthickness.
4. Take a large heavy-duty bag resealable zip bags and add the squash wedges,curry paste, butter and salt and seal it using the immersionmethod.
5. Submerge it underwater and let it cook for 1 ½hour.
6. Once cooked, remove the bag from water and give it a slight squeeze until it issoft.
7. If it is not soft, then add to the water once again and cook for 40 minutesmore.
8. Transferthe cooked dishto a serving plateand drizzle with abitofcurry buttersauce from the bag.
9. Top your squash with a bit of cilantro, lime wedges andserve!

Nutritional Value Per Serving:

Calories 197, Carbohydrates 27 g, Fats 9 g, Protein 2 g

Balsamic Mushroom &

Prep time: 15 minutes, Cook time: 1 hour, Serves: 4

Ingredients

- 1-pound cremini mushrooms with the stems removed
- 1 tablespoon extra-virgin olive oil
- 1 tablespoon apple balsamic vinegar
- 1 minced garlic clove
- 1 teaspoon kosher salt
- 1 teaspoon freshly ground black pepper
- 1 teaspoon minced fresh thyme

Instructions:

1. Prepare the Sous-vide water bath using your immersion circulator and raisethe temperature to 138°F.
2. Add the listed ingredients to your resealable zipbag.
3. Seal using the immersion method and let it cook for 1hour.
4. Once cooked, transfer the contents to a platter andserve!

Nutritional Value Per Serving:

Calories 414, Carbohydrates 51 g, Fats 18 g, Protein 12 g

Currant & Braised Cabbage

Prep time: 15 minutes, Cook time: 2 hours, Serves: 4

Ingredients

- 1 ½ pounds red cabbage
- ¼ cup currants
- 1 thinly sliced shallot
- 3 thinly sliced garlic clove
- 1 tablespoon apple balsamicvinegar
- 1 tablespoon unsalted butter
- ½ a teaspoon kosher salt

Instructions:

1. Prepare the Sous-vide water bath using your immersion circulator and raisethe temperature to 185°F.
2. Take the cabbage and slice the cabbage into quarters, make sure to discard thecore.
3. Chop them up into 1 ½-inch pieces.
4. Take 2 heavy-duty resealable zipper bags and divide the cabbages between thetwo bags.
5. Divide as well the remaining ingredients equally between thebags
6. Seal using the immersion method. Submerge underwater and cook for 2hours.
7. Once done, remove the bag and transfer to abowl.
8. Add the cooking juices and season with a bit of salt andvinegar.
9. Serve!

Nutritional Value Per Serving:

Calories 178, Carbohydrates 6 g, Fats 14 g, Protein 7 g

Sous-vide Pennies

Prep time: 15 minutes, Cook time: 3 hours, Serves: 4

Ingredients

- 1-pound carrots, peeled up and sliced into ¼ inch thick rounds
- ¼ cup dried apricots, thinly sliced up
- ¼ cup freshly squeezed orange juice
- 2 tablespoons freshly squeezed lemonjuice
- 1 tablespoon unsalted vegan butter
- 2 teaspoons beet sugar
- ½ a teaspoon kosher salt
- ¼ teaspoon orange zest
- ¼ teaspoon freshly ground black pepper
- 1/8 teaspoon ground cinnamon

Instructions:

1. Prepare the Sous-vide water bath using your immersion circulator and raisethe temperature to 183°F.
2. Add the listed ingredients to your resealable zip bag and seal using theimmersion method. Submerge underwater and cook for 3hours.
3. Transferthe carrotsto a serving platterwith cooking liquid and season with saltand pepper.
4. Garnish with the additional lemon juice andserve!

Nutritional Value Per Serving:

Calories 256, Carbohydrates 35 g, Fats 12 g, Protein 2 g

Pomme Purée

Prep time: 10 minutes, Cook time: 30 minutes, Serves: 4

Ingredients

- 1½ lb. potatoes, peeled
- 15-ounce vegan butter
- 8-ounce coconut milk
- A pinch of salt
- White pepper

Instructions:

1. Prepare your Sous-vide water bath using your immersion circulator and raisethe temperature to 194°F.
2. Slice the potatoes to 1 cm thickslices
3. Take your heavy-duty resealable zipper bag and add the potatoes, coconut milk,vegan butter and salt
4. Submerge underwater and let it cook for 30minutes
5. Strainthe mixture through a metal mesh/sieve and allowthe butter mixture to pour into a bowl
6. Puree the potatoes by blending them or mashing them using aspoon
7. Pour the puree into the butterbowl
8. Season with pepper and serve!

Nutritional Value Per Serving:

Calories 57, Carbohydrates 2 g, Fats 5 g, Protein 1 g

Sous-vide Golden Beets

Prep time: 20 minutes, Cook time: 1 hour 30 minutes, Serves: 2

Ingredients

- 1 lb. golden beets, cut up into ¼ inch thick slices 1
- cup freshly squeezed orange juice
- ¼ cup freshly squeezed lemon juice
- 4 tablespoons unsalted vegan butter
- 1 tablespoon agave nectar
- 1 teaspoon freshly ground black peppercorns
- 1 teaspoon kosher salt

Instructions:

1. Prepare the Sous-vide water bath using your immersion circulator and raisethe temperature to 180°F.
2. Add the listed ingredients to a resealable zip bag and seal using the immersion method. Cook for 1 ½ hours
3. Once done, remove the bag and take the beets out and set themaside.
4. Pour the cooking liquid into a saucepan and bring it to a simmer overmedium-high heat.
5. Keep simmering until the liquid is lowered by half.
6. Remove from the heat and stir in beets.
7. Serve!

Nutritional Value Per Serving:

Calories 176, Carbohydrates 7 g, Fats 16 g, Protein 1 g

Fingerling Cooked Potatoes

Prep time: 10 minutes, Cook time: 45 minutes, Serves: 3

Ingredients

- 8 ounces fingerling potatoes
- Salt, and pepper to taste
- 1 tablespoon unsalted veganbutter
- 1 sprig rosemary

Instructions:

1. Prepare the Sous-vide water bath using your immersion circulator and raisethe temperature to 178°F.
2. Takethe potatoes and season itwith saltand pepperand transferthem to aresealable zip bag.
3. Seal using the immersion method and submerge it underwater and cook for 45minutes.
4. Once cooked, remove the bag andpotatoes.
5. Cut the potatoes in half(lengthwise).
6. Take a large skillet and put it over medium-highheat.
7. Add the butter and allow it to melt, add the rosemary andpotatoes.
8. Cook for 3 minutes and transfer to aplate.
9. Serve by seasoning it with a bit of salt ifneeded

Nutritional Value Per Serving:

Calories 150, Carbohydrates 19 g, Fats 6 g, Protein 5 g

Daikon Radishes

Prep time: 10 minutes, Cook time: 30 minutes, Serves: 4

Ingredients

- ½ cup white winger vinegar
- 3 tablespoons beet sugar
- 2 teaspoons kosher salt
- 1 large size Daikon radish, trimmed and sliced up

Instructions:

1. Prepare the Sous-vide water bath using your immersion circulator and raisethe temperature to 180°F.
2. Take a large bowl and mix in vinegar, salt, and beetsugar.
3. Transfer to a Sous-vide zip bag and seal using the immersionmethod.
4. Submerge underwater and cook for 30minutes
5. Once cooked, remove the bag and transfer to an icebath.
6. Serve!

Nutritional Value Per Serving:

Calories 166, Carbohydrates 19 g, Fats 6 g, Protein 9 g

Green Beans in Tomato

Prep time: 10 minutes, Cook time: 3 hours, Serves: 4

Ingredients

- 1 lb. trimmed green beans
- 1 can whole crushed tomatoes
- 1 thinly sliced onion
- 3 garlic cloves, peeled and thinly sliced
- Kosher salt, to taste
- Extra-virgin olive oil

Instructions:

1. Prepare the Sous-vide water bath using your immersion circulator and raisethe temperature to 183°F
2. Take a large heavy-duty resealable zip bag and add the tomatoes, green beans,garlic, and onion
3. Seal using the immersion method. Submerge underwater and lct it cook for 3hours.
4. Once cooked, transfer the contents of the bag to a largebowl.
5. Serve with a seasoning of salt and a drizzle of oliveoil.

Nutritional Value Per Serving:

Calories 275, Carbohydrates 6 g, Fats 19 g, Protein 20 g

French Fries

Prep time: 20 minutes, Cook time: 25 minutes, Serves: 10

Ingredients

- 2 quarts' water
- 2 tablespoons kosher salt
- 1 teaspoon beet sugar
- 1 teaspoon baking powder
- 2 ½ pounds russet potatoes, cut up into French fry shapes

Instructions:

1. Prepare the Sous-vide water bath using your immersion circulator and raisethe temperature to 194°F.
2. Take a large bowl and add the water, sugar, kosher salt, and bakingpowder.
3. Give everything a nice mix until everything dissolves.
4. Add the sliced-up potatoes to the mixture and transfer it to a heavy-duty resealable zipper bag.
5. Seal using the immersion method. Submerge underwater and let it cook for 25minutes.
6. Once done, remove the bag and pre-heat your Air Fryer to a temperature of260°F.
7. Let the fries cool for 20 minutes and Air Fry them for 8minutes.
8. Transfer them to a freezer and let them chill for 60minutes.
9. Preheat your fryer to 735°F and cook them again for 2minutes.
10. Serve!

Nutritional Value Per Serving:

Calories 345, Carbohydrates 67 g , Fats 5 g, Protein 8 g

Moroccan Chickpeas

Prep time: 10 minutes, Cook time: 3 hours, Serves: 4

Ingredients

- 1 cup chickpeas, soaked overnight in cold saltywater
- 3 cups water
- 2 tablespoons extra-virgin oliveoil
- 1 teaspoon kosher salt
- ½ teaspoon ground cumin
- ½ teaspoon groundcoriander
- ¼ teaspoon ground cinnamon
- 1/8 teaspoon ground cloves
- 1/8 teaspoon cayennepepper
- Fresh cilantro for garnishing, chopped
- Harissa, to taste

Instructions:

1. Preparethe Sous-videwater bath usingyour immersioncirculatorand increasethe temperature to 190°F.
2. Then, drain the soaked chickpeas and transfer them to a resealable bag with the soaking water
3. Add in the cumin, salt, olive oil, cloves, cinnamon, coriander, and cayennepepper.
4. Seal using the immersion method. Submerge underwater and let it cook for 3hours.
5. Drain the chickpeas from the liquid and transfer them to abowl.
6. Season with a bit ofsalt.
7. Take a small bowl and add the olive oil andharissa.
8. Drizzle the mixture over thechickpeas.
9. Serve with a garnish ofcilantro.

Nutritional Value Per Serving:

Calories 189, Carbohydrates 29 g, Fats 5 g, Protein 7 g

Pickle in A Jar

Prep time: 30 minutes, Cook time: 15 minutes, Serves: 6

Ingredients

- 1 cup white wine vinegar
- ½ cup beet sugar
- 2 teaspoons kosher salt
- 1 tablespoon pickling spice
- 2 English cucumbers sliced up into ¼ inch thick slices
- ½ white onion, thinly sliced

Instructions:

1. Prepare the Sous-vide water bath using your immersion circulator and raisethe temperature to 180°F.
2. Take a large bowl and add the vinegar, sugar, salt, pickling spice and whisk themwell.
3. Transfer to a heavy-duty resealable zipper bag alongside the cucumber andsliced onions and seal using the immersionmethod.
4. Submerge underwater and let it cook for 15minutes.
5. Transfer the bag to an ice bath
6. Pour the mixture into a 4-6-ounce masonjar
7. Serve or store!

Nutritional Value Per Serving:

Calories 121, Carbohydrates 27 g, Fats 1 g, Protein 1 g

Sous Vide Glazed Carrots

Prep time: 4 minutes, Cook time: 20 minutes, Serves: 3

Ingredients:

- 4-5 carrots of different colors, peeled, sliced
- ½ cup of chopped pumpkin or sweet potato
- 1 tsp of dried thyme
- 1 tbsp of salted butter
- Salt/Pepper

Instructions:

1. Prepare your Sous Vide water bath by attaching the immersion circulator and setting the temperature to 194°F.
2. Place the carrots in a pouch and seal using the vacuum sealer or the water displacement method.
3. Let cook in the water bath for 25 minutes.
4. Remove the carrots from the pouch and glaze in a pan with the butter and thymeuntil they get a sleek golden sheen and serve

Nutritional Value Per Serving:

Calories 98, Carbohydrates 14.7 g, Protein 1.73 g, Fats 6 g

Eggplant Parmesan

Prep time: 5 minutes, Cook time: 1 hour, Serves: 2

Ingredients:

- 1 large eggplant, sliced
- 2 large eggs, beaten
- ¼ cup parmesan cheese, grated
- 1 cup, tomato sauce
- ½ cup, bread crumbs
- ⅓ cup, white flour
- 4 tablespoons olive oil
- Salt/pepper

Instructions:

1. Prepare your Sous Vide water bath by attaching the immersion circulator and setting the temperature to 183°F.
2. Place the eggplants on water, pinch with a fork and let them release their bitterness in the water for 10 minutes. Drain, season with salt, pepper, and setaside.
3. Place and distribute the eggplant slices into 2-3 pouches, while these are lying flat. Seal using the water displacement method or the vacuum sealer (while placing the pouch horizontally so that eggplants are not on top of eachother).
4. Submerge into the water and let cook for 40minutes.
5. In three separate small bowls, divide the beaten eggs, the breadcrumbs, and the flour. Season everything with salt and pepper.
6. Once the eggplants are cooked, dip each slice into the flour, then to the eggs and thento the breadcrumb mixture.
7. Heat the olive oil in a medium pan (over medium heat) and place the breadedeggplant slices. Cook for 2-3 minutes on each side, or until goldenbrown.
8. Transfer the eggplants into a baking dish or pyrex and pour over the tomato sauceand the grated mozzarella cheese.
9. Pop these into the oven and cook for 15-20 minutes (or until cheese ismelted)
10. Serve hot

Nutritional Value Per Serving:

Calories 679.9, Carbohydrates 66.5 g, Fats 39.1 g, Protein 15.5 g

Sous Vide Balsamic Onions

Prep time: 3 minutes, Cook time: 2 hours, Serves: 2

Ingredients:

- 2 medium white onions, sliced julienne
- 1 tbsp, balsamic vinegar
- 2 tbsp, brown sugar
- 2 tbsp, olive oil
- Salt/Pepper to taste

Instructions:

1. Prepare your Sous Vide water bath by attaching the immersion circulator and setting the temperature to 185°F.
2. Mix the onions with the rest of the ingredients in a sealable plastic bag and seal using a vacuum sealer or the water displacement method.
3. Submerge into the bath water and allow cooking for 2hours.
4. Remove, transfer into a mason jar, cool and keep in the fridge for up to 12 hoursbefore serving.

Nutritional Value Per Serving:

Calories 186.7, Carbohydrates 15.5 g, Fats 13.5 g, Protein 0.8 g

Sous Vide Turmeric and Cumin

Ingredients:

- 1 pack, firm tofu, drained and cut to ½ inch thick pieces 3
- cloves, garlic, minced
- 1 tbsp, turmeric
- 1 tsp, cumin
- 2 tbsp, lime
- 3 tablespoons oliveoil
- Kosher salt/Pepper

Instructions:

1. Prepareyour Sous Vide water bath by attaching the immersion circulator and setting the temperature to 180°F.
2. Arrange the tofu pieces on a flat surface (you can use a baking tray) and place onthe fridge for 15 minutes.
3. In a small bowl, combine all the rest of the ingredients to make amarinade.
4. Takethe tofu pieces out of the fridge and dip into the marinade, making sure all pieces are well coated.
5. Transfer the marinated tofu on a sealable pouch (lying flat) and seal using avacuum sealer or the water displacementmethod.
6. Submerge into the water bath and let cook for 2hours.
7. Take out of the pouch carefully and serve as it is or with lettuce or Roca leaves as a garnish.

Nutritional Value Per Serving:

Calories 220, Carbohydrates 5.4 g, Fats 16.9 g, Protein 11.7 g

Garlic Mushrooms with Truffle

Prep time: 5 minutes, Cook time: 1 hour, Serves: 2

Ingredients:

- 10 mediums to large button mushrooms
- 2 cloves, garlic, minced
- 3 tbsp, olive oil
- 2 tbsp of truffle oil
- 1 tbsp of fresh thyme, chopped
- Salt/Pepper

Instructions:

1. Prepare your Sous Vide water bath by attaching the immersion circulator and setting the temperature to 185°F.
2. Mix the olive oil with the truffle oil and the rest of the ingredients. Add the mushrooms and make sure that they are well coated with the oilmixture.
3. Place the mushrooms into a sealable plastic pouch and seal using a vacuum sealer or the water displacement method.
4. Place into the water bath and cook for 1 hour.
5. Once the mushrooms are cooked, remove from the bag, drain and toss in a grillingpan to sear, until golden brown.
6. Serve hot and garnish optionally with some extra thyme ontop.

Nutritional Value Per Serving:

Calories 330, Carbohydrates 4.4 g, Fats 34.1 g, Protein 1.5 g

Chapter 8: Vegetables And Fruits

Tangerine Ice Cream

Prep time: 10 minutes, Cook time: 24 hours and 30 minutes, Serves: 6

Ingredients:

- 1 cup mandarin (only juice and pulp)
- 2 cups heavy cream
- 6 fresh egg yolks
- ½ cup milk
- ½ cup white sugar
- ¼ cup sweet condensed milk
- A pinch of salt

Instructions:

1. In a big bowl, combine all ingredients and whisk well untileven.
2. Carefully pour the mixture into the vacuum bag and sealit.
3. Cook for 30 minutes in the water bath, previously preheated to185°F.
4. When the time is up, quick chill the vacuum bag without opening it. To do this, putit into big bowl or container, filled with ice andwater.
5. Refrigerate the vacuum bag with ice-cream for 24hours.
6. Carefully transfer the mixture to an ice-cream machine and cook according to the instructions.

Nutritional Value Per Serving:

Calories 152, Carbohydrates 17 g, Fats 8 g, Protein 3 g

Citrus Confit

Prep time: 10 minutes, Cook time: 1 hour, Serves: 15

Instructions:

- 2 lemons, sliced
- 1 orange, sliced
- 1 lime, sliced
- ½ cup sugar
- ½ cup salt

Instructions:

1. In a big bowl, combine all ingredients and mix well, making sure that fruits are evenly covered with salt and sugar.
2. Carefully put the mixture into the vacuum bag and seal it.
3. Cook for 1 hour in the water bath, previously preheated to 185°F.
4. This confit is very rich in vitamins and can be stored in the fridge for at least 1 month.

Nutritional Value Per Serving:

Calories 90, Carbohydrates 17 g, Fats 2 g, Protein 1 g

Strawberry Jam

Prep time: 10 minutes, Cook time: 1 hour 30 minutes, Serves: 10

Ingredients:

- 2 cups strawberries, coarselychopped
- 1 cup white sugar
- 2 tbsp orange juice

Instructions:

1. Put the ingredients into the vacuum bag and sealit.
2. Cook for 1 hour 30 minutes in the water bath, previously preheated to180°F.
3. Serve over ice cream or cheese cake, or store in the fridge in an airtightcontainer.

Nutritional Value Per Serving:

Calories 131, Carbohydrates 13 g, Fats 7 g, Protein 4 g

Peach and Orange Jam

Prep time: 10 minutes, Cook time: 2 hours, Serves: 10

Ingredients:

- 2 cups peaches, coarsely chopped
- 1 ½ cup white sugar
- 1 cup water
- Zest and juice of 1 orange

Instructions:

1. Put the ingredients into the vacuum bag and sealit.
2. Cook for 2 hours in the water bath, previously preheated to190°F.
3. Serve over ice cream or cake, or store in the fridge in an airtightcontainer.

Nutritional Value Per Serving:

Calories 135, Carbohydrates 14 g, Fats 7 g, Protein 4 g

Blueberry Jam

Prep time: 10 minutes, Cook time: 1 hour 30 minutes, Serves: 10

Ingredients:

- 2 cups blueberries
- 1 cup white sugar
- 2 tbsp lemonjuice

Instructions:

1. Preheat the water bath to 180°F.
2. Put the ingredients into the vacuum bag and sealit.
3. Cook for 1 hour 30 minutes in the waterbath.
4. Serve over ice cream or cake, or store in the fridge in an airtightcontainer.

Nutritional Value Per Serving:

Calories 74, Carbohydrates 13 g, Fats 2 g, Protein 1 g

Steamed Asparagus with Hollandaise

Prep time: 5 minutes, Cook time: 25 minutes, Serves: 3

Ingredients:

- 20 spears white asparagus, trimmed
- 2 tablespoons butter
- ¼ cup orange juice
- 2 orange slices
- 1 teaspoon salt

Hollandaise sauce:

- 2 eggs
- ¼ cup butter
- ½ tablespoon lemon juice
- Salt and pepper, to taste

Instructions:

1. Set the cooker to 185°F.
2. Place the asparagus, butter, orange juice, orange slices, and salt in a vacuum sealbag.
3. Seal the bag and submerge in a water bath. Cook 25minutes.
4. Heat large skillet over medium-highheat.
5. Remove the asparagus from the bag and transfer to the skillet. Cook 30 secondsand remove.
6. Makethe sauce; place the egg yolks in aheat-proofbowl. Setthe bowl over simmering water.
7. Melt butter over medium heat. Gradually add butter to egg yolks, whiskingrapidly. Continue until all butter isincorporated.
8. Stir in the lemon juice. Season to taste.
9. Serve asparagus and drizzle with sauce.

Nutritional Value Per Serving:

Calories 132.5, Carbohydrates 5.6 g, Fats 10.1 g, Protein 4.8 g

Colorful Veggies with Tomato

Prep time: 15 minutes, Cook time: 12 minutes, Serves: 4

Ingredients:

- 8 carrots,halved
- 12 spears greenasparagus
- 1 cup fresh peas
- 3 tablespoons olive oil
- Salt and pepper, to taste

Sorbet:

- ¼ cup water
- 2 tablespoons sugar
- 4 ripe tomatoes, peeled
- 2 tablespoons fresh lemon juice
- 1 tablespoon tomato paste
- Salt and black pepper, to taste

Instructions:

1. Make the sorbet; in a food blender, blend the tomatoes untilpureed.
2. Bring water, sugar, and basil to a boil in a saucepan. Remove from heat and allow to cool. Pour in thetomatoes and add tomato paste. Stirto combine. Season to taste with salt and pepper.
3. Place the sorbet into a freezer. Freeze 2-4 hours or untilfirm.
4. Make the vegetables; peel and trimasparagus.
5. Place the asparagus in one Souse vide bag and add 1 tablespoon oliveoil.
6. In a separate bag, place carrots and peas. Drizzle with olive oil. Vacuum seal bothbags.
7. Set the Sous Vide to 190°F.
8. Cook the carrots and peas 12 minutes in heated water. After the carrots have been cooked 8 minutes, add asparagus.
9. Remove the bags from Sous Vide. Unpack the bags and arrange veggies onto aserving plate. Season to taste.
10. Serve veggies with a scoop of tomato sorbet.

Nutritional Value Per Serving:

Calories 243.4, Carbohydrates 30.8 g, Fats 11 g, Protein 5.3 g

Okra with Chili Yogurt

Prep time: 15 minutes, Cook time: 1 hour, Serves: 6

Ingredients:

- 2.5lb. fresh okra
- 4 tablespoons olive oil
- 1 ½ tablespoon lime zest
- 2 cloves garlic, crushed
- Salt and white pepper, to taste

Yogurt:

- 1 cup Greek yogurt
- 2 teaspoons chili powder
- ¼ cup chopped cilantro

Instructions:

1. Preheat your Sous Vide to 178°F.
2. Divide the fresh okra among two cooking bags.
3. Drizzle the okra with 2 ½ tablespoons olive oil (divided per bag), lime zest, and season to taste. Add one clove garlic per pouch.
4. Vacuum seal the bags and submerge in water.
5. Cook the okra 1 hour. Remove from a water bath and drain the accumulated liquid in a bowl. Place the okra in a separate bowl.
6. In a medium bowl, combine Greek yogurt, chili powder, cilantro, and accumulated okra water. Stir to combine.
7. Heat remaining olive oil in a skillet over medium-high heat.
8. Fry okra in the heated oil for 2 minutes.
9. Serve warm, with chili yogurt.

Nutritional Value Per Serving:

Calories 189.3, Carbohydrates 16.5 g, Fats 10.5 g, Protein 7.2 g

Honey Glazed Purple Carrots

Prep time: 10 minutes, Cook time: 45 minutes, Serves: 4

Ingredients:

- 1lb. purple carrots, scrubbed
- ¾ cup orange juice
- 2 tablespoons acacia honey
- 2 teaspoons orange zest
- 1 sprig mint
- 1 teaspoon cumin
- Salt and pepper, to taste

Instructions:

1. Preheat your sous Vide to 185°F.
2. Combine all ingredients into a Sous Vide bag.
3. Vacuum seal the bag and submerge carrots in the heated water.
4. Cook the carrots 45 minutes.
5. Remove the bag from the Sous Vide appliance.
6. Open and serve warm.

Nutritional Value Per Serving:

Calories 78.2, Carbohydrates 17.7 g, Fats 0.2 g, Protein 1.4 g

Sous Vide Ratatouille

Prep time: 10 minutes, Cook time: 30 minutes, Serves: 4

Ingredients:

- 2 red bell peppers, seeded, sliced
- 2 yellow bell peppers, seeded, sliced
- 2 green bell peppers, seeded, sliced 4
- small green zucchinis, sliced
- 4 yellow zucchinis, sliced
- 4 shallots, sliced
- 4 cloves garlic
- 10 brown mushrooms
- 6 small tomatoes, sliced
- 2 tablespoons soy sauce
- 4 tablespoons chopped mixed herbs, parsley, coriander, mint
- 2 pinches sugar
- 2 pinches black pepper
- ½ cup olive oil
- Salt, to taste

Instructions:

1. Before you start, cut the vegetables into equal-size pieces. This way you will ensure all ingredients are cooked at the same time.
2. Preheat your Sous Vide to 150°F.
3. Combine all ingredients in a large bowl. Toss gently to coat with oil.
4. Divide the veggies between four cooking bags.
5. Vacuum seal the bags and submerge under heated water.
6. Cook the vegetables 30 minutes.
7. Heat some oil in a wok pan.
8. Add in the veggies and stir-fry 30 seconds.
9. Serve warm.

Nutritional Value Per Serving:

Calories 366.7, Carbohydrates 25.5 g, Fats 26.3 g, Protein 7 g

Potato Salad

Prep time: 10 minutes, Cook time: 1 hour 30 minutes, Serves: 6

Ingredients:

- 1 ½ pounds yellow potatoes or red potatoes
- ½ cup chicken stock
- Salt and pepper to taste
- 4 oz. thick cut bacon, sliced into about ¼-inch slices
- ½ cup chopped onion
- 1/3 cup cider vinegar
- 4 scallions, thinly sliced

Instructions:

1. Set Sous Vide cooker to 185°F.
2. Cut potatoes in ¾-inch thick cubes.
3. Place potatoes and chicken stock to the zip-lock bag, making sure they are in asingle layer; seal using immersion watermethod.
4. Place potatoes in a water bath and cook for 1 hour 30minutes.
5. Meanwhile, in last 15 minutes heat non-stick skillet over medium-high heat. Addbacon and cook until crisp; remove bacon and add chopped onions. Cook until soften for 5-7 minutes.
6. Add vinegar and cook until reduced slightly.
7. Remove potatoes from the water bath and place them in skillet, with the cookingwater.
8. Continue cooking for few minutes until liquidthickens.
9. Remove potatoes from the heat and stir in scallions; toss tocombine.
10. Serve while stillhot.

Nutritional Value Per Serving:

Calories 108.8, Carbohydrates 19.9 g, Fats 1.6 g, Protein 3.7 g

Rosemary Fava Beans

Prep time: 10 minutes, Cook time: 70 minutes, Serves: 4

Ingredients:

- 1.25lb. fava beans, cleaned
- ½ teaspoon salt
- 2 sprigs rosemary
- ¼ teaspoon caraway seeds
- 1 pinch black pepper
- 3 tablespoons cold butter

Instructions:

1. Preheat your Sous Vide to 176°F.
2. Blanche the fava beans in simmering water 1 minute. Drain and dividebetween two Sous Vide bags.
3. Season the beans with salt, pepper, and caraway seeds.
4. Add 1 tablespoon butter per bag, and vacuum seal thebags.
5. Submerge the bags in water and cook 70minutes.
6. Remove the veggies from thebag.
7. Heat remaining butter in a skillet. Toss in the beans and coat the beans withbutter.
8. Servewarm.

Nutritional Value PerServing:

Calories 342.2, Carbohydrates 43.8 g, Fats 9.8 g, Protein 19.7 g

Garlic Parmesan Broccolini

Prep time: 10 minutes, Cook time: 30 minutes, Serves: 4

Ingredients:

- 1 bunch broccolini, washed and trimmed
- 1 tablespoon butter
- 1 clove garlic, crushed
- ¼ teaspoon salt
- ¼ teaspoon pepper
- 2 tablespoons grated Parmesan

Instructions:

1. Preheat the water bath to 185 ℉.
2. Combine broccolini, butter, garlic, salt, and pepper in a bag. Seal and place inwater bath.
3. Cook 30 minutes. Remove to plate and sprinkle withParmesan.

Nutritional Value Per Serving:

Calories 70, Carbohydrates 4.75 g, Fats 3.57 g, Protein 4.73 g

Tomato Confit

Prep time: 15 minutes , Cook time: 20 minutes , Serves: 4

Ingredients:

- 1.25lb. cherry tomatoes
- 1 pinch Fleur de sel
- 6 black peppercorns
- 1 teaspoon cane sugar
- 2 tablespoons Bianco AcetoBalsamico
- 2 sprigs rosemary

Instructions:

1. Preheat Sous Vide to 126 °F.
2. Heat water in a pot and bring tosimmer.
3. Make a small incision at the bottom of eachtomato.
4. Place the tomatoes into simmering water and simmer 30seconds.
5. Remove from the water and peel theirskin.
6. Divide the tomatoes between two Souse Videbags.
7. Sprinklethetomatoeswithsalt,peppercorns,sugar,and Aceto Balsamico. Add 1 sprig rosemary per bag.
8. Vacuum-seal the bags, but just to 90%. Tomatoes are soft, and they can turn intomush.
9. Submerge tomatoes in water and cook 20minutes.
10. Remove the tomatoes from Sous Vide cooker and submerge in ice-cold water for5 minutes.
11. Transfer the tomatoes to a bowl, and serve with freshmozzarella.

Nutritional Value Per Serving:

Calories 34.3, Carbohydrates 6.6 g, Fats 0.3 g, Protein 1.3 g

Pears in Pomegranate Juice

Prep time: 20 minutes , Cook time: 30 minutes , Serves: 8

Ingredients:

- 8 pears
- 5 cups pomegranate juice
- ¾ cup sugar
- 1 cinnamon stick
- ¼ teaspoon nutmeg
- ¼ teaspoon ground cloves
- ¼ teaspoon allspice

Instructions:

1. Preheat Sous Vide cooker to 176°F.
2. Combine all ingredients, except thepears.
3. Simmer until the liquid is reduced byhalf.
4. Strain and place aside.
5. Gently scrub the pears or peel ifdesired.
6. Place each pear is sous Vide bag, and pour in some poaching liquid. Make sureeach pear has the same level of poachingliquid.
7. Vacuum seal the pears and submerge inwater.
8. Cook 30 minutes.
9. Open bags and remove pears carefully. Slice the pears and place onto aplate.
10. Cook the juices in a saucepan untilthick.
11. Drizzle overpears.
12. Servewarm.

Nutritional Value PerServing:

Calories 243.5, Carbohydrates 59.4 g, Fats 0.3 g, Protein 0.8 g

Whiskey Infused Apples

Prep time: 10 minutes , Cook time: 1 hour , Serves: 4

Ingredients:

- 4 Gala apples
- 2 tablespoons brown sugar
- 2 tablespoons maple whiskey

Instructions:

1. Preheat your Sous Vide cooker to 175°F
2. Peel, core, and slice apples.
3. Place the apple slices, sugar, and whiskey into Sous Videbag.
4. Vacuum seal and submerge in water.
5. Cook 1 hour.
6. Remove the bag from the water.
7. Serve apples with ice cream while hot.

Nutritional Value Per Serving:

Calories 86.9, Carbohydrates 20.4 g, Fats 0.5 g, Protein 0.2 g

Apricot Dates Compote

Prep time: 10 minutes , Cook time: 30 minutes , Serves: 4

Ingredients:

- 10oz. fresh apricots
- 6oz. pitted dates
- 1-star anise
- 1 tablespoon Pernod
- 4 tablespoons brown sugar 1
- tablespoon unsalted butter 2
- tablespoons maplesyrup

Instructions:

1. Set the Sous Vide cooker to 180°F.
2. In a large Sous Vide bag, combine allingredients.
3. Shake gently.
4. Vacuum seal the bag and submerge inwater.
5. Cook the figs and dates 30minutes.
6. Remove the bag from the Sous Videcooker.
7. Open the bag and transfer the content to thebowl.
8. Allow cooling before serving.

Nutritional Value Per Serving:

Calories 260.3, Carbohydrates 55.2 g, Fats 3.5 g, Protein 2 g

Stuffed Apples

Prep time: 20 minutes , Cook time: 90 minutes , Serves: 4

Ingredients:

- 4 golden apples
- ¼ cup palm sugar + 1 ½ tablespoons
- 1 tablespoon chopped dates
- 3 tablespoons raisins
- 2 tablespoons butter
- ¼ teaspoon cinnamon
- 1/3 cup organic apple juice
- 1 ½ tablespoons whipping cream

To garnish:

- A handful of chopped walnuts

Instructions:

1. Preheat your Sous Vide cooker to 185°F.
2. Core the apples, leaving the bottom intact.
3. In a bowl, combine sugar, raisins, dates, butter, and cinnamon.
4. Fill the apples with prepared mixture.
5. Place each apple in Sous Vide bag and vacuum seal.
6. Cook the apples 90 minutes.
7. Combine the remaining sugar with apple juice in a saucepan.
8. Simmer until sauce is thick, for 10 minutes. Stir in the whipping cream.
9. Remove the apples from bags and serve on a plate.
10. Drizzle with sauce and sprinkle with walnuts.

Nutritional Value Per Serving:

Calories 153.2, Carbohydrates 20.7 g, Fats 7.6 g, Protein 0.5 g

Vanilla Poached Peaches

Prep time: 15 minutes , Cook time: 1 hour , Serves: 4

Ingredients:

- 4 peaches, halved, stone removed
- ½ cup white rum
- ¾ cup brown sugar
- 2 tablespoons lemon juice
- ½ vanilla bean, seeds scraped
- ¼ cup Greek yogurt
- 2 tablespoons honey
- ¼ cup chopped pistachios

Instructions:

1. Heat Sous Vide cooker to 165°F.
2. In a Sous Vide bag, combine peaches, rum, ¼ cup brown sugar, lemon juice,and vanilla.
3. Vacuum seal the bag and cook the peaches in the cooker for 1hour.
4. In a small bowl, combine Greek yogurt andhoney.
5. Open the bag and pour the poaching liquid into a saucepan. Add brown sugarand simmer 6-7 minutes or untilthickened.
6. Servepeacheson aplate. Fillthecavities with Greek yogurtand drizzle all with the syrup.
7. Serve.

Nutritional Value Per Serving:

Calories 240, Carbohydrates 51 g, Fats 2.5 g, Protein 3.5 g

Orange Compote

Prep time: 10 minutes , Cook time: 3 hours , Serves: 4

Ingredients:

- 4 blood oranges, quartered and thinly sliced
- 2 cups granulated sugar
- 1 lemon, juice and zest
- ½ vanilla seed pod
- 1 teaspoon beef gelatin powder or agar agar

Instructions:

1. Set the Sous Vide cooker to 190°F.
2. Combine all ingredients in a Sous Vide bag.
3. Seal using water immersion technique.
4. Cook the oranges 3 hours.
5. Remove the bag from the cooker and place into an ice-cold waterbath.
6. Once cooled transfer into a food processor.
7. Add the gelatin and process until smooth.
8. Allow cooling completely before serving.

Nutritional Value Per Serving:

Calories 502.7, Carbohydrates 123.1 g, Fats 0.3 g, Protein 1.9 g

Yogurt & Caraway Soup

Prep time: 25 minutes, Cook time: 2 hours 8 minutes, Serves: 4

Ingredients

- 1 tablespoon extra-virgin olive oil
- 1½ teaspoons caraway seeds
- 1 medium onion, diced
- 1 leek, halved and thinlysliced
- Kosher salt
- 2 pounds red beets, peeled,chopped
- 1 bay leaf
- 3 cups chicken broth
- ½ cup whole milk yogurt
- Apple cider vinegar
- Fresh dill fronds

Instructions:

1. Prepare your Sous Vide water bath using your immersion circulator and raisethe temperature to 185°F
2. Add the oil in a large skillet and heat it over mediumheat
3. When the oil is shimmering, add your caraway seeds
4. Toast them for about 1 minute
5. Put the onion, pinch of salt and leek, and sauté them for 5-7 minutes until the leekand onion are tender
6. Put the bay leaf, beets, and ½ teaspoon of salt into a large bowl and mix themwell
7. Dividethemixturebetweentwo heavy-duty, resealablezipperbagsand sealthem using the displacement/water immersion method
8. Submerge the bag under water for about 2hours
9. Once done, take the bags out and pour the contents to a large-sized bowl orpot.
10. Add the chicken broth and blend the whole mixture using an immersionblender
11. Stir in the yogurt, with some extra water or broth if you want a differentconsistency
12. Season the soup with some salt andvinegar
13. Serve with a garnish of dillfronds!

Nutritional Value Per Serving:

Calories 208, Carbohydrates 16 g, Fats 12 g, Protein 9 g

Miso Roasted Celeriac

Prep time: 30 minutes, Cook time: 2 hours, Serves: 6

Ingredients

- 1 tablespoon miso paste
- 1 whole celeriac
- 6 clovesgarlic
- 5 sprigsthyme
- 1 teaspoon onion powder
- 3 tablespoon fetacheese
- 1 tablespoon mustard seeds
- Juice of ¼ a largelemon
- 5 cherry tomatoes roughly cut
- Chopped up parsley
- 8-ounce vegan butter
- 1 tablespoon olive oil
- 8-ounce cooked quinoa

Instructions:

1. Prepare the Sous Vide water bath using your immersion circulator and raisethe temperature to 185°F
2. Take a large-sized pan and place it over medium heat, add the garlic, thyme,feta cheese, and dry fry them for 1 and a ½minute
3. Add the butter and keep stirring until slightly browned
4. Add the onion powder and keep the mixture on the side and allow it to cool atroom temperature
5. Add the celeriac to a zip bag alongside the cooled buttermixture
6. Submerge and cook for 1½ to 2 hours
7. Transfer the mixture to a hot pan (place over medium heat) and stirring it until golden brown
8. Season with miso paste
9. Add the oil to another pan and place it over medium heat, add the tomatoes,mustard seeds and re-heat the quinoa
10. Carefully add the lemon and parsley to the previously made tomatomixture
11. Assemble your platter by transferring the celeriac and tomatomix
12. Serve!

Nutritional Value Per Serving:

Calories 203, Carbohydrates 5 g, Fats 15 g, Protein 12 g

Whiskey & Poached

Prep time: 15 minutes, Cook time: 30 minutes, Serves: 4

Ingredients

- 2 peaches, pitted, quartered
- ½ cup rye whiskey
- ½ cup ultrafine sugar
- 1 teaspoon vanillaextract
- A pinch of salt

Instructions:

1. Prepare your Sous Vide water bath using your immersion circulator and raisethe temperature to 180°F
2. Place all the ingredients in a heavy-duty zipbag
3. Seal it using immersion method and submerge it in the hotwater
4. Let it cook for about 30minutes
5. Once the timer runs out, take the bag out and transfer it to an icebath
6. Serve!

Nutritional Value Per Serving:

Calories 727, Carbohydrates 162 g, Fats 3 g, Protein 13 g

Curried Apples

Prep time: 5 minutes, Cook time: 1 hour, Serves: 4

Ingredients

- 2 tart apples, cored, peeled, sliced
- 1 tablespoon Madras curry powder
- 2 tablespoons coconut cream

Instructions:

1. Prepare your Sous Vide water bath using your immersion circulator and raise the temperature to 185°F
2. Put all the ingredients into a heavy-duty resealable bag and seal it using the immersion method
3. Submerge and cook for 60 minutes
4. Remove the apples and transfer to a large bowl
5. Divide them among the serving plates and serve!

Nutritional Value Per Serving:

Calories 376, Carbohydrates 70 g, Fats 8 g, Protein 6 g

Cardamom Apricots

Prep time: 15 minutes, Cook time: 1 hour, Serves: 4

Ingredients

- 1-pint small apricots, halved
- 1 tablespoon unsalted butter
- 1 teaspoon cardamom seeds, freshly ground
- ½ teaspoon ground ginger
- A pinch of smoked sea salt
- Fresh basil for garnishing, chopped

Instructions:

1. Prepareyour Sous Vide water bath by increasing the temperature to 180°F Fahrenheit using an immersion circulator
2. Put the butter, apricots, ginger, cardamom, and salt in a large, heavy-duty plasticbag, and mix them well
3. Carefully seal the bag using the immersion method and submerge it in the hotwater
4. Let it cook for 60 minutes and remove the bag oncedone
5. Put the apricots in serving bowls
6. Garnish by topping it up with basil
7. Serve!

Nutritional Value Per Serving:

Calories 244, Carbohydrates 60 g, Fats 0 g, Protein 1 g

Honey Kumquats

Prep time: 15 minutes, Cook time: 1 hour, Serves: 4

Ingredients

- 1 lb. kumquats
- ¼ cup honey
- ¼ teaspoon kosher salt

Instructions:

1. Prepare your Sous Vide water bath using your immersion circulator and raisethe temperature to 194°F
2. Sliceyour Kumquats into ⅛ inch thick slices, carefully remove the stems and de-seed them
3. Put the honey, kumquat, and salt in a heavy-duty, resealable bag and seal it usingthe immersion method/water displacement method
4. Submerge it in the hot water and cook for 60minutes
5. Prepare an ice bath and put the bag in thebath
6. Cool and serve!

Nutritional Value Per Serving:

Calories 402, Carbohydrates 28 g, Fats 30 g, Protein 5 g

Squash Casseroles

Prep time: 30 minutes, Cook time: 1 hour, Serves: 4

Ingredients

- 2 tablespoons unsalted butter
- ¾ cup onion, chopped
- 1½ lbs. zucchini, quartered lengthwise and sliced into ¼ inch thick pieces
- Kosher salt
- Ground black pepper
- ½ cup whole milk
- 2 large whole eggs
- ½ cup crumbled plain potato chips for serving

Instructions:

1. Prepare your water bath using your Sous Vide immersion circulator and raisethe temperature to 176°F
2. Take 4 x 1-pint canning jars and greasethem
3. Take a large skillet and put it over medium heat. Add the butter, melt thebutter
4. Add the onions and sauté for 7minutes
5. Add the zucchini and sauté for 10 minutes and season with pepper andsalt
6. Divide the zucchini mix into the greased jars and allow them tocool
7. Whisk the milk, salt, and eggs in abowl
8. Grind some pepper and mixwell
9. Divide the mixture amongst the jars and place the lids loosely ontop
10. Submerge underwater and cook for 60minutes
11. Allow to cool for few minutes and serve over potatochips

Nutritional Value Per Serving:

Calories 327, Carbohydrates 29 g, Fats 19 g, Protein 10 g

Potato Confit

Prep time: 15 minutes, Cook time: 1 hour, Serves: 4

Ingredients

- 1 lb. small red potatoes
- 1 teaspoon kosher salt
- ¼ teaspoon ground white pepper
- 1 teaspoon chopped fresh rosemary
- 2 tablespoons whole butter
- 1 tablespoon corn oil

Instructions:

1. Prepare the Sous Vide water bath using your immersion circulator and increase the temperature to 190°F
2. Then cut the potatoes in half, carefully season the potatoes with rosemary, salt and pepper
3. Mix the potatoes with butter and oil
4. Transfer them to a heavy-duty, resealable bag and seal using the immersion method
5. Submerge underwater and cook for 60 minutes
6. Once done, add them into a large bowl, add the extra butter and serve

Nutritional Value Per Serving:

Calories 334, Carbohydrates 53 g, Fats 10 g, Protein 8 g

Cauliflower Mash

Prep time: 10 minutes, Cook time: 2 hours, Serves: 4

Ingredients

- 1 lb. trimmed cauliflower
- ½ teaspoon garlic powder
- 1 teaspoon kosher salt
- 1 tablespoon butter
- 1 tablespoon heavy whipping cream

Instructions:

1. Prepare the Sous Vide water bath using your immersion circulator and increase the temperature to 183°F
2. Add the cauliflower, salt, garlic powder, and heavy whipping cream in alarge resealable bag and seal using the immersion method
3. Cook for about 2 hours
4. Pour the contents into a blender and purée
5. Season and serve!

Nutritional Value Per Serving:

Calories 336, Carbohydrates 14 g, Fats 28 g, Protein 7 g

Garlic & Rosemary Mashed Potatoes

Prep time: 25 minutes, Cook time: 1 hour 30 minutes, Serves: 4

Ingredients

- 2 lbs. Russet potatoes
- 5 pieces' garlic cloves, peeled, mashed
- 8 oz. unsalted butter, melted
- 1 cup whole milk
- 3 sprigs rosemary
- Kosher salt
- White pepper

Instructions:

1. Prepare your water bath using your Sous Vide immersion circulator and raisethe temperature to 194°F
2. Rinse the potatoes well under coldwater
3. Peel the potatoes and slice them into ⅛ inch thickrounds
4. Put the potatoes, garlic, butter, 2 teaspoons of salt, and rosemary into aheavy-duty, resealable bag and seal using the immersionmethod
5. Cook for 1½ hours
6. Strain the mixture and pour into a medium-sizedbowl
7. Transfer the potatoes to a large-sized bowl and mash them using a potatomasher
8. Stir the melted butter and milk into your mashedpotatoes
9. Season with salt and pepper
10. Garnish with rosemary and serve!

Nutritional Value Per Serving:

Calories 102, Carbohydrates 6 g, Fats 6 g, Protein 6 g

Persimmon Chutney

Prep time: 25 minutes, Cook time: 1 hour 30 minutes, Serves: 4

Ingredients

- 2 lbs. fuyu persimmons, peeled, diced into smallpieces
- 1 small onion, diced
- ½ cup light brown sugar
- ¼ cup raisins
- 2 tablespoons apple cider vinegar
- 2 tablespoons freshly squeezed lemon juice
- 1½ teaspoons yellow mustard seeds
- 1½ teaspoons coriander seeds
- ½ teaspoon kosher salt
- ¼ teaspoon curry powder
- ¼ teaspoon dried ginger
- ⅛ teaspoon cayenne

Instructions:

1. Prepare your Sous Vide water bath using your immersion circulator and raisethe temperature to 183°F
2. Put all the ingredients into a large, heavy-duty resealablebag
3. Seal it using the immersion method andsubmerge
4. Cook for 90 minutes
5. Once done, remove the bag and transfer it to a storagecontainer
6. Serve cool

Nutritional Value Per Serving:

Calories 333, Carbohydrates 79 g, Fats 1 g, Protein 2 g

Vegetable Frittata

Prep time: 35 minutes, Cook time: 1 hour, Serves: 5

Ingredients

- 1 tablespoon extra-virgin olive oil
- 1 medium onion, chopped
- Kosher salt
- 4 cloves garlic, minced
- 1 small rutabaga, peeled, diced
- 2 medium-sized carrots, peeled, diced
- 1 medium-sized parsnip, peeled, diced
- 1 cup butternut squash, peeled,diced
- 6 oz. oyster mushrooms, roughly chopped, trimmed
- ¼ cup fresh parsley leaves, minced
- A pinch of red pepper flakes
- 5 large whole eggs
- ¼ cup whole milk

Instructions:

1. Prepare your Sous Vide water bath using your immersion circulator and raisethe temperature to 176°F
2. Grease your canning jars withoil
3. Take a large-sized skillet and add the oil in it and place over a medium highheat
4. Add your onions to the heated skillet, stir cook for about 5 minutes, season withsome salt
5. Add the garlic and stir cook for few moreminutes
6. Add the carrots, rutabaga, mushrooms, butternut squash and parsnips, season withsome salt and cook for 10-15 moreminutes
7. Stir in the pepper flakes andparsley
8. Take a large liquid measuring cup and whisk in eggs and milk, season the mix withsalt
9. Divide the egg mixture amongst the jars together with thevegetables
10. Wipe off the tops, using a damp cloth, and tighten the lids using the fingertipmethod
11. Place the jars in your water bath and cook them for 60minutes
12. Once done, remove the jars from your water bath and remove thelids
13. Allow to cool and serve!

Nutritional Value Per Serving:

Calories 459, Carbohydrates 34 g, Fats 23 g, Protein 29 g

Peas & Shallots

Prep time: 5 minutes, Cook time: 1 hour, Serves: 8

Ingredients

- 1 lb. fresh sweet peas
- 1 cup heavy cream
- ¼ cup butter
- 1 tablespoon cornstarch
- ¼ teaspoon ground nutmeg
- 4 cloves
- 2 bay leaves
- Freshly ground black pepper

Instructions:

1. Prepare your water bath using your Sous Vide immersion circulator and raisethe temperature to 184°F
2. Put the cornstarch, butter, nutmeg and cream into a smallbowl
3. Whisk well until the cornstarch has fully dissolved
4. Put the mixture into a zip bag together with the peas, black pepper, cloves, bayleaves, and seal using the immersion method
5. Submerge underwater and cook for 1 hour
6. Discard the bay leaf and serve!

Nutritional Value Per Serving:

Calories 155, Carbohydrates 17 g, Fats 7 g, Protein 6 g

Apple & Cauliflower Soup

Prep time: 30 minutes, Cook time: 1 hour, Serves: 8

Ingredients

- 2 tablespoons extra-virgin olive oil
- 1 large onion, diced
- 2 garlic cloves, thinly sliced
- Kosher salt as needed
- ⅛ teaspoon crushed red chili flakes
- 1 large cauliflower head, chopped into medium florets
- 1 apple, peeled and diced
- 4-6 cups vegetable broth

Instructions:

1. Prepare the Sous Vide water bath using your immersion circulator and increase the temperature to 183°F
2. Place a medium-sized skillet over a medium heat, add the oil and allow the oil to shimmer
3. Add the onion, ¼ teaspoon of salt, and garlic and sauté for 7 minutes until theyare tender
4. Add the chili flakes and stirwell
5. Once done, turn-off the heat and allow the mixture tocool
6. Divide the apple, the onion mix, cauliflower, and ¼ teaspoon of salt betweentwo individual resealable bags
7. Seal the bags using the immersion method, submerge and cook for 1hour
8. Once done, remove the bag and place the contents in a largepot
9. Add the vegetable broth and blend well using an immersionblender
10. Add a bit more broth for a thickerconsistency
11. Season with salt and serve

Nutritional Value Per Serving:

Calories 207, Carbohydrates 19 g, Fats 11 g, Protein 8 g

Honey Miso Butter Corn

Prep time: 15 minutes, Cook time: 30 minutes, Serves: 4

Ingredients

- 4 ears, corn
- 6 tablespoons butter
- 3 tablespoons red miso paste
- 1 teaspoon honey
- Togarashi
- Sesame oil
- 1 scallion, thinly sliced
- 1 teaspoon toasted sesame seeds

Instructions:

1. Prepare the Sous Vide water bath using your immersion circulator and increase the temperature to 183°F
2. First remove the husks, then the silks from the corn and cut the ears inhalf
3. Slather 2 teaspoons of butter on each of thecorn
4. Transfer the corn to sous vide resealable bag and seal using the immersionmethod
5. Put 4 tablespoons of butter, 2 tablespoons of miso paste, 1 teaspoon of honey,the sesame oil and Togarashi in abowl
6. Whisk well. Allow to rest for 30minutes
7. Once the corns are ready, broil the corn for a Nice char* and spread the misohoney mixture on top
8. Sprinkle with sesame seeds andscallions
9. Serve!

Nutritional Value Per Serving:

Calories 263, Carbohydrates 36 g, Fats 11 g, Protein 5 g

Honey Poached Pears

Prep time: 5 minutes, Cook time: 45 minutes, Serves: 2

Ingredients

- 1 pear, thinly sliced
- 1 lb. honey
- ½ cup of walnuts
- 4 tablespoons shaved Parmesan
- 2 cups rocket leaves
- Salt and pepper
- 2 tablespoons lemon juice
- 2 tablespoons extra-virgin olive oil

Instructions:

1. Prepare your water bath using your Sous Vide immersion circulator and raisethe temperature to 158.8°F
2. Put the honey, smeared pears in a heavy-duty resealablebag
3. Seal using the immersion method and submerge
4. Cook for 45 minutes
5. Put the contents of the bag in abowl
6. Add the remaining dressing ingredients and tosswell
7. Serve!

Nutritional Value Per Serving:

Calories 208, Carbohydrates 16 g, Fats 12 g, Protein 9 g

Pear & Walnut Salad

Prep time: 10 minutes, Cook time: 30 minutes, Serves: 4

Ingredients

- 2 tablespoons honey
- 2 pears, cored, halved, thinly sliced
- ½ cup walnuts, lightly toasted, roughly chopped
- ½ cup shaved parmesan
- 4 cups arugula
- Sea salt and pepper
- Garlic Dijon Dressing
- ¼ cup olive oil
- 1 tablespoon white wine vinegar
- 1 teaspoon Dijon mustard
- 1 garlic clove, minced
- Salt

Instructions:

1. Prepare your Sous Vide water bath using your immersion circulator and raisethe temperature to 159°F
2. Put the honey in a heat-proofbowl
3. Heat for 20 seconds
4. Put the pears in the honey and mixwell
5. Put them in a heavy-duty resealable bag and seal using the immersionmethod
6. Cook for 30 minutes and plunge the bag into an ice water bath for 5minutes
7. Chill in your fridge for 3hours
8. Add all of the dressing ingredients and give the jar a niceshake
9. Leave it in your fridge for awhile
10. Serve by placing the walnuts, arugula, and parmesan in a largebowl
11. Add your drained pear slices and thedressing
12. Toss everything well and season with pepper andsalt

Nutritional Value Per Serving:

Calories 370, Carbohydrates 56 g, Fats 14 g, Protein 5 g

Red Onions Balsamic Glaze

Prep time: 20 minutes, Cook time: 1 hour 30 minutes, Serves: 1

Ingredients

- 3 medium-sized red onions
- 1 tablespoon unsalted butter
- Salt and pepper
- 2 tablespoons balsamic vinegar
- 1 tablespoon honey
- 2 teaspoons, fresh thyme leaves

Instructions:

1. Prepare the Sous Vide water bath using your immersion circulator and raisethe temperature to 185°F
2. Peel the skin of the onion, making sure to keep the rootsintact
3. Cut the onion into wedges through the rootend
4. Put a large skillet over a medium/highheat
5. Add the butter and allow to heat up andmelt
6. Add the onion and season with pepper and salt, cook for about 10 minutes untilnicely browned
7. Put the balsamic vinegar and simmer on low heat for 1minute
8. Remove from the heat and carefully stir in thehoney
9. Transfer the onions to a large, heavy-duty zipperbag
10. Seal the bag using the immersion method andsubmerge
11. Cook for 90 minutes
12. Once done, remove from the water and arrange the onions on a servingplate
13. Sprinkle with fresh thyme and serve with pizza or asandwich

Nutritional Value Per Serving:

Calories 150, Carbohydrates 19 g, Fats 6 g, Protein 5 g

Gnocchi Pillows with Parmesan

Prep time: 20 minutes, Cook time: 1 hour 30 minutes, Serves: 2

Ingredients

- 1 pack store-bought gnocchi
- 1 tablespoon unsaltedbutter
- ½ thinly sliced sweet onion
- Salt and black pepper
- ½ cup frozen peas
- ¼ cup heavy cream
- ½ cup grated parmesan
- Salt and pepper

Instructions:

1. Prepare your water bath using your Sous Vide immersion circulator and raisethe temperature to 183°F
2. Put the gnocchi in a heavy-duty resealablebag
3. Seal using the immersion method and cook for 1½hours
4. Once done, place a cast iron skillet over a mediumheat
5. Add the butter and allow to melt
6. Add the onion and season with salt. Sauté for 3minutes
7. Add the frozen peas and cream, and bring to asimmer
8. Stir in the gnocchi and grated parmesan, to coat with the creamsauce
9. Season with pepper and salt
10. Transfer to a plate andserve!

Nutritional Value Per Serving:

Calories 208, Carbohydrates 16 g, Fats 12 g, Protein 9 g

Momofuku Styled Brussels

Prep time: 20 minutes, Cook time: 50 minutes, Serves: 2

Ingredients

- 2 lbs. Brussels sprouts, stems trimmed, sliced inhalf
- 2 tablespoons extra-virgin oliveoil
- ¼ teaspoon kosher salt
- ¼ cup fish sauce
- 2 tablespoons water
- 1½ tablespoons granulated sugar
- 1 tablespoon rice vinegar
- 1½ teaspoons lime juice
- 12 pieces thinly sliced Thai chilis
- 1 small minced garlic clove
- Chopped fresh mint
- Chopped fresh cilantro

Instructions:

1. Prepare the Sous Vide water bath using your immersion circulator and raisethe temperature to 183°F
2. Put the Brussel sprouts, olive oil and salt in a heavy-duty, resealablebag
3. Seal using the immersion method
4. Cook for 50 minutes
5. Putthe fish sauce, sugar, water, rice vinegar, lime juice, garlic, and chilis in a small bowl and mix them to prepare the vinaigrette
6. Once done, put the Brussels on an aluminum foil, lined baking sheet and heat upyour broiler
7. Broil the Brussels for 5 minutes until they arecharred
8. Transfer to a medium-sized bowl and add the vinaigrette
9. Toss well and sprinkle with mint and cilantro

Nutritional Value Per Serving:

Calories 237, Carbohydrates 38 g, Fats 5 g, Protein 10 g

Cauliflower Puree

Prep time: 20 minutes, Cook time: 45 minutes, Serves: 4

Ingredients

- 1 head cauliflower
- 1 cup chicken stock
- 3 tablespoons unsalted butter
- ¾ teaspoon salt

Instructions:

1. Preparethe Sous Vide water bath using your immersion circulator and increase the temperature to 185°F
2. Remove a few leaves from the bottom part of the cauliflower core and cut into ¼ inch small slices
3. Put the cauliflower, butter and chicken stock in a heavy-duty, resealablebag
4. Seal using the immersion method
5. Submerge underwater and cook for 45 minutes
6. Once cooked, remove the bag and strain the contents through a metalmesh
7. Save the cooking liquid
8. Put the cauliflower to a blender and puree untilsmooth
9. Add some of the cooking liquid, season with salt andserve!

Nutritional Value Per Serving:

Calories 189, Carbohydrates 29 g, Fats 5 g, Protein 7 g

Sweet Corn Soup

Prep time: 15 minutes, Cook time: 1 hour, Serves: 4

Ingredients

- 4 ears, corn, shucked*
- 4 tablespoons unsalted butter
- 1 cup whole milk
- 1 bay leaf
- Kosher salt
- Ground white pepper
- 4 slices crispy cooked bacon
- 2 tablespoons minced chives

Instructions:

1. Preparethe Sous Videwaterbath usingyourimmersioncirculatorandincreasethe temperature to 185°F
2. Put the corn kernels, corn cobs, milk, 1 tablespoon of salt, 1 tablespoon of white pepper, and bay leaf into a heavy-duty, resealable bag and seal using theimmersion method
3. Submerge the bag and allow it to cook for 1 hour
4. When ready, discard the corn cobs and bay leaf, and transfer the remaining mix toa blender
5. Puree for about 1 minute
6. Add some milk if you want to change theconsistency
7. Season it with salt and pepper and serve with a garnish of bacon andchive

NutritionalValuePerServing:

Calories 460, Carbohydrates 11 g, Fats 32 g, Protein 32 g

Butter Radish

Prep time: 15 minutes, Cook time: 45 minutes, Serves: 4

Ingredients

- 1 lb. radish, halved
- 3 tablespoons unsaltedbutter
- 1 teaspoon sea salt
- ½ teaspoon freshly ground black pepper

Instructions:

1. Prepare the Sous Vide water bath using your immersion circulator and raisethe temperature to 180°F
2. Put all the listed ingredients into a medium-sized zipbag
3. Seal using the immersion method and allow it to cook underwater for about 45minutes
4. Once done, remove the bag and transfer the contents to aplatter
5. Serve!

Nutritional Value Per Serving:

Calories 237, Carbohydrates 56 g, Fats 1 g, Protein 1 g

Cinnamon Poached Pears

Prep time: 40 minutes, Cook time: 30 minutes, Serves: 8

Ingredients

- 4 Bosc pears
- 1 cup tawny port
- ½ cup granulated sugar
- 2 wide strips orange zest, 2 inches long and ½ inchwide 2
- wide strips lemon zest, 2 inches long and ½ inchwide
- ½ teaspoon ground cinnamon
- Ice cream for flavor

Instructions:

1. Set your Sous Vide immersion circulator to a temperature of 180°F, and prepareyour water bath
2. Peel the pears and add them in a heavy-duty zip bag, together with theremaining ingredients
3. Seal using the immersion method and cook for 30minutes
4. Cool for 30 minutes and pour the liquid into a pan. Place it over medium heatand reduce the liquid by 2/3
5. Remove the heat and wait until the liquid iscooled
6. Core the pears diagonally and create fanshapes
7. Carefully transfer the pears to your serving plate and pour the previouslyprepared sauce on top
8. Serve with a topping of your favorite icecream

Nutritional Value Per Serving:

Calories 392, Carbohydrates 97 g, Fats 0 g, Protein 1 g

Mexican Street Corn

Prep time: 5 minutes, Cook time: 30 minutes, Serves: 2

Ingredients

- 2 ears of corn, shucked
- 2 tablespoons cold butter
- Kosher salt
- Fresh ground pepper
- ¼ cup mayonnaise
- ½ tablespoon Mexican style chili powder
- ½ teaspoon grated lime zest
- ¼ cup crumbled Queso Fresco
- ¼ cup chopped, fresh cilantro

Instructions:

1. Prepare the Sous Vide water bath using your immersion circulator and increase the temperature to 183°F
2. Put the corn ears and butter in a zipbag
3. Season with salt and pepper and seal using the immersionmethod
4. Cook for 30 minutes
5. Once done, remove the corn
6. Add the mayo, lime zest, and chili powder into a small bag andmix
7. Place the Queso Fresco on a smallplate
8. Spread 1 tablespoon of mayonnaise mixture on top of the corn ears, and roll themon the cheese
9. Sprinkle with salt and fresh cilantro and serve!

Nutritional Value Per Serving:

Calories 396, Carbohydrates 30 g, Fats 24 g, Protein 15 g

Schmaltzy Brussels Sprouts

Prep time: 10 minutes, Cook time: 30 minutes, Serves: 4

Ingredients

- 1 lb. Brussels sprouts
- ¼ cup schmaltz
- ½ teaspoon salt
- Pepper

Instructions:

1. Prepare the Sous Vide water bath using your immersion circulator and increase the temperature to 183°F
2. Trim the Brussels to halve and quarter them
3. Put them in a zip bag and season with salt and pepper
4. Add the schmaltz and mix well
5. Seal the bag using the immersion method
6. Submerge and cook for 30 minutes
7. Remove from the bag and serve!

Nutritional Value Per Serving:

Calories 257, Carbohydrates 23 g, Fats 13 g, Protein 12 g

Green Beans & Mandarin

Prep time: 5 minutes, Cook time: 60 minutes, Serves: 9

Ingredients

- 1 lb. green beans,trimmed
- 2 small mandarin oranges
- 2 tablespoons butter
- ½ teaspoon salt
- 2 oz. toasted hazelnuts

Instructions:

1. Prepare the Sous Vide water bath using your immersion circulator and increase the temperature to 185°F
2. Put the green beans, butter, and salt in a zip bag
3. Zest one of the mandarins into the bag and keep the other for later use
4. Cut the zested mandarin in half and squeeze the juice into the bag
5. Use the immersion method to seal the bag
6. Submerge and cook for 60 minutes
7. Pre-heat your oven to 400°F and toast the hazelnuts for 7 minutes
8. Remove the skin and chop roughly
9. Serve by putting the beans on a platter and topping them up with a garnish of toasted hazelnut and the remaining mandarin zest

Nutritional Value Per Serving:

Calories 514, Carbohydrates 48 g, Fats 18 g, Protein 40 g

Sous Vide Cactus

Prep time: 15 minutes, Cook time: 1 hour, Serves: 4

Ingredients

- 2 tablespoons freshly squeezed lime juice
- 1 tablespoon canola oil
- 1 clove garlic, thinly sliced 1
- teaspoon ground coriander 1
- teaspoon ground cumin
- 1 teaspoon salt
- 4 cactus paddles, thorns removed

Instructions:

1. Prepare the Sous Vide water bath using your immersion circulator and increase the temperature to 175°F
2. Whisk the lime juice, garlic, oil, coriander, cumin and salt in a smallbowl
3. Transfer to a zip bag and add thecactus
4. Seal using the immersion method and cook for 60minutes
5. Once cooked, remove the bag from the water and take out thecactus
6. Discard the cooking liquid
7. Remove the skin from the cactus with a vegetable peeler and slice into thinstrips
8. Serve!

Nutritional Value Per Serving:

Calories 70, Carbohydrates 11 g, Fats 2 g, Protein 2 g

Asparagus Vinaigrette

Prep time: 20 minutes, Cook time: 15 minutes, Serves: 2

Ingredients

- 1 Bunch large asparagus
- Salt and pepper
- ¼ cup extra-virgin olive oil
- 1 teaspoon Dijon mustard
- 1 teaspoon red wine vinegar
- 1 hard-boiled egg, cooled, roughly chopped
- Fresh parsley, chopped

Instructions:

1. Prepare the Sous Vide water bath using your immersion circulator and increase the temperature to 185°F
2. Slice up the fibrous bottom of the asparagus and discardit
3. Peel the bottom three-quarters of the stalks and place them, in a single layer, in a zip bag
4. Season with salt and pepper and seal using the immersion method and cook for15 minutes
5. For the vinaigrette, put the olive oil, vinegar and Dijon mustard in a bowl and mixthem well
6. Season with salt and transfer to a mason jar. Seal tightly and shake untilemulsified
7. Remove the bag and transfer to an icebath
8. Discard the cooking liquid and serve with a topping of egg, parsley, and thevinaigrette

Nutritional Value Per Serving:

Calories 146, Carbohydrates 9 g, Fats 10 g, Protein 5 g

Ma Po Tofu

Prep time: 15 minutes, Cook time: 1 hour 30 minutes, Serves: 6

Ingredients

- 1 cup vegetable broth
- 2 tablespoons tomato paste
- 1 tablespoon grated ginger
- 1 tablespoon rice wine vinegar
- 1 tablespoon agave nectar
- 2 teaspoons sriracha sauce
- 3 cloves minced garlic
- 1 teaspoon soy sauce
- 2 boxes cubed silken tofu

Instructions:

1. Prepare the Sous Vide water bath using your immersion circulator and increase the temperature to 185°F
2. Whisk all of the listed ingredients in a bowl, except the tofu
3. Put the tofu in a zip bag and add the mixture
4. Seal the bag using the immersion method and cook for 1½ hours
5. Serve!

Nutritional Value Per Serving:

Calories 590, Carbohydrates 83 g, Fats 14 g, Protein 33 g

Buttered Beets & Orange

Prep time: 15 minutes, Cook time: 1 hour 30 minutes, Serves: 4

Ingredients

- 1 lb. medium red beets, peeled,quartered
- 2 tablespoons unsalted butter
- 2 peeled oranges, cut intoSupreme
- 1 tablespoon honey
- 3 tablespoons balsamic vinegar
- 4 tablespoons extra virgin oliveoil
- Kosher salt and blackpepper
- 6 oz. baby romaine leaves
- ½ cup pistachios, chopped, roasted
- ½ cup Parmigiano Reggiano/Parmesan Cheese

Instructions:

1. Prepare the Sous Vide water bath using your immersion circulator and increase the temperature to 180°F
2. Put the beets in a plastic zip bag and add thebutter
3. Seal using the immersion method, and cook for 90minutes
4. Once cooked, take the beets out from the bag and discard the cookingliquid
5. Whisk the honey, oil and vinegar, with a seasoning of salt and pepper, in abowl
6. Toss the romaine leaves, orange, beets and vinaigrette, and divide the wholemixture amongst fourplatters
7. Top the servings with pistachio and Parmigiano Reggiano cheese andserve!

Nutritional Value Per Serving:

Calories 134, Carbohydrates 17 g, Fats 6 g, Protein 3 g

Chapter 9: Desserts

Apple & Cinnamon Pie

Prep time: 10 minutes, Cook time: 2 hours 20 minutes, Serves: 4

Instructions:

- 2 pounds green, cored, peeled and sliced
- 3/4 cup sugar
- 2 tbsp cornstarch
- 2 tbsp butter
- 2 tsp ground cinnamon
- 1 pack puff pastry
- 2 tbsp milk
- 2 tbsp sugar

Instructions:

1. Preheat the water bath to 160°F.
2. Put the sliced apples, cornstarch, sugar, cinnamon and butter in the vacuum bag andset the cooking time for 1 hour 30minutes.
3. When the time is up, cool down the filling to the roomtemperature.
4. In the meantime, preheat the oven to 375°F, grease a baking pan, and roll out 1 sheetof the pastry.
5. Pourthe filling overthe sheet, andcover it with another sheet, seal the sheets on the edges with your fingers.
6. Bake in the preheated oven for 35minutes.

Nutritional Value Per Serving:

Calories 276, Carbohydrates 30 g, Fats 16 g, Protein 3 g

Spicy Custard Crème

Prep time: 10 minutes, Cook time: 1 hour 30 minutes, Serves: 4

Ingredients:

- 2 cups heavycream
- 1 cup milk
- 3 tsp ginger root,sliced
- 4 fresh egg yolks
- ½ cup brown sugar
- A pinch of salt

Instructions:

1. Before preheating the water bath, arrange the ramekins: install the rack half-inch below the water surface.
2. Place 4 ramekins on the rack. Make sure the water level is not higher than 2/3 ofthe ramekins. Remove the ramekins and setaside.
3. Combine the heavy cream, milk and sliced ginger in a small saucepan and heatthe mixture but do not bring it to boil. Cover the pan and set aside for 30minutes.
4. In 30 minutes, strain the liquid, return it to the pan, and reheatagain.
5. Whisk the egg yolks with salt and sugar, and carefully pour the cream mixture intothe yolk mixture. Whisk well untileven.
6. Pour the custards into the 4 ramekins, wrap them with plastic and return back onthe rack.
7. Set the timer for 50minutes.
8. When the time is up, cool the ramekins to the room temperature then refrigerate until cold and serve.

Nutritional Value Per Serving:

Calories 61.8, Carbohydrates 8 g, Fats 3 g, Protein 0.7 g

Crème Brulee

Prep time: 10 minutes, Cook time: 2 hours, Serves: 4

Ingredients:

- 2 cups heavy cream
- ½ tsp vanilla powder
- 1 cinnamon stick
- 4 fresh eggyolks
- ½ cup brown sugar
- A pinch of salt

Instructions:

1. Install the rack in the water bath half-inch below the watersurface.
2. Place 4 ramekins on the rack. Make sure the water level is not higher than 2/3 ofthe ramekins. Remove the ramekins and setaside.
3. Combine the heavy cream, vanilla powder and cinnamon stick in a small saucepanand heat the mixture but do not bring it to boil. Cover the pan and set aside for 10minutes.
4. In 10 minutes, strain the cream and return it to thepan.
5. Whisk the egg yolks with salt and sugar, and carefully pour the cream mixture intothe yolk mixture. Whisk well untileven.
6. Pour the custards into the 4 ramekins, wrap them with plastic and return back tothe rack.
7. Set the timer for 90minutes.
8. When the time is up, cool the ramekins to the room temperature, then refrigerate until cold and serve.

Nutritional Value Per Serving:

Calories 61.8, Carbohydrates 8 g, Fats 3 g, Protein 0.7 g

Apricot and Cranberry Pie

Prep time: 10 minutes, Cook time: 2 hours 20 minutes, Serves: 4

Instructions:

- 2 pounds ripe apricots, bone removed, halved
- ½-pound cranberries
- 3/4 cup sugar
- 2 tbsp cornstarch
- 2 tbsp butter
- 2 tsp ground cinnamon
- 1 pack puff pastry
- 2 tbsp milk
- 2 tbsp sugar

Instructions:

1. Preheat the water bath to 160°F.
2. Put the apricots, cornstarch, cranberries, sugar, cinnamon and butter in the vacuumbag and set the cooking time for 1 hour 30minutes.
3. When the time is up, cool down the filling to the roomtemperature.
4. In the meantime, preheat the oven to 375°F, grease a baking pan, and roll out 1 sheetof the pastry.
5. Pour the filling over the sheet, and cover it with another sheet, seal the sheets on the edges with your fingers.
6. Bake in the preheated oven for 35minutes.

Nutritional Value Per Serving:

Calories 276, Carbohydrates 30 g, Fats 16 g, Protein 3 g

White Chocolate Mousse

Prep time: 10 minutes, Cook time: 24 hours and 7 hours, Serves: 4

Ingredients:

- 2/3 cup white chocolate, chopped
- ½ cup milk
- ½ cup double cream
- ½ tsp gelatin powder
- 2 tbsp cold water

Instructions:

1. Preheat your Sous Vide machine to 194°F.
2. Place the chopped white chocolate in the vacuumbag.
3. Seal the bag, put it into the water bath and set the timer for 6hours.
4. When the time is up, pour the chocolate into a bowl and stir with aspoon.
5. Pour the milk into a pan and warm it over mediumheat.
6. Soak the gelatin powder in 2 tbsp cold water and dissolve it in the warmmilk.
7. Carefully stir the milk-gelatin mixture into the chocolate paste until even and refrigerate for 25 minutes.
8. Remove from the fridge, stir again and refrigerate for another 25minutes.
9. Beat the cream to peaks and combine with white chocolatemixture.
10. Pour into single serve cups and refrigerate for 24 hours beforeserving.

Nutritional Value Per Serving:

Calories 227, Carbohydrates 19 g, Fats 15 g, Protein 4 g

Dark Chocolate Mousse

Prep time: 10 minutes, Cook time: 24 hours + 7 hours, Serves: 4

Ingredients:

- 2/3 cup dark chocolate, chopped
- ½ cup milk
- ½ cup double cream
- ½ tsp gelatin powder
- 2 tbsp cold water

Instructions:

1. Preheat your Sous Vide machine to 194°F.
2. Place the chopped dark chocolate in the vacuumbag.
3. Seal the bag, put it into the water bath and set the timer for 6hours.
4. When the time is up, pour the chocolate into a bowl and stir with aspoon.
5. Pour the milk into a pan and warm it over mediumheat.
6. Soak the gelatin powder in 2 tbsp cold water and dissolve it in the warmmilk.
7. Carefully stir the milk-gelatin mixture into the chocolate paste until even and refrigerate for 25 minutes.
8. Remove from the fridge, stir again and refrigerate for another 25minutes.
9. Beat the cream to peaks and combine with white chocolatemixture.
10. Pour into single serve cups and refrigerate for 24 hours beforeserving.

Nutritional Value Per Serving:

Calories 227, Carbohydrates 19 g, Fats 15 g, Protein 4 g

Sous Vide Crème Brulee

Prep time: 10 minutes, Cook time: 1 hour, Serves: 4

Ingredients:

- ¼ cup sugar
- 1 pinch salt
- 1 cup heavy cream
- 3 large egg yolks
- Brown sugar, to sprinkle

Instructions:

1. Preheat Sous Vide cooker to 181°F.
2. Combine all ingredients in a foodblender.
3. Blend until smooth.
4. Transfer the content into Sous Videbag.
5. Fold the edges, and remove as much as airpossible.
6. Clip the bag to the side of your pot. Submerge the bag into a water bath and cook60 minutes. Make sure you remove the bag after 30 minutes and shakegently.
7. Remove the bag from thecooker.
8. Divide the bag content between four ramekins. Sprinkle the egg custard withbrown sugar.
9. Caramelize the sugar with atorch.
10. Serve.

Nutritional Value Per Serving:

Calories 196, Carbohydrates 13.8 g, Fats 14.5 g, Protein 2.6 g

Chocolate Chili Cake

Prep time: 20 minutes, Cook time: 1 hour 20 minutes, Serves: 6

Ingredients:

- 4 large eggs
- 4oz. unsalted butter
- 2 tablespoons cocoa powder
- ½ lb. chocolate chips
- ½ teaspoon chili powder
- ¼ cup brown sugar

Instructions:

1. Preheat the Sous Vide cooker to 115°F.
2. Place the chocolate chips, and butter into Sous Vide bag.
3. Submerge in water and cook 15 minutes.
4. Remove the bag and set the cooker to 170°F.
5. Prepare 6 4oz. Mason jars by coating with cooking spray.
6. Beat the eggs with brown sugar until fluffy.
7. Stir in the chocolate, cocoa powder, and chili powder.
8. Divide the mixture between prepared mason jars and apply the lid on finger tightonly.
9. Submerge the jars in a water bath for 1 hour.
10. Remove the jars and place onto wire rack to cool completely.
11. Invert the cake onto a plate.
12. Serve with raspberry ice cream.

Nutritional Value Per Serving:

Calories 420.5, Carbohydrates 29.8 g, Fats 30.1 g, Protein 7.6 g

Chocolate Chip Cookies

Prep time: 30 minutes, Cook time: 30 minutes, Serves: 12

Ingredients:

- ½ cup flour
- ½ teaspoon baking powder
- 1 pinch salt
- 3 tablespoons unsalted softenedbutter
- 1/3 cup granulated sugar
- 1 small egg
- ½ cup mini chocolate chips
- 1 teaspoon vanilla paste

Instructions:

1. Set the cooker to 195°F.
2. In a small bowl, combine flour, baking powder, andsalt.
3. In a separate large bowl, cream butter and sugar untilfluffy.
4. Fold in the egg and vanilla paste, and stir untilsmooth.
5. Mix in the flour mixture and stir until just combined. Fold in the chocolatechips.
6. Roll the dough between two pieces of baking paper and cut out the cookies usinga cookie cutter.
7. Divide the cookies between two Sous Vide cookingbags.
8. Vacuum seal the cookies and submerge in a waterbath.
9. Cook 30 minutes.
10. Remove the bag from the waterbath.
11. Cool completely beforeopening.
12. Remove the cookies from the bag andserve.

Nutritional Value Per Serving:

Calories 46, Carbohydrates 9.7 g, Fats 0.4 g, Protein 0.9 g

Strawberry Mousse

Prep time: 10 minutes, Cook time: 45 minutes, Serves: 4

Ingredients:

- ½ lb. strawberries
- 1 ½ tablespoons lemon juice
- 3 tablespoons fine sugar
- ½ cup heavy cream
- ½ teaspoon vanilla paste

Instructions:

1. Set the cooker to 180°F.
2. Combine the strawberries, lemon juice, and sugar into Sous videbag.
3. Seal the bag using water immersiontechnique.
4. Submerge the bag into a water bath and cook 45minutes.
5. Remove the bag from the Sous Videcooker.
6. Transfer the strawberries to a food blender. Blend untilsmooth.
7. Let the mixture cool to a roomtemperature.
8. In the meantime, beat the heavy cream and vanilla until stiff peaksform.
9. Stir in the strawberry puree.
10. Divide the mousse between four serving bowls. Refrigerate 1 hour beforeserving.

Nutritional Value Per Serving:

Calories 110.6, Carbohydrates 13.9 g, Fats 5.8 g, Protein 0.7 g

Cookie Dough

Prep time: 10 minutes, Cook time: 10 minutes, Serves: 6

Ingredients:

- ½ cup softened butter
- ¾ cup brown sugar
- 1 teaspoonmolasses
- 1 medium egg
- 1 ¼ cups almond flour
- ½ cup salted caramel chips

Instructions:

1. Preheat your cooker to 171°F.
2. Cream the butter with sugar in a largebowl.
3. Fold in molasses and egg. Stir untilsmooth.
4. Fold in the almond flour and mix until just combined. Add caramel chips and mixuntil incorporated.
5. Refrigerate 1 hour.
6. Remove the dough from the fridge and shape into 12balls.
7. Place the balls into Sous Vide bag and press each to ½-inchthick.
8. Vacuum seal the bag and submerge inwater.
9. Cook the dough 10 minutes.
10. Remove the bag from the water bath and chill in a fridge 10minutes.
11. Open the bag carefully and serve the cookiedough.

Nutritional Value Per Serving:

Calories 259.3, Carbohydrates 19.9 g, Fats 18.9 g, Protein 2.4 g

Pistachio Ice Cream

Prep time: 20 minutes, Cook time: 1 hour, Serves: 6

Ingredients:

- 1 cup shelled pistachios
- ½ cup brown sugar
- ¾ cup heavy cream
- 1 cup almond milk 5
- medium egg yolks
- ¼ teaspoon pistachio extract

Instructions:

1. Set the cooker 180°F.
2. Process the pistachios and sugar in a food processor until you have a finepowder.
3. Combine the pistachio mixture with heavy cream, and milk in asaucepan.
4. Bring to a simmer and remove from the heat. Cover and let the milk infuse 1hour.
5. Strain the milk and discard any solids.
6. Pour the milk into a food blender. Add eggs and pistachio extract. Blend untilfrothy.
7. Transferthemilk mixtureinto aSous Videbag. Sealthebag usingwater immersion technique.
8. Submerge the bag into a water bath and cook 1 hour. Make sure you shake thebag every 20 minutes.
9. Remove the bag from the water bath and transfer into the ice-cold waterbath.
10. Once cooled churn into ice creammachine.
11. Serve.

Nutritional Value Per Serving:

Calories 368.6, Carbohydrates 20.7 g, Fats 28.8 g, Protein 8 g

Lemon and Crème Brulee

Prep time: 10 minutes, Cook time: 1 hour 10 minutes, Serves: 4

Ingredients:

- 6 large egg yolks
- 1 and 1/3 cup, superfine sugar
- 3 cups of heavy whipcream
- 2 lemon zest
- 4 tablespoon, freshly squeezed lemon juice
- 1 teaspoon, vanilla extract
- 1 cup, fresh blueberries

Instructions:

1. Set up your Sous Vide immersion circulator to a temperature of 195°F and prepareyour water bath
2. Take an electric mixer and whisk in egg yolks, sugar until you have a creamymixture, keep it on the side
3. Take a medium saucepan and place it over medium heat, add cream and heat itup
4. Add lemon zest, lemon juice, vanilla and stir simmer for 4-5 minute over lowheat
5. Remove the cream mixture from heat and allow it to cool, once cooled transfer a small amount into egg mix and whisk well
6. Add remaining cream mixture into the egg and stir
7. Divide the blueberries among six pieces of mini mason jars and pour the egg cream mix over the blueberries divide the mixture amongst thejars
8. Tightly seal the lid and submerge, cook for 45minutes
9. Remove the jars from water bath and chill for 5hours
10. Caramelize a layer of sugar on top using a blowtorch andserve!

Nutritional Value Per Serving:

Calories 154, Carbohydrates 5 g, Fats 10 g, Protein 11 g

Coconut Milk Kheer

Prep time: 10 minutes, Cook time: 3 hours, Serves: 5

Ingredients:

- 5 heaping tablespoon, basmati rice
- 2 cans, full-fat coconut milk
- 1 cup, water
- 3 tablespoons, granulated sugar
- Pinch, kosher salt
- 10 green cardamom pods,crushed
- Chopped shelled pistachios
- Slivered almonds
- Rosewater

Instructions:

1. Set up your Sous Vide immersion circulator to a temperature of 180°F and prepareyour water bath
2. Divide the rice evenly amongst 5 half-pintjars
3. Take a large bowl and add coconut milk, sugar, water, salt and divide themixture amongst the cans aswell
4. Add 2 cardamom pods to each jar and seallightly
5. Submerge and cook for 3 hours
6. Remove the jars from water bath and transfer to coolingrack
7. Remove the lids and stir thepudding
8. Allow them to cool and chill for 4hours
9. Remove the lid and stir
10. Serve with a topping of pistachio, almond or few drops of rosewater

Nutritional Value Per Serving:

Calories 220, Carbohydrates 6 g, Fats 16 g, Protein 13 g

Pumpkin Pie Jars

Prep time: 10 minutes, Cook time: 1 hour, Serves: 6

Ingredients:

- 1 large sized can,pumpkins
- 1 egg + 3 egg yolks
- 2 tablespoons, flour
- ½ teaspoon, kosher salt
- 1 tablespoon, pumpkin pie spice
- 1 can, evaporated milk
- ½ cup, white and brown sugar
- Whipped cream
- Candied nuts

Instructions:

1. Set up your Sous Vide immersion circulator to a temperature of 175°F and prepareyour water bath
2. Add 1 large can of pumpkin, 2 tablespoons of flour, ½ a teaspoon of kosher salt, 1 tablespoon of pumpkin pie spice, 1 egg and 3 egg yolks alongside the 1 can of evaporated milk
3. Mix well
4. Pour the mixture into 6 - 4-ounce jars and seal themtightly
5. Cook for 1 hour
6. Remove the jars and chill for 8hours
7. Garnish with whipped cream and candied nuts andserve!

Nutritional Value Per Serving:

Calories 325, Carbohydrates 6 g, Fats 25 g, Protein 19 g

Genuine Cheesecake for the

Prep time: 10 minutes, Cook time: 1 ½ hours, Serves: 6, Serves: 6

Ingredients:

- 12-ounce, cream cheese at room temperature
- ½ cup, sugar
- ¼ cup, creole cream cheese
- 2 eggs
- Zest, 1 lemon
- ½ tablespoon, vanilla extract

Instructions:

1. Set up your Sous Vide immersion circulator to a temperature of 176°F and prepareyour water bath
2. Take a bowl and add cream cheese, sugar, yogurt and mixwell
3. Gradually add the eggs one by one and keep beating until wellcombined
4. Add zest and vanilla and mix well
5. Pour the cheesecake mix into jars and distributeevenly
6. Seal the jars with lid and submerge them, cook for 1 hour and 30minutes
7. Remove from water bath and chill for awhile
8. Serve chilled with a topping of fresh fruitcompote

Nutritional Value Per Serving:

Calories 321, Carbohydrates 5 g, Fats 25 g, Protein 19 g

Mind Boggling Peach

Prep time: 15 minutes, Cook time: 3 hours, Serves: 6

Ingredients:

- 1 cup of self-rising flour 1
- cup of granulated sugar 1
- cup of whole milk
- 1 teaspoon of vanilla extract
- 8 tablespoons of unsalted melted butter
- 2 cups of roughly chopped peaches

Instructions:

1. Set up your Sous Vide immersion circulator to a temperature of 195 °F andprepare your water bath
2. Prepare 6 half pint canning jars withbutter
3. Whisk flour, sugar in a large bowl, whisk in milk and vanilla andmix
4. Stir in butter and peaches
5. Divide the batter between jars and wipe sides, sealgently
6. Cook for 3 hours
7. Remove the jars and place on cooling rack, rest for 10 minutes andenjoy!

Nutritional Value Per Serving:

Calories 329, Carbohydrates 7 g, Fats 25 g, Protein 19 g

Sweet Corn Gelato

Prep time: 1 hour, Cook time: 30 minutes, Serves: 6

Ingredients

- 4 ears shuckedcorn
- 3 cups whole milk
- 1 cup heavy cream
- 1 cup granulated sugar
- 1 teaspoon kosher salt
- 6 large egg yolks
- ¼ cup crème fraiche

Instructions:

1. Set up your Sous Vide immersion circulator to a temperature of 180 °F andprepare your water bath.
2. Take the corn cobs and slice off the kernels, transfer to asaucepan.
3. Add the milk, cream, salt, and sugar.
4. Lower down the heat and allow the mixture to simmer, remove the heat, allowit to steep for 30 seconds.
5. Strain the mixture out and discard corn andcobs.
6. Add the corn-infused milk and egg to the blender and purée for 30 seconds until itgets a frothy texture.
7. Transferthe whole mixture to a resealable bag and seal using the immersion method. Cook for 30 minutes.
8. Chill the bag in ice bath. Once the mixture is cool, mix in crème fraiche and churn the mixture in an ice cream maker.
9. Freeze and serve!

Nutritional Value Per Serving:

Calories 823, Carbohydrates 102 g, Fats 39 g, Protein 16 g

Raspberry Mousse

Prep time: 15 minutes, Cook time: 45 minutes, Serves: 8

Ingredients

- 1 lb. raspberries
- ¼ cup ultrafine sugar
- 3 tablespoons fresh squeezed lemon juice
- ½ teaspoon kosher salt
- ¼ teaspoon ground cinnamon
- 1 cup heavy cream
- 1 teaspoon vanilla extract

Instructions:

1. Set up your Sous Vide immersion circulator to a temperature of 180°F and prepareyour water bath.
2. Add the raspberries, sugar, salt, lemon juice and cinnamon to a resealable bag and seal using the immersion method. Cook for 45 minutes.
3. Once done, take the bag out from the water bath and pour the contents into ablender.
4. Purée until it gets smooth.
5. Take a large mixing bowl and mix in cream, vanilla until stiff peaksform.
6. Fold in raspberry purée and mix.
7. Divide among 8 serving bowls, chill and serve!

Nutritional Value Per Serving:

Calories 402, Carbohydrates 30 g, Fats 30 g, Protein 3 g

Strawberry Mousse

Prep time: 45 minutes, Cook time: 45 minutes, Serves: 8

Ingredients

- 1 lb. strawberries, stemmed, halved
- ¼ cup packed light brown sugar
- 3 tablespoons freshly squeezed lemon juice
- ½ teaspoon kosher salt
- ¼ teaspoon ground cinnamon
- 1 cup heavy cream
- 1 teaspoon vanilla extract
- 1 cup crème fraiche

Instructions:

1. Set up your Sous Vide immersion circulator to a temperature of 180°F and prepareyour water bath.
2. Addthe strawberries, brownsugar, lemonjuice, salt, andcinnamon to a largeresealable zipper bag.
3. Seal using the immersion method and cook for 45minutes.
4. Once done, remove the bag and pour the contents to a foodprocessor.
5. Purée for a few seconds until you have a smoothmixture
6. Take a large chilled mixing bowl and add the heavy cream and vanilla, whisk welluntil stiff peaks form.
7. Fold in strawberry purée and crème fraiche.
8. Whisk them well and divide it among 8 servingbowls.
9. Serve chilled!

Nutritional Value Per Serving:

Calories 257, Carbohydrates 22 g, Fats 17 g, Protein 4 g

Blueberry & Lemon Compote

Prep time: 15 minutes, Cook time: 1 hour, Serves: 8

Ingredients

- ½ cup ultrafine sugar
- 1 tablespoon freshly squeezed lemonjuice
- 1 tablespoon lemon zest
- 1 tablespooncornstarch
- 1 lb. blueberries

Instructions:

1. Set up your Sous Vide immersion circulator to a temperature of 180°F and prepareyour water bath.
2. Take a medium-sized bowl and mix in sugar, lemon juice, lemon zest, andcornstarch.
3. Add the blueberries and toss well to coatthem.
4. Transfer the mixture to a resealable zip bag and seal using the immersionmethod.
5. Cook for 60 minutes.
6. Once done, remove the bag and transfer the contents to a servingdish.
7. Servewarm!

Nutritional Value PerServing:

Calories 201, Carbohydrates 47 g, Fats 1 g, Protein 1 g

Chocolate & Ricotta Mousse

Prep time: 30 minutes, Cook time: 1 hour, Serves: 8

Ingredients

- 2 quarts' whole milk
- 6 tablespoons white wine vinegar
- 4 oz. semisweet chocolate chips
- ¼ cup powdered sugar
- Grand Marnier liquor
- 1 tablespoon orange zest
- 2 oz. ricotta

Instructions:

1. Set up your Sous Vide immersion circulator to a temperature of 172°F and prepareyour water bath.
2. Put the milk and vinegar to a resealable zipbag.
3. Seal using the immersion method and cook for 1 hour.
4. Once done, remove the bag and skim the curds from top and transfer to a strainerlined with cheesecloth. Discard any remaining liquid.
5. Let it sit and drain the curd for about 10 minutes. Then chill for 1hour.
6. Prepareyour double broilerby setting a bowl over a small saucepan filled with 1 inch of water
7. Bring the water to a low simmer over mediumheat.
8. Add the chocolate chips to a bowl of the double boiler and cook until it hasmelted.
9. Transfer to a food processor.
10. Add the sugar, orange zest, grand mariner, ricotta, and then process untilsmooth
11. Transfer to individual bowls and serve!

Nutritional Value Per Serving:

Calories 487, Carbohydrates 37 g, Fats 35 g, Protein 6 g

Brioche Bread Pudding

Prep time: 30 minutes, Cook time: 2 hours, Serves: 4

Ingredients

- 1 cup whole milk
- 1 cup heavy cream
- ½ cup granulated sugar
- ¼ cup maple syrup
- 2 tablespoons orangejuice
- 1 tablespoon orange zest
- 1 teaspoon vanilla bean paste
- ½ teaspoon kosher salt
- 4 cups brioche, cut up into 1-inch cubes

Instructions:

1. Set up your Sous Vide immersion circulator to a temperature of 170°F and prepareyour water bath.
2. Take a large bowl and add the milk, heavy cream, sugar, maple syrup, orangezest, juice, vanilla bean paste, and salt.
3. Mix well and add the brioche. Toss well
4. Divide the mixture among 4 mason jars of 4-ounces size and gently seal them usingthe finger-tip method
5. Cook for 2 hours underwater.
6. Heat up your broiler and place the jars in thebroiler.
7. Brown for 2-3 minutes (with lids removed) andserve.

Nutritional Value Per Serving:

Calories 248, Carbohydrates 19 g, Fats 16 g, Protein 7 g

Spiced Coconut Ice Cream

Prep time: 1 hour, Cook time: 30 minutes, Serves: 4

Ingredients

- 1 can full-fat coconut milk
- ¾ cup sugar
- ½ teaspoon kosher salt
- 2 teaspoons vanilla extract
- ½ teaspoon ground cinnamon
- ¼ teaspoon nutmeg
- ¼ teaspoon coriander
- 4 large egg yolks

Instructions:

1. Set up your Sous Vide immersion circulator to a temperature of 180°F and prepareyour water bath.
2. Take a medium-sized saucepan and add the coconut milk, salt, sugar,cinnamon, vanilla, nutmeg, coriander and bring it to asimmer.
3. Once done, remove the heat and allow it to steep for 30minutes.
4. Transfer to a blender and purée the mixture alongside the egg yolks for 30seconds
5. Transferthe mixture to a resealable zip bag and seal using the immersion method.
6. Cook for 30 minutes, making sure to agitate the bag from time totime.
7. Chill the bag in an ice bath and churn the mixture in an ice creammaker.
8. Freeze and serve!

Nutritional Value Per Serving:

Calories 720, Carbohydrates 36 g, Fats 60 g, Protein 9 g

Rhubarb Mousse

Prep time: 30 minutes, Cook time: 1 hour, Serves: 6

Ingredients

- 1 oz. trimmed rhubarb cut up into 1-inch pieces
- ½ cup packed light brown sugar
- 1/3 cup freshly squeezed orange juice
- 1 tablespoon Grand Marnier
- ½ teaspoon kosher salt
- ¼ teaspoon ground cinnamon
- 2 large-sized eggs, separated
- ½ cup heavy cream
- 1 teaspoon vanilla extract

Instructions:

1. Set up your Sous Vide immersion circulator to a temperature of 180°F and prepareyour water bath.
2. Put the rhubarb, ¼ cup of brown sugar, orange juice, salt, Grand Marnier,and cinnamon to a resealable zip bag.
3. Seal using the immersion method. Cook for 1 hour.
4. Once cooked, remove the bag from the water bath and pour the contents to ablender.
5. Then, transfer the rhubarb mixture to a large saucepan and place it over mediumheat.
6. Mix in egg yolks and ¼ cup of brown sugar.
7. Cook for 3 minutes until the mixture isthick.
8. Once cooked, transfer the contents to a large bowl and allow it tocool.
9. Take another bowl and mix in egg whites until stiff peaksforms.
10. Fold the egg whites into rhubarb mixture and then stir tocombine.
11. Take another bowl and mix in the cream and vanilla, mix until stiff peakforms.
12. Fold cream into rhubarb egg mixture andcombine.
13. Spoon into serving cups, chill and serve!

Nutritional Value Per Serving:

Calories 591, Carbohydrates 54 g, Fats 39 g, Protein 6 g

Chocolate Pots De Crème

Prep time: 45 minutes, Cook time: 45 minutes, Serves: 12

Ingredients

- 1 cup fruit-forward red wine
- ½ cup granulated sugar
- 12 oz. semisweet chocolate chips
- 8 ounces unsweetened dark chocolate, finely chopped up
- 1 cup whole milk
- ½ cup heavy cream
- 8 large egg yolks
- A pinch of kosher salt

Instructions:

1. Set up your Sous Vide immersion circulator to a temperature of 180°F and prepareyour water bath.
2. Take a medium-sized saucepan and place it over medium-highheat.
3. Add the wine and sugar and bring the mixture to a boil, reduce heat to medium-lowand simmer for 20 minutes. Remove and allow it to cool for 10minutes.
4. Transfer to a food processor and add the chocolate chips, unsweetened darkchocolate, milk, cream, salt, and egg yolks. Blend well until smooth.
5. Then, transfer the mixture to a resealable bag and seal using the immersion method, cook for 45 minutes.
6. Once cooked, remove the bag and transfer the contents to a foodprocessor.
7. Blend for 2 minutes.
8. Divide the mixture among 12 ramekins and cover them with plasticwrap.
9. Chill for 4 hours and serve!

Nutritional Value Per Serving:

Calories 834, Carbohydrates 56 g, Fats 62 g, Protein 13 g

Champagne Zabaglione

Prep time: 15 minutes, Cook time: 45 minutes, Serves: 6

Ingredients

- 1 cup heavy cream
- ½ cup champagne
- ½ cup ultrafine sugar
- 4 large egg yolks
- 1 teaspoon vanilla extract
- A pinch of kosher salt

Instructions:

1. Set up your Sous Vide immersion circulator to a temperature of 180°F and prepareyour water bath.
2. Add all the listed ingredients to a blender and purée for 30seconds.
3. Transfer to a resealable zip bag and seal using the immersionmethod.
4. Cook for 45 minutes and once done, transfer the bag to an icebath.
5. Serve immediately!

Nutritional Value Per Serving:

Calories 371, Carbohydrates 28 g, Fats 27 g, Protein 4 g

Orange Curd

Prep time: 15 minutes, Cook time: 45 minutes, Serves: 6

Ingredients

- 1 cup ultrafine sugar
- 8 tablespoons unsalted butter, melted
- 6 egg yolks
- ¼ cup freshly squeezed orange juice
- A pinch of kosher salt

Instructions:

1. Set up your Sous Vide immersion circulator to a temperature of 180°F and prepareyour water bath.
2. Add the listed ingredients to a blender and pulse the mixture for 20seconds
3. Transfer to a resealable bag and seal using the immersionmethod.
4. Submerge it underwater and cook for 45 minutes. Keep agitating the bag from timeto time.
5. Once cooked, remove the bag from the water bath and transfer to an icebath.
6. Chill for 2 hours and serve!

Nutritional Value Per Serving:

Calories 434, Carbohydrates 54 g, Fats 22 g, Protein 5 g

Rice & Cardamom

Prep time: 15 minutes, Cook time: 2 hours, Serves: 8

Ingredients

- ½ cup raisins
- ½ cup dark rum
- 5 tablespoons unsalted butter
- 1/3 cup light brown sugar
- 4 cups cooked wild rice blend
- 1 cup whole milk
- 1 cup heavy cream
- 3 strips lemon peel
- 3 crushed cardamom pods, crushed and wrapped in cheese cloth
- 1 teaspoon vanilla extract
- Cinnamon

Instructions:

1. Set up your Sous Vide immersion circulator to a temperature of 181°F and prepareyour water bath.
2. Put the raisins and rum into a small microwave bowl and heat for 1minute.
3. Allow it to cool and remove the raisins using slottedspoon.
4. Take a medium non-stick skillet and place it over medium-highheat.
5. Add the butter and then brown sugar and heat itup.
6. Stir until it has melted and simmer for 5minutes.
7. Add the cooked rice, milk, cream, lemon peel, cardamom and vanilla to buttermixture and bring the mixture to a boil.
8. Lower down the heat to low and simmer for about 2minutes.
9. Remove from the heat and stir in raisins, spoon the mixture into resealable zip bag and seal using the immersion method.
10. Cook for 2 hours underwater.
11. Once cooked, take the bag out from the water bath and pour the mixture into alarge bowl. Stir well and discard cardamom pod bundle alongside the lemonpeels.
12. Sprinkle cinnamon and serve!

Nutritional Value Per Serving:

Calories 365, Carbohydrates 50 g, Fats 13 g, Protein 12 g

Lemon Curd

Prep time: 8 hours 10 minutes, Cook time: 45 minutes, Serves: 3

Ingredients

- 6 tablespoons unsalted butter, melted, cooled
- 4 lemon juice
- 6 large egg yolks at room temperature
- 1 cup granulated sugar

Instructions:

1. Set up your Sous Vide immersion circulator to a temperature of 179°F and prepare your water bath.
2. Mix the sugar, butter, and lemon juice in a bowl.
3. Keep mixing until the sugar has dissolved and then add the egg yolks, mix them well.
4. Transfer the egg mixture to a resealable bag and seal using the immersion method.
5. Cook for 45 minutes underwater.
6. Transfer the bag to an ice bag and shake well.
7. Once the curd is cool, chill overnight.
8. Then, pour the curd into a bowl and whisk.
9. Serve and use as needed.

Nutritional Value Per Serving:

Calories 184, Carbohydrates 15 g, Fats 12 g, Protein 4 g

Kiwi & Vanilla Fresh Mint

Prep time: 10 minutes, Cook time: 20 minutes, Serves: 2

Ingredients

- 2 peeled, sliced kiwis
- 2 tablespoons granulated sugar
- 1 tablespoon freshly squeezed lemon juice
- 2 generous tablespoons yogurt/ vanilla icecream
- Fresh mint leaves forgarnishing

Instructions:

1. Set up your Sous Vide immersion circulator to a temperature of 176°F and prepareyour water bath.
2. Take a medium bowl and add the kiwi slices, sugar, lemon juice andstir.
3. Transfer the mixture to a resealable zipper bag and seal using the immersionmethod.
4. Cook for 20 minutes and remove the bag from the waterbath.
5. Divide the mixture between 2 servingplates.
6. Scoop yogurt/ vanilla ice cream onto the plate next to your kiwi and garnish withsome mint leaves.
7. Serve!

Nutritional Value Per Serving:

Calories 149, Carbohydrates 21 g, Fats 5 g, Protein 5 g

Cinnamon Spiced Apples

Prep time: 20 minutes, Cook time: 2 hours, Serves: 4

Ingredients

- 4 tart peeled apples
- 1 lemon juice
- 3 tablespoons unsalted butter
- 2 tablespoons light brown sugar
- 2 whole fresh dates pitted
- 2 tablespoons raisins
- 1 tablespoon ground cinnamon
- ¼ teaspoon fine sea salt
- ¼ teaspoon grated nutmeg
- 1/9 teaspoon vanilla extract
- Freshly whipped ice cream

Instructions:

1. Set up your Sous Vide immersion circulator to a temperature of 183°F and prepareyour water bath.
2. Core the apples and toss the apples with lemonjuice.
3. Take a medium bowl and add the butter, brown sugar, dates, raisins, cinnamon,salt, vanilla, and nutmeg.
4. Take a fork and mash the mixture into a chunkypaste.
5. Divide the mixture and fill the applecores.
6. Transferthe appleto aresealable zipperbag and seal using the immersion method. Cook for 2 hours.
7. Remove the bags from the water bath. Take the apples out from the bag and placethem on serving plates.
8. Serve apples with whipped cream/icecream.

Nutritional Value Per Serving:

Calories 210, Carbohydrates 30 g, Fats 10 g, Protein 0 g

Vanilla & Butter Pears

Prep time: 10 minutes, Cook time: 30 minutes, Serves: 2

Ingredients

- 2 peeled ripe pears
- 1 vanilla bean
- 2 tablespoons dark brown sugar
- 1/8 teaspoon flaky sea salt
- 1 tablespoon unsalted butter
- Vanilla ice cream for serving

Instructions:

1. Set up your Sous Vide immersion circulator to a temperature of 175°F and prepareyour water bath.
2. Slice the pears in halflengthwise.
3. Scoop out the core using a spoon, divide the pear halves between two resealablebags.
4. Then, cut/slice the vanilla bean in halfand use the back ofthe spoon to scrape its seeds into a small bowl.
5. Add the brown sugar and salt.
6. Then, rub the vanilla bean seed into sugar using your fingers andcombine.
7. Divide the mixture between the resealable bags and add 1 tablespoon of butter andone half of your vanilla pod into eachbag.
8. Seal using the immersion method. Cook for 30minutes.
9. Remove the bag from the water bath. Take the pears out from the bag and thentransfer to serving bowls.
10. Drizzle the butter sauce from the bag over the pears and serve with vanilla icecream.

Nutritional Value Per Serving:

Calories 449, Carbohydrates 109 g, Fats 1 g, Protein 1 g

Lemon Raspberry Ricotta

Prep time: 8 hours 30 minutes, Cook time: 2 hours, Serves: 12

Ingredients

- 9 oz. ricotta cheese
- 1 cup granulated sugar
- 7 oz. soft creamcheese
- ½ cup full-fat Greek yogurt
- ½ cup heavy cream
- 2 large eggs + 1 large eggyolk
- Finely grated zest one lemon + 2 tablespoons freshly squeezed juice 2
- tablespoons all-purpose flour
- ¼ teaspoon vanilla extract
- Fine sea salt
- 1 ½ cup graham crackers
- 1/3 cup unsaltedbutter
- 2 pints' fresh raspberries

Instructions:

1. Set up your Sous Vide immersion circulator to a temperature of 170°F and prepareyour water bath.
2. Preheat your oven to 375°F
3. Take a large bowl and mix in ricotta cheese, 2/3 cup of sugar, cream cheese, Greek yogurt, heavy cream, egg yolks, eggs, lemon zest, juice, 1 tablespoon of flour,vanilla, and ½ a teaspoon of salt.
4. Transfer to a resealable bag and seal using the immersion method. Cook for 2hours.
5. Make the crust by taking another medium bowl and add the graham crackercrumbs, butter, 1/3 cup of sugar, pinch of salt and 1 tablespoon offlour.
6. Whisk well until fully combined and press the mixture into the bottom of a9-inch springform pan.
7. Bake in your oven until the crust is browned, should take about 7-10minutes.
8. Once cooked, remove the bag from the water bath and pat itdry.
9. Cut off one corner of the resealable bag. Pipe contents of bag carefully into the baked crust.
10. Press raspberries onto the surface and chill for 8 hours beforeserving.

Nutritional Value Per Serving:

Calories 259, Carbohydrates 27 g, Fats 15 g, Protein 4 g

Doce De Banana

Prep time: 10 minutes, Cook time: 40 minutes, Serves: 4

Ingredients

- 5 small ripe bananas, firm, ripe, peeled and cut up into chunks 1
- cup brown sugar
- 2 cinnamonsticks
- 6 whole cloves
- Whipped cream
- Vanillaice-cream

Instructions:

1. Set up your Sous Vide immersion circulator to a temperature of 176°F and prepareyour water bath.
2. Put the bananas, brown sugar, cinnamon sticks, and cloves to a resealablebag.
3. Seal using the immersion method and cook for 30-40minutes.
4. Remove the bag and allow the contents tocool.
5. Open the bag and remove the cinnamon sticks andcloves.
6. Serve warm in a bowl with a topping of whipped cream and vanilla icecream.

Nutritional Value Per Serving:

Calories 324, Carbohydrates 80 g, Fats 0 g, Protein 1 g

Maple Raisin Rice Pudding

Prep time: 10 minutes, Cook time: 2 hours, Serves: 4

Ingredients

- 3 cups skim milk
- 2 tablespoons butter
- 2 cups Arborio rice
- ½ cup maple syrup
- 2 teaspoons ground cinnamon
- ½ teaspoon ground ginger
- Ground cinnamon/cinnamon sugar for serving

Instructions:

1. Set up your Sous Vide immersion circulator to a temperature of 140°F and prepareyour water bath.
2. Add all the listed ingredients except for the cinnamon to your resealable bag and stir well.
3. Seal using the immersion method. Submerge underwater and cook for 2hours.
4. Once done, remove from the water bath and stir theingredients.
5. Transfer the pudding to serving bowls.
6. Sprinkle cinnamon over the bowls and servewarm.

Nutritional Value Per Serving:

Calories 292, Carbohydrates 49 g, Fats 8 g, Protein 6 g

Lavender Poached Honey

Prep time: 10 minutes, Cook time: 20 minutes, Serves: 4

Ingredients

- 2 halved, pitted peaches
- 1 tablespoon dried lavender buds
- ¼ cup water
- ¼ cup honey

For Whipped MascarponeCheese

- 1/3 cup mascarponecheese
- ½ cup coconut cream
- 1 tablespoon maple syrup
- Just a drop lavenderextract

Instructions:

1. Set up your Sous Vide immersion circulator to a temperature of 185°F and prepareyour water bath.
2. Add the peaches and the remaining ingredients (except the whipped Mascarpone) toa resealable bag and seal using the immersionmethod.
3. Submerge underwater and cook for 20minutes.
4. Once cooked, transfer the bag to an ice bath and place it in your fridge and allow itto chill for 1 hour
5. Take a medium-sized bowl and add the coconut cream and mascarpone cheese,mix well until a soft peakform
6. Add the syrup and lavender to the bowl and keep whipping until you see thestable peaks
7. Serve the peach with a dollop of the whipped mascarpone and a drizzle of thebag liquid
8. Garnish with dried lavender and serve!

Nutritional Value Per Serving:

Calories 727, Carbohydrates 162 g, Fats 3 g, Protein 13 g

Citrus Yogurt

Prep time: 15 minutes, Cook time: 3 hours, Serves: 4

Ingredients

- ½ cup yogurt
- ½ tablespoon orange zest
- ½ tablespoon lemon zest
- ½ tablespoon lime zest
- 4 cups full cream milk

Instructions:

1. Set up your Sous Vide immersion circulator to a temperature of 113°F and prepareyour water bath.
2. Heat the milk on stove top to a temperature of180°F
3. Transfer to an ice bath and allow it to cool down to110°F.
4. Stir in yogurt.
5. Fold in the citruszest.
6. Pour the mixture into 4-ounce canning jars and lightly close thelid.
7. Submerge underwater and cook for 3 hours.
8. Remove the jars and serveimmediately!

Nutritional Value Per Serving:

Calories 182, Carbohydrates 35 g, Fats 2 g, Protein 6 g

Sweet Candied Potatoes

Prep time: 45 minutes, Cook time: 2 hours, Serves: 8

Ingredients

- 2 lbs. sweet potatoes, peeled up and cut into ¼slices
- ½ cup unsalted butter
- ¼ cup maple syrup
- 2 oranges, juice and zest
- 1 teaspoon kosher salt
- 1 cup chopped walnuts
- 1 cinnamon stick
- ¼ cup brown sugar

Instructions:

1. Set up your Sous Vide immersion circulator to a temperature of 155°F and prepareyour water bath.
2. Take a resealable bag and add the sweet potatoes and ¼ cup ofbutter.
3. Seal using the immersion method and cook for 2hours.
4. Preheat your oven to 350°F
5. Remove the potatoes from the bag and patdry.
6. Arrange the potatoes evenly in a bakingdish.
7. Take a medium saucepan and bring ¼ cup of butter, brown sugar, maple syrup,orange zest, juice, walnuts, salt, and cinnamon stick to aboil.
8. Remove from heat and pour over sweet potatoes, discard the cinnamonstick
9. Bake for 30 minutes and servewarm!

Nutritional Value Per Serving:

Calories 325, Carbohydrates 67 g, Fats 5 g, Protein 3 g

Mocha Pot De Crème

Prep time: 15 minutes, Cook time: 30 minutes, Serves: 8

Ingredients

- 1/3 cup espresso
- ¾ cup milk
- 1 cup heavy cream
- 6 oz. chopped chocolate
- 1/3 cup sugar
- ¼ teaspoon fine salt
- Whipped cream
- Cinnamon powder
- 4 large egg yolks

Instructions:

1. Set up your Sous Vide immersion circulator to a temperature of 180°F and prepareyour water bath.
2. Take a medium-sized saucepan and heat it up over mediumheat.
3. Add the heavy cream, espresso, milk and bring to aboil.
4. Once done, turn-off the heat and stir in chocolate. Then, cook once again overmedium heat and occasionally stir for 15minutes.
5. Take a medium bowl and add in the egg yolks, salt, and sugar. Stir well and addthe chocolate crème mixture.
6. Once mixed together, cool the mixture for 10-15minutes.
7. Add the contents to a resealable zipper bag and seal using the immersionmethod.
8. Cook for 30 minutes.
9. Spoon the mixture into small ramekins and garnish with cinnamon powder orwhipped cream.
10. Chill for 2 hours and serve!

Nutritional Value Per Serving:

Calories 231, Carbohydrates 45 g, Fats 3 g, Protein 6 g

Baked Ricotta

Prep time: 50 minutes, Cook time: 1 hour, Serves: 6

Ingredients

- 2 quarts whole milk
- 6 tablespoons white wine vinegar
- 2 large eggs
- 2 tablespoons extra virgin olive oil
- 1 ½ teaspoon smoked salt
- 1 teaspoon fresh ground smoked black pepper

Instructions:

1. Set up your Sous Vide immersion circulator to a temperature of 172°F and prepareyour water bath.
2. Add the milk and vinegar to a resealable zipbag.
3. Seal using the immersion method and cook for 1 hour.
4. Preheat your oven to 350°F
5. Remove the bag and skim the curd off thetop.
6. Then, pass the mixture through a strainer lined with a cheesecloth and discardany remaining liquid.
7. Drain the curd for 10 minutes.
8. Transfer drained curds to food processor alongside the eggs, salt, olive oil, andpepper.
9. Process for 20 seconds.
10. Divide the ricotta mixture between 6 oven proof ramekins and bake for 30 minutesuntil golden brown.
11. Serve!

Nutritional Value Per Serving:

Calories 142, Carbohydrates 3 g, Fats 10 g, Protein 10 g

Chapter 10: Cocktails And Infusions

Infused Blackberry Syrup

Prep time: 10 minutes, Cook time: 2 hours, Serves: 8

Ingredients:

- 1.5lb. blackberries
- 4 cups water
- 4 cups sugar
- 4 sprigs basil

Instructions:

1. Preheat Sous vide to 135°F.
2. In a Sous Vide bag combine all ingredients.
3. Seal the bag and submerge in a water bath.
4. Cook 2 hours.
5. Remove the bag from the cooker.
6. Place the bag in an ice-cold water and cool 30 minutes.
7. Strain the infusion into a glass jar.
8. Serve or store in a fridge.

Nutritional Value Per Serving:

Calories 441.2, Carbohydrates 108.2 g, Fats 0.4 g, Protein 1.2 g

Sweet Basil Syrup

Prep time: 5 minutes, Cook time: 1 hour, Serves: 4

Ingredients:

- 2 cups water
- 2 cups basil
- 2 cups sugar
- 1 lime, use the rind only

Instructions:

1. Set the Sous vide cooker to 180ºF.
2. Combine all the ingredients into Sous Vide bag and seal using a waterimmersion technique.
3. Cook the syrup 1 hour.
4. Prepare ice-cold water bath.
5. Remove the bag from the cooker and place into ice-cold water bath 30minutes.
6. Strain the syrup into a clean glassjar.
7. Serve or store in afridge.

Nutritional Value Per Serving:

Calories 411.3, Carbohydrates 102.1 g, Fats 0.1 g, Protein 0.5 g

Ginger Syrup

Prep time: 15 minutes, Cook time: 55 minutes, Serves: 10

Ingredients:

- 1 cup Ginger, sliced thinly 1
- large White Onion, peeled 2
- ½ cups Water
- ¼ cup Monk Fruit Powder

Instructions:

1. Make a water bath, place a Sous Vide cooker in it, and set it at 185°F. Place the onion in a vacuum-sealable bag.
2. Release air by the water displacement method, seal and submerge the bag in the water bath. Set the timer for 40 minutes.
3. Once the timer has stopped, remove and unseal thebag.
4. Transfer the onion with 4 tablespoons of water to a blender and puree tosmooth.
5. Place a pot over medium heat, add the onion puree and the remaining listedingredients. Bring to a boil for 15 minutes.
6. Turn off heat, cool, and strain through a finesieve.
7. Store in a jar, refrigerate, and use for up to 14 days. Use it as a spice in otherfoods.

Nutritional Value Per Serving:

Calories 33.3, Carbohydrates 8.27g, Fats 0.01 g, Protein 0.04 g

Honey Lemon Thyme

Prep time: 5 minutes, Cook time: 1 ½ hours, Serves: 10

Ingredients:

- 2 cups water
- 2 organic lemons, sliced
- 2 cups honey
- 2 bunches lemon thyme

Instructions:

1. Preheat sous Vide cooker to 135°F.
2. Combine all ingredients into Sous vide bag.
3. Seal the bag using water immersion technique.
4. Cook the syrup 1 ½ hours.
5. Prepare ice-cold water bath.
6. Remove the bag from the cooker and place into the waterbath.
7. Chill the syrup 30 minutes.
8. Strain into a clean glass jar and serve.

Nutritional Value Per Serving:

Calories 229.2, Carbohydrates 57 g, Fats 0 g, Protein 0.3 g

Tom Collins Cocktail

Prep time: 10 minutes, Cook time: 1 hour, Serves: 20

Ingredients:

- 7 cups gin
- 1 cup lemon juice
- 2 cups lemon rind
- 1 ½ cups granulated sugar
- Soda water, to servewith

Instructions:

1. Preheat Sous Vide to 131°F.
2. In a large Sous vide bag, combine gin, lemon juice, lemon rind, andsugar.
3. Fold the edges of the bag few times and clip to the side of yourpot.
4. Cook the cocktail 1 hour.
5. Strain the cocktail into a large glassjug.
6. Place aside to cool completely beforeuse.
7. Serve over ice, and finish off with a sodawater.
8. Garnish the cocktail with lemon rind or freshthyme.

Nutritional Value Per Serving:

Calories 71.8, Carbohydrates 17.2 g, Fats 0.2 g, Protein 0.3 g

Cherry Manhattan

Prep time: 10 minutes, Cook time: 1 hour, Serves: 8

Ingredients:

Bourbon infusion:

- 2 cups bourbon
- ¼ cup raw cacao nibs
- 1 cup dried cherries

To finish:

- 4oz. sweet vermouth
- Chocolate bitters, as desired

Instructions:

1. Make the infusion; preheat Sous Vide to 122°F.
2. In a Sous Vide bag combine bourbon, cacao nibs, andcherries.
3. Seal the bag, and cook 1 hour
4. Remove the bag from the water bath and let cool. Strain the content into ajar.
5. Fill the tall glasses withice.
6. Add chocolate bitters (3 dashes per serving) and 1/8 of the infusedbourbon.
7. Skewer the Sous vide cherries andgarnish.

Nutritional Value Per Serving:

Calories 22.1, Carbohydrates 2.2 g, Fats 1.3 g, Protein 0.4 g

Lavender Syrup

Prep time: 5 minutes, Cook time: 1 hour, Serves: 4

Ingredients

- 1 cupwater
- 1 cup sugar
- 1 tablespoon culinary grade dried lavender

Instructions:

1. Prepare your Sous Vide water bath using your immersion circulator and raisethe temperature to 135°F
2. Take a heavy-duty resealable zipper bag and add the water, lavender, andsugar.
3. Seal it using the immersionmethod.
4. Submerge it underwater and cook for about 1hour.
5. Once done, let it cool down to room temperature and strain through a metalmesh.
6. Serve chilled!

Nutritional Value Per Serving:

Calories 404, Carbohydrates 101 g, Fats 0 g, Protein 0 g

Thyme Liqueur

Prep time: 15 minutes, Cook time: 1 hour 30 minutes, Serves: 12

Ingredients

- Zest, 8 large oranges
- 4 sprigs fresh thyme
- 1 cup ultrafine sugar
- 1 cup water
- 1 cup vodka

Instructions:

1. Prepare your Sous Vide water bath using your immersion circulator and raisethe temperature to 180°F.
2. Add all the listed ingredients to a heavy-duty resealable zip bag and seal usingthe immersion method.
3. Cook for 90 minutes.
4. Strain the mixture and serve chilled!

Nutritional Value Per Serving:

Calories 520, Carbohydrates 110 g, Fats 8 g, Protein 2 g

Pineapple Rum

Prep time: 15 minutes, Cook time: 2 hours, Serves: 12

Ingredients

- 1 peeled and cored pineapple cut into 1-inch pieces
- 1 bottle dark rum
- 1 cup granulated sugar

Instructions:

1. Prepare your Sous Vide water bath using your immersion circulator and raisethe temperature to 135°F.
2. Take a resealable zipper bag and add the pineapple, rum, sugar, and seal usingthe immersion method.
3. Submerge underwater and cook for about 2hours.
4. Once done, strain the mixture through a metal mesh strainer into a mediumbowl.
5. Chill overnight and serve!

Nutritional Value Per Serving:

Calories 184, Carbohydrates 45 g, Fats 0 g, Protein 1 g

Vodka Lemon Meyer

Prep time: 15 minutes, Cook time: 2 hours, Serves: 6

Ingredients

- 1 cup vodka
- 1 cup granulated sugar
- 1 cup freshly squeezed Meyer lemon
- Zest, 3 Meyer lemons

Instructions:

1. Prepare your Sous Vide water bath using your immersion circulator and raisethe temperature to 135°F.
2. Take a resealable zip bag and add all the listedingredients.
3. Seal the bag using the immersion method. Submerge and cook for about 2hours.
4. Once done, strain the mixture through a fine metal mesh strainer into a mediumbowl.
5. Chill the mixture overnight andserve!

Nutritional Value Per Serving:

Calories 192, Carbohydrates 48 g, Fats 0 g, Protein 0 g

Rosemary & Lemon Vodka

Prep time: 10 minutes, Cook time: 3 hours, Serves: 5

Ingredients

- 1 bottle vodka
- Zest, 6 large lemons
- 5 sprigs fresh rosemary

Instructions:

1. Prepare your Sous Vide water bath using your immersion circulator and raisethe temperature to 145°F.
2. Take a heavy-duty resealable zip bag and add all the listedingredients.
3. Seal using the immersion method and cook for 3 hours.
4. Once done, transfer the contents through a strainer and allow it tocool.
5. Serve!

Nutritional Value Per Serving:

Calories 244, Carbohydrates 23 g, Fats 16 g, Protein 2 g

Bloody Mary Vodka

Prep time: 20 minutes, Cook time: 3 hours, Serves: 20

Ingredients

- 1 bottle vodka
- 6 quartered roma tomatoes
- 1 Anaheim pepper, stemmed, seeds removed, sliced into ½ inch pieces
- ¼ onion, peeled, sliced into ½-inch pieces
- 6 whole garlic cloves, peeled
- 1 thinly sliced jalapeno pepper
- 1 tablespoon whole black peppercorns
- Zest of 3 large limes

Instructions:

1. Prepare your Sous Vide water bath using your immersion circulator and raisethe temperature to 145°F.
2. Add all the listed ingredients to your resealable zipperbag.
3. Seal using the immersion method.
4. Cook for about 3 hours and transfer the contents through a meshstrainer.
5. Serve!

Nutritional Value Per Serving:

Calories 384, Carbohydrates 77 g, Fats 4 g, Protein 10 g

Coffee Liquor

Prep time: 10 minutes, Cook time: 3 hours, Serves: 20

Ingredients

- 1 bottle vodka
- 32 oz. strong black coffee
- 2 cups granulated sugar
- ½ cup coffee beans
- 2 split vanilla beans

Instructions:

1. Prepare your Sous Vide water bath using your immersion circulator and raisethe temperature to 145°F.
2. Take a heavy-duty large resealable zip bag and add all the listedingredients.
3. Seal the bag using the immersionmethod.
4. Cook for about 3 hoursunderwater.
5. Once done, transfer the contents through a fine mesh strainer and let itcool.
6. Serve!

Nutritional Value Per Serving:

Calories 228, Carbohydrates 25 g, Fats 12 g, Protein 5 g

Honey Ginger Shrub

Prep time: 10 minutes, Cook time: 120 minutes, Serves: 6

Ingredients

- 1 cup water
- ½ cup honey
- ½ cup balsamic vinegar
- 1 tablespoon freshly grated ginger
- Bourbon whiskey
- Club soda
- Lemon wedges

Instructions:

1. Prepare your Sous Vide water bath using your immersion circulator and raisethe temperature to 134°F.
2. Take a resealable zipper bag and add the water, vinegar, honey, ginger, and seal itusing the immersion method.
3. Submerge and cook for about 2 hours.
4. Once cooked, strain the mixture through a fine metal mesh strainer into amedium bowl.
5. Chill the mixture overnight.
6. Serve with one-part whiskey and one-part club soda in a glass overice.
7. Garnish with a lemon wedge and serve!

Nutritional Value Per Serving:

Calories 220, Carbohydrates 54 g, Fats 0 g, Protein 1 g

Cherry Bourbon

Prep time: 20 minutes, Cook time: 2 hours, Serves: 8

Ingredients

- 1 lb. fresh cherries
- 1½ cup bourbon

Instructions:

1. Prepare your Sous Vide water bath using your immersion circulator and raisethe temperature to 135°F.
2. Then, pit the cherries using a cherrypitter.
3. Add the cherries and bourbon to a resealable zipperbag.
4. Seal using the immersion method and mash the cherries. Cook for 2hours.
5. Let the mixture cool and strain it to a bowl through a fine metalmesh
6. Pour in the bottles and servechilled!

Nutritional Value Per Serving:

Calories 438, Carbohydrates 65 g, Fats 18 g, Protein 4 g

Raspberry Cordial

Prep time: 15 minutes, Cook time: 2 hours, Serves: 14

Ingredients

- 2 cups freshraspberries
- 2 cups sugar
- 3 cups vodka

Instructions:

1. Prepare your Sous Vide water bath using your immersion circulator and raisethe temperature to 135°F.
2. Add the raspberries and sugar to a resealable zipbag.
3. Mash the berries by hand.
4. Open the bag and add the vodka.
5. Seal using the immersion method.
6. Cook for 2 hours and allow it to come to roomtemperature.
7. Pour into bottles and serve chilled!

Nutritional Value Per Serving:

Calories 391, Carbohydrates 41 g, Fats 23 g, Protein 5 g

Bacon Vodka

Prep time: 20 minutes, Cook time: 45 minutes, Serves: 10

Ingredients

- 2 cups vodka
- 8 oz. bacon
- 3 tablespoons reserved bacon grease

Instructions:

1. Prepare your Sous Vide water bath using your immersion circulator and raisethe temperature to 150°F.
2. Bake the bacon for 16 minutes at400°F.
3. Allow the mixture tocool.
4. Add all the ingredients to a resealable bag and seal using the immersionmethod.
5. Cook for 45 minutes.
6. Strain the liquid into bowl and chill until a fat layerform.
7. Remove and skim off the fat layer, strain using a cheesecloth onceagain.
8. Serve chilled!

Nutritional Value Per Serving:

Calories 209, Carbohydrates 9 g, Fats 17 g, Protein 5 g

Spiced Rum

Prep time: 5 minutes, Cook time: 2 hours, Serves: 10

Ingredients

- 1 bottle rum
- 1 vanilla bean, splitlengthwise
- 2 whole cloves
- ½ cinnamon stick
- 2 whole black peppercorns
- ½ piece star anise
- 2 pieces of 3-inch fresh orange zest

Instructions:

1. Prepare your Sous Vide water bath using your immersion circulator and raisethe temperature to 153°F.
2. Add all the listed ingredients to a resealable zipperbag.
3. Seal using the immersion method and cook for 2hours.
4. Once cooked, transfer it to an ice bath andchill.
5. Strain to bottle and serve thedrink!

Nutritional Value Per Serving:

Calories 4, Carbohydrates 1 g, Fats 0 g, Protein 0 g

Mulled Wine

Prep time: 15 minutes, Cook time: 1 hour, Serves: 2

Ingredients

- ½ bottle red wine
- Juice, 2 oranges, peel of 1
- 1 cinnamon stick
- 1 bay leaf
- 1 vanilla pod, sliced in halflengthways
- 1-star anise
- 2 oz. caster sugar

Instructions:

1. Prepare your Sous Vide water bath using your immersion circulator and raisethe temperature to 140°F.
2. Add all the listed ingredients to a largebowl.
3. Dividethemixtureacrosstworesealablezipbagsand sealusing the immersion method. Cook for 1 hour.
4. Serve chilled!

Nutritional Value Per Serving:

Calories 72, Carbohydrates 17 g, Fats 0 g, Protein 1 g

Hot Spiced Cider

Prep time: 5 minutes, Cook time: 1 hour, Serves: 6

Ingredients

- 2 bottles apple cider
- 1 cinnamon stick
- 1 tablespoon maple syrup
- ½ teaspoon black peppercorns
- 2 tablespoons orange juice

Instructions:

1. Prepare your Sous Vide water bath using your immersion circulator and raisethe temperature to 140°F.
2. Add all the listed ingredients to a resealable zipbag.
3. Seal using the immersion method.
4. Cook for 1 hour.
5. Strain and serve chilled!

Nutritional Value Per Serving:

Calories 96, Carbohydrates 24 g, Fats 0 g, Protein 0 g

Mint Julep & Coconut

Prep time: 10 minutes, Cook time: 1 hour 30 minutes, Serves: 2

Ingredients

- 2 cups water
- 2 cups bourbon
- 1 ½ cups coconut sugar
- 2 cups fresh mint

Instructions:

1. Prepare your Sous Vide water bath using your immersion circulator and raise the temperature to 135°F.
2. Add the water, coconut sugar, bourbon, and mint to a resealable zipbag.
3. Seal using the immersion method.
4. Cook for 1 ½ hour.
5. Strain and serve chilled!

Nutritional Value Per Serving:

Calories 20, Carbohydrates 5 g, Fats 0 g, Protein 0 g

Grand Marnier

Prep time: 5 minutes, Cook time: 1 hour 30 minutes, Serves: 12

Ingredients

- Zest, 8 large orange
- 2 cups brandy
- ½ cup ultrafine sugar

Instructions:

1. Prepare your Sous Vide water bath using your immersion circulator and raise the temperature to 180°F.
2. Add all the listed ingredients to a resealable zip bag.
3. Seal using the immersion method.
4. Cook for 90 minutes.
5. Strain and discard the orange zest.
6. Allow it to chill and serve when needed!

Nutritional Value Per Serving:

Calories 190, Carbohydrates 39 g, Fats 2 g, Protein 4 g

Red Wine Plum Shrub

Prep time: 15 minutes, Cook time: 1 hour 30 minutes, Serves: 8

Ingredients

- 2 cups red plum, pitted,diced
- 1 cup ultrafine sugar
- 1 cup red wine
- 1 cup red wine vinegar
- 1 cinnamon stick
- 1 clove
- ½ teaspoon vanilla bean paste

Instructions:

1. Prepare your Sous Vide water bath using your immersion circulator and raisethe temperature to 180°F.
2. Add all the listed ingredients to a resealablebag.
3. Seal using the immersion method and cook for 90minutes.
4. Strain and discard the cinnamon stick, clove, andplums.
5. Chill and serve!

Nutritional Value Per Serving:

Calories 28, Carbohydrates 2 g, Fats 0 g, Protein 5 g

Sous Vide Classic Creamy

Prep time: 10 minutes, Cook time: 60 minutes, Serves: 8

Ingredients

- 6 large whole eggs
- 1-quart whole milk
- 1 cup heavy cream
- ½ cup bourbon
- ½ cup brandy
- ½ cup ultrafine sugar
- 1 teaspoon vanilla bean paste
- ½ teaspoon freshly ground nutmeg
- ½ teaspoon freshly ground cinnamon
- A pinch of salt

Instructions:

1. Prepare your Sous Vide water bath using your immersion circulator and raisethe temperature to 144°F.
2. Add all the listed ingredients to a blender and puree, pour the mixture to a zipbag
3. Seal using the immersion method
4. Submerge underwater and cook for 1 hour, making sure to agitate abit
5. Transfer the bag to an ice bath
6. Serve chilled and add a bit of bourbon if youdesire.

Nutritional Value Per Serving:

Calories 438, Carbohydrates 34 g, Fats 30 g, Protein 8 g

Tomato Shrub

Prep time: 15 minutes, Cook time: 1 hour 30 minutes, Serves: 12

Ingredients

- 2 cups diced tomatoes 2
- cups granulated sugar 2
- cups red wine vinegar 1
- cup water

Instructions:

1. Prepare your Sous Vide water bath using your immersion circulator and raisethe temperature to 180°F.
2. Add all the listed ingredients to a resealable zip bag and seal using the immersion method.
3. Cook for 1 ½ hour.
4. Once done, remove and strain the contents into abowl.
5. Discard any solids and transfer to storingjar.
6. Serve as needed!

Nutritional Value Per Serving:

Calories 124, Carbohydrates 30 g, Fats 0 g, Protein 1 g

Strawberry & Rhubarb Shrub

Prep time: 15 minutes, Cook time: 1 hour 30 minutes, Serves: 12

Ingredients

- 2 cups granulated sugar
- 2 cups balsamic vinegar
- 1 cup diced rhubarb
- 1 cup strawberries, diced
- 1 cup water

Instructions:

1. Prepare your Sous Vide water bath using your immersion circulator and raisethe temperature to 180°F.
2. Add all the listed ingredients to a large-sized heavy-duty zipbag
3. Seal using the immersion method and cook for 1 ½ hour.
4. Remove the bag and strain the contents to abowl.
5. Save the fruit forlater.
6. Transfer to liquid storage, chill and serve!

Nutritional Value Per Serving:

Calories 145, Carbohydrates 30 g, Fats 1 g, Protein 4 g

Rhubarb & Thyme Syrup

Prep time: 15 minutes, Cook time: 1 hour 30 minutes, Serves: 12

Ingredients

- 2 cups diced rhubarb
- 1 cup ultrafine sugar
- 1 cup water
- 5 sprigs thyme

Instructions:

1. Prepare your Sous Vide water bath using your immersion circulator and raisethe temperature to 180°F.
2. Add all the listed ingredients to a heavy-duty zipbag
3. Seal using the immersion method
4. Submerge underwater and cook for 1 ½hour.
5. Remove the bag and strain the contents to abowl.
6. Transfer to liquid storage, chill and serve!

Nutritional Value Per Serving:

Calories 192, Carbohydrates 47 g, Fats 0 g, Protein 1 g

Chili Agave Liqueur

Prep Time: 10 minutes, Cook time: 45 minutes, Serves: 8

Ingredients

- 2 cups vodka
- ½ cup water
- ½ cup light agave nectar
- 3 dried Guajillo chili peppers
- 1-piece Serrano pepper, sliced in half, seeded
- 1 Fresno pepper, sliced in half, seeded
- Zest, 1 lemon
- 1 cinnamon stick
- 1 teaspoon black peppercorns

Instructions:

1. Prepare your Sous Vide water bath using your immersion circulator and raisethe temperature to 180°F.
2. Add all the listed ingredients to a heavy-duty zipbag.
3. Seal using the immersion method and cook for 45minutes.
4. Once done, remove the bag and strain the contents to abowl.
5. Transfer to liquid storage, chill and serve!

Nutritional Value Per Serving:

Calories 152, Carbohydrates 37 g, Fats 0 g, Protein 1 g

Bourbon Grape & Ginger Beer

Prep time: 30 minutes, Cook time: 2 hours, Serves: 8

Ingredients

- 2-3 cups sliced seedless red grapes
- 1 ¼ cups vanilla sugar
- ½ cup bourbon
- ½ vanilla bean, split
- 1 lemon, peeled
- 1-star anise pod
- 1 cardamom pod
- ½ cup ginger beer
- Fresh mint leaves
- Lemon twists
- Sliced grapes for garnishing

Instructions:

1. Prepare your Sous Vide water bath using your immersion circulator and raisethe temperature to 167°F.
2. Add the grapes, sugar, vanilla, bourbon, star anise, lemon peel, and cardamom toa large resealable zip bag.
3. Seal using the immersion method and cook for 2hours.
4. Once done, remove the bag and transfer to an ice bath, once the grape mix iscool, transfer to the refrigerator andchill.
5. Strain the grape mixture through a metal mesh strainer over a bowl and reserve the fruit for later use.
6. Then, fill a rocks glass with ice and add ½ cup ginger beer, 1 ½ ounce ofinfused bourbon.
7. Garnish with mint and lemon twist.
8. Serve with a garnish of slicedgrapes.

Nutritional Value Per Serving:

Calories 92, Carbohydrates 23 g, Fats 0 g, Protein 0g

Sous Vide Gin

Prep time: 10 minutes, Cook time: 1 minute 30 seconds, Serves: 1

Ingredients

- 3 oz. vodka
- Zest, small orange
- 8 juniper berries
- 10-12 coriander seeds
- 2 cardamom pods
- 8-10 grains of paradise
- 1 Tasmanian pepper berry

Instructions:

1. Prepare your Sous Vide water bath using your immersion circulator and raisethe temperature to 176°F.
2. Add all the listed ingredients to a resealable bag and seal using the immersionmethod.
3. Cook for 90 seconds.
4. Once done, take the bag out from the water bath and transfer it to an icebath.
5. Massage the bag to infuse the gincarefully.
6. Cool down the mixture and strain the mixture through a metal mesh strainer and pourit to a medium-sized bowl
7. Serve!

Nutritional Value Per Serving:

Calories 68, Carbohydrates 17 g, Fats 0 g, Protein 0 g

Limoncello Vodka Cocktail

Prep time: 20 minutes, Cook time: 3 hours, Serves: 5

Ingredients

- 1 bottle vodka
- Grated zest/peel, 10-15 thoroughly washed lemons
- 1 cup granulated sugar
- 1 cup water

Instructions:

1. Prepare your Sous Vide water bath using your immersion circulator and raisethe temperature to 135°F.
2. Add the vodka and lemon zest to a large zip bag and seal using the immersionmethod. Cook for 2-3 hours.
3. Take a saucepan and put it over medium-highheat
4. Add the sugar and water and stir until the sugar dissolves to prepare thesyrup
5. Once done, take the bag out from the water bath and strain through metal mesh intoa bowl.
6. Stir in syrup.
7. Pour Limoncello into bottles and serve!

Nutritional Value Per Serving:

Calories 248, Carbohydrates 61 g, Fats 0 g, Protein 1 g

Swedish Rosemary Snaps

Prep time: 10 minutes, Cook time: 2 hours, Serves: 10

Ingredients

- 1 bottle vodka
- 3 sprigs fresh rosemary + plus extra for storage
- 4 strips, fresh orange peel

Instructions:

1. Prepare your Sous Vide water bath using your immersion circulator and raisethe temperature to 135°F.
2. Add the vodka, 3 sprigs rosemary, and 3 strips of orange peel to a resealable zipbag.
3. Seal using the immersion method. Cook for 2hours.
4. Once done, take the bag out from the water bath and pass through metal meshstrainer into large bowl.
5. Put one fresh sprig of rosemary and one strip of orange peel intobottle.
6. Pour the prepared snaps into bottle.
7. Chill and serve!

Nutritional Value Per Serving:

Calories 83, Carbohydrates 14 g, Fats 3 g, Protein 0 g

Strawberry Basil Shrub

Prep time: 10 minutes, Cook time: 2 hours, Serves: 12

Ingredients

- 1 lb. fresh strawberries,trimmed
- 1 lb. ultrafine sugar
- 2 cups balsamicvinegar
- 1 cup water
- 1 cup fresh basil leaves

Instructions:

1. Prepare your Sous Vide water bath using your immersion circulator and raisethe temperature to 135°F.
2. Add all the listed ingredients to a resealable zipbag.
3. Seal using the immersion method. Cook for 2hours.
4. Once cooked, take the bag out from the water bath and pass through metalmesh strainer into large bowl.
5. Chill and serve!

Nutritional Value Per Serving:

Calories 176, Carbohydrates 36 g , Fats 0 g, Protein 8 g

Drambuie

Prep time: 15 minutes, Cook time: 30 minutes, Serves: 8

Ingredients

- 1 cup scotch
- ½ cup water
- ½ cup honey
- 2 teaspoons fresh rosemary
- 2 teaspoons whole fennel seeds

Instructions:

1. Prepare your Sous Vide water bath using your immersion circulator and raisethe temperature to 180°F.
2. Add all the above ingredients to a resealable zipbag.
3. Seal using the immersion method.
4. Cook for 30minutes.
5. Once done, take the bag out from the water bath and pass through metal meshstrainer into a large bowl.
6. Chill and serve!

Nutritional Value Per Serving:

Calories 186, Carbohydrates 24 g, Fats 6 g, Protein 9 g

Bacon Infused Bourbon

Prep time: 1 hour 20 minutes, Cook time: 1 hour, Serves: 8

Ingredients

- 2 cups bourbon
- 8 oz. smoked bacon, cooked until crisp
- 3 tablespoon bacon fat reserved fromcooking
- 3 tablespoons light brownsugar

Instructions:

1. Prepare your Sous Vide water bath using your immersion circulator and raisethe temperature to 150°F.
2. Add all the listed ingredients to a resealable zipbag.
3. Seal using the immersion method. Cook for 1hour.
4. Once done, take the bag out from the water bath and strain the contents through afine-mesh strainer into a largebowl
5. Transferthe bourbon to the refrigeratorand chilluntil the pork fatsolidifies ontop. Skim off the fat
6. Then, strain the bourbon a second time through a cheesecloth-linedstrainer.
7. Pass it to a storage container and store in therefrigerator.

Nutritional Value Per Serving:

Calories 251, Carbohydrates 14 g, Fats 19 g, Protein 6 g

Lemongrass Syrup

Prep time: 15 minutes, Cook time: 1 hour, Serves: 4

Ingredients

- 4 stalks lemongrass, cut into 1-inchpieces
- 1 cup water
- 1 cup ultrafine sugar

Instructions:

1. Prepare your Sous Vide water bath using your immersion circulator and raisethe temperature to 180°F.
2. Add all the above ingredients to a resealable zipbag.
3. Seal using the immersionmethod.
4. Cook for about 1 hour.
5. Once cooked, remove the bag from the water bath and transfer it to an ice-coldbath.
6. Strain into a large bowl and transfer to acontainer
7. Serve chilled!

Nutritional Value Per Serving:

Calories 291, Carbohydrates 54 g, Fats 7 g, Protein 3 g

Thai Basil Drink

Prep time: 15 minutes, Cook time: 1 hour, Serves: 4

Ingredients

- 1 bunch, Thai basil rinsed
- 1 cup water
- 1 cup ultrafine sugar

Instructions:

1. Prepare your Sous Vide water bath using your immersion circulator and raisethe temperature to 180°F.
2. Add all the listed ingredients to a resealable zipperbag.
3. Seal using the immersionmethod.
4. Submerge underwater and cook for 1hour.
5. Once done, take the bag out from the water bath and transfer to an icebath.
6. Strain into a large bowl and transfer to acontainer
7. Serve chilled!

Nutritional Value Per Serving:

Calories 175, Carbohydrates 19 g, Fats 7 g, Protein 9 g

Jalapeno Vodka

Prep time: 10 minutes, Cook time: 2 hours, Serves: 5

Ingredients

- 2 jalapeno peppers
- 1 bottle vodka

Instructions:

1. Prepare your Sous Vide water bath using your immersion circulator and raisethe temperature to 147°F.
2. Cut the peppers and remove the stem, veins andseeds.
3. Add the ingredients to a resealable zipperbag.
4. Seal using the immersion method. Cook for 2hours.
5. Once done, take the bag out from the water bath and transfer to an icebath.
6. Strain into a large bowl and transfer to acontainer
7. Serve chilled!

Nutritional Value Per Serving:

Calories 52, Carbohydrates 1 g, Fats 4 g, Protein 3 g

Apple & Cardamom Gin

Prep time: 10 minutes, Cook time: 2 hours, Serves: 4

Ingredients

- 1 cup Gin
- 1 pink lady apple cored, sliced into rings
- 1 green cardamom pod

Instructions:

1. Prepare your Sous Vide water bath using your immersion circulator and raisethe temperature to 136.4°F.
2. Add all the above ingredients to a resealable zipbag.
3. Seal using the immersion method. Cook for 2hours.
4. Once done, take the bag out from the water bath and transfer to an icebath.
5. Strain into a large bowl and transfer to acontainer
6. Serve chilled!

Nutritional Value Per Serving:

Calories 185, Carbohydrates 22 g, Fats 9 g, Protein 4 g

Ginger Brandy

Prep time: 10 minutes, Cook time: 2 hours, Serves: 1

Ingredients

- 4 ½ oz. fresh ginger
- 1 ½ cup brandy
- 5 oz. sugar
- 1 cup water

Instructions:

1. Prepare your Sous Vide water bath using your immersion circulator and raisethe temperature to 135°F.
2. Peel and grate the ginger.
3. Add the ginger and brandy to a resealable zip bag and seal using theimmersion method. Cook for 2 hours.
4. Then, take a saucepan and place it over medium heat. Add the water and sugarand allow the sugar to dissolve.
5. Strain the brandy and ginger mixture into a clean bottle and add all the sugarsyrup.
6. Serve!

Nutritional Value Per Serving:

Calories 232, Carbohydrates 57 g, Fats 0 g, Protein 1 g

Chapter 11: Stocks, Sauces, Broth And Spice Rubs

Beef Broth

Prep time: 3 minutes, Cook time: 14 hours 15 minutes, Serves: 6

Ingredients:

- 3 lb. Beef Feet
- 1 ½ lb. Beef Bones
- ½ lb. Grounded Beef
- 5 cups Tomato Paste, unsweetened
- 6 medium Sweet Onions
- 3 heads Garlic
- 6 tbsp Black Pepper Powder
- 5 sprigs Thyme
- 4 Bay Leaves
- 10 cups Water

Instructions:

1. Preheat an oven to 425°F.
2. Place beef bones and beef feet in a roasting pan and rub them withthe
3. tomato paste. Add garlic and onion. Placeaside.
4. Place and crumble ground beef in another roastingpan.
5. Place the roasting pans in the oven and roast until darkbrown.
6. Once done, drain fat from the roastingpans.
7. Make a water bath in a large container, place a Sous Vide cooker in it, and set it at 195°F.
8. Separate the ground beef, roasted vegetables, black pepper, thyme, and bay leaves in3 vacuum bags.
9. Deglaze the roasting pans with water and add it to thebags.
10. Fold the top of the bags 2 to 3times.
11. Place the bags in the water bath and clip it to the Sous Videcontainer.
12. Set the timer for 13 hours.
13. Once the timer has stopped, remove the bags and transfer the ingredients to apot.
14. Bring the ingredients to a boil over highheat.
15. Cook for 15 minutes.
16. Turn off heat and strain.
17. Use the stock as a soupbase.

Nutritional Value Per Serving:

Calories 32.42, Carbohydrates 2.88 g, Fats 0.22 g, Protein 4.73 g

Chicken Stock

Prep time: 20 minutes, Cook time: 12 hours 10 minutes, Serves: 3

Ingredients:

- 2 lb. Chicken, any parts – thighs, breasts
- 5 cups Water
- 2 Celery Sticks, chopped
- 2 White Onions, chopped

Instructions:

1. Make a water bath, place a Sous Vide cooker in it, and set it at194°F.
2. Separate the listed ingredients in 2 vacuum bags, fold the top of the bags 2 – 3times.
3. Place them in the water bath and clip it to the Sous Videcontainer.
4. Set the timer for 12hours.
5. Once the timer has stopped, remove the bag and transfer the ingredients to apot.
6. Boil the ingredients over high heat for 10minutes.
7. Turn off heat and strain. Use the stock as a soupbase.

Nutritional Value Per Serving:

Calories 68, Carbohydrates 4.47 g, Fats 2.88 g, Protein 6.05 g

Fish Broth

Prep time: 10 minutes, Cook time: 10 hours 5 minutes, Serves: 4

Ingredients:

- 5 cups Water
- ½ lb Fish fillets, skin
- 1 lb. Fish Head
- 5 medium Green Onions
- 3 Sweet Onion
- ¼ lb. Black Seaweed (Kombu)

Instructions:

1. Make a water bath, place a Sous Vide cooker in it, and set it at194°F.
2. Separate all the listed ingredients equally into2 vacuum bags, fold the top of the bags 2 times.
3. Place them in the water bath and clip it to the Sous Vide container. Set the timer for 10 hours.
4. Once the timer has stopped, remove the bag and transfer the ingredients to apot.
5. Boil the ingredients over high heat for 5minutes
6. Turn off heat and strain.
7. Refrigerate and use for up to 14days.

Nutritional Value Per Serving:

Calories 105, Carbohydrates 0.98 g, Fats 1.46 g, Protein 22 g

Seafood Stock

Prep time: 10 minutes, Cook time: 10 hours, Serves: 6

Ingredients:

- 1 lb. Shrimp Shells, with heads and tails
- 3 cups Water
- 1 tbsp Olive Oil
- 2 tsp Salt
- 2 sprigs Rosemary
- ½ head Garlic, crushed
- ½ cup Celery Leaves, chopped

Instructions:

1. Make a water bath, place a Sous Vide cooker in it, and set it at180°F.
2. Toss the shrimp with the olive oil. Place the shrimp with the remaining listed ingredients in a vacuum-sealable bag.
3. Release air, seal and submerge the bag into the water bath, and set the timer for 10 hours.
4. Once the timer has stopped, remove and unseal the bag. Strain the ingredients. Cooland use frozen for up to 2 weeks.

Nutritional Value Per Serving:

Calories 53, Carbohydrates 0 g, Fats 5 g, Protein 2 g

Vegetable Stock

Prep time: 15 minutes, Cook time: 12 hours 20 minutes, Serves: 10

Ingredients:

- 1 ½ cups Celery Root, diced
- 1 ½ cups Leeks, diced
- ½ cup Fennel, diced
- 4 cloves Garlic, crushed
- 1 tbsp Olive Oil
- 6 cups Water
- 1 ½ cups Mushrooms
- ½ cup Parsley, chopped 1
- tbsp Black Peppercorns 1
- Bay Leaf

Instructions:

1. Make a water bath, place a Sous Vide cooker in it, and set it at 180°F. Preheat an oven to 450°F. Place the leeks, celery, fennel, garlic, and olive oil in a bowl. Toss them. Transfer to a roasting pan and tuck them in the oven. Roast for 20minutes.
2. Place the roasted vegetables with its juices, water, parsley, peppercorns, mushrooms, and bay leaf in a vacuum-sealable bag.
3. Release air, seal and submerge the bag into the water bath and set the timer for 12 hours.
4. Cover the water bath's container with a plastic wrap to reduce evaporation and keep adding water to the bath to keep the vegetablescovered.
5. Once the timer has stopped, remove and unseal the bag. Strain the ingredients. Cooland use frozen for up to 1 month.

Nutritional Value Per Serving:

Calories 12, Carbohydrates 3 g, Fats 0 g, Protein 0 g

Spicy BBQ Sauce

Prep time: 10 minutes, Cook time: 1 hour, Serves: 10

Ingredients:

- 1 ½ lb. small Tomatoes
- ¼ cup Apple Cider Vinegar
- ¼ tsp Monk Fruit Powder
- 1 tbsp low-carb Worcestershire Sauce
- ½ tbsp Liquid Hickory Smoke
- 2 tsp Smoked Paprika
- 2 tsp Garlic Powder
- 1 tsp Onion Powder
- Salt to taste
- ½ tsp Chili Powder
- ½ tsp Cayenne pepper
- 4 tbsp Water

Instructions:

1. Make a water bath, place a Sous Vide cooker in it, and set it at185°F.
2. Separate the tomatoes into two vacuum sealablebags.
3. Release air by the water displacement method, seal and submerge the bags in the water bath. Set the timer for 40 minutes.
4. Once the timer has stopped, remove and unseal thebag.
5. Transfer the tomatoes to a blender and puree until smooth and thick. Do not addwater.
6. Put a pot over medium heat, add the tomato puree and the remaining listedingredients. Bring to a boil, stirring continuously for 20 minutes. A thick consistency should be achieved.
7. Use as a sauce forbarbecuing.

Nutritional Value Per Serving:

Calories 30.9, Carbohydrates 4.5 g, Fats 0.9 g, Protein 1.2 g

Peri Peri Sauce

Prep time: 7 minutes, Cook time: 30 minutes, Serves: 15

Ingredients:

- 2 lb. Red Chili Peppers
- 4 cloves Garlic, crushed
- 2 tsp Smoked Paprika
- 1 cup Cilantro Leaves, chopped
- ½ cup Basil Leaves, chopped
- 1 cup Olive Oil
- 2 Lemons' Juice

Instructions:

1. Make a water bath, place a Sous Vide cooker in it, and set it at185°F.
2. Place the peppers in a vacuum-sealable bag.
3. Release air by the water displacement method, seal and submerge the bag in the water bath. Set the timer for 30minutes.
4. Once the timer has stopped, remove and unseal thebag.
5. Transfer the pepper and the remaining listed ingredients to a blender and pureeto smooth.
6. Store in an airtight container, refrigerate, and use for up to 7days.

Nutritional Value Per Serving:

Calories 27.8, Carbohydrates 5.6 g, Fats 0.2 g, Protein 0.9 g

Jalapeno Seasoning

Prep time: 5 minutes, Cook time: 55 minutes, Serves: 6

Ingredients:

- 2 Jalapeno Peppers
- 2 Green Chili Peppers
- 2 cloves Garlic, crushed
- 1 medium Onion, peeled only
- 3 tsp Oregano Powder
- 3 tsp Black Pepper Powder
- 2 tsp Rosemary Powder
- 10 tsp Aniseed Powder

Instructions

1. Make a water bath, place a Sous Vide cooker in it, and set it at 185°F. Place the peppers and onion in a vacuum-sealable bag.
2. Release air by the water displacement method, seal and submerge the bag in the water bath. Set the timer for 40 minutes. Once the timer has stopped, remove and unseal the bag. Transfer the pepper and onion with 2 tablespoons of water to a blender andpuree to smooth.
3. Place a pot over low heat, add the pepper puree and the remaining listedingredients. Simmer for 15 minutes. Turn off heat andcool.
4. Store in a spice jar, refrigerate, and use for up to 7 days. Use it as a spice in other foods.

Nutritional Value Per Serving:

Calories 3.6, Carbohydrates 0 g, Fats 0 g, Protein 0.9 g

Garlic Basil Rub

Prep time: 15 minutes, Cook time: 40 minutes, Serves: 15

Ingredients:

- 2 heads Garlic, crushed
- 2 tsp Olive Oil
- A pinch Salt
- 1 head Fennel
- 2 Lemons, zested and juiced
- ¼ Monk Fruit
- 25 Basil Leaves

Instructions:

1. Make a water bath, place a Sous Vide cooker in it, and set it at185°F.
2. Place the fennel and monk fruit in a vacuum-sealablebag.
3. Release air by the water displacement method, seal and submerge the bag in the water bath. Set the timer for 40 minutes. Once the timer has stopped, remove and unseal the bag.
4. Transfer the fennel, monk fruit, and remaining listed ingredients to a blender and puree to smooth.
5. Store in a spice container and use up to a week withrefrigeration.

Nutritional Value Per Serving:

Calories 18.13, Carbohydrates 1.22 g, Fats 0.05 g, Protein 3.2 g

Ancho Chili Oil

Prep time: 15 minutes , Cook time: 1 hour, Serves: 12

Ingredients:

- 1 cup, canola oil
- 2 dried ancho chilies, with removed stems and seeds, and turned into 1-inchpieces 1
- tablespoon, red wine vinegar
- 2 crushed garlic cloves
- 1 teaspoon, kosher salt

Instructions:

1. Prepare your Sous Vide water bath to a temperature of180°F
2. Add everything to a zip bag
3. Seal using immersion method
4. Cook for 1 hour
5. Serve or store in container for up to 2weeks

Nutritional Value Per Serving:

Calories 209, Carbohydrates 11 g, Fats 17 g, Protein 3 g

Cool Garlic Confit

Prep time: 10 minutes, Cook time: 2 hours, Serves: 8

Ingredients:

- 1 cup, peeled garlic cloves
- ¼ cup, extra virgin olive oil
- 1 tablespoon, kosher salt

Instructions:

1. Prepare your Sous Vide water bath to a temperature of190°F
2. Add the ingredients to a large sized zip bag and seal using immersionmethod
3. Submerge and cook for 2 hours
4. Transfer to storage and use asneeded

Nutritional Value Per Serving:

Calories 150, Carbohydrates 28 g, Fats 2 g, Protein 5 g

Very Hot Chili Oil

Prep time: 10 minutes, Cook time: 3 hours, Serves: 8

Ingredients:

- 2 habanero peppers, sliced upcrosswise
- 2 jalapeno peppers, sliced up crosswise
- 2 cups, milk olive oil

Instructions:

1. Prepare your Sous Vide water bath to a temperature of131°F
2. Add the listed ingredients to your Zip bag and seal using immersionmethod
3. Cook for 3 hours
4. Transfer bag to ice bath and allow it tocool
5. Discard the peppers
6. Store in airtight container and serve asneeded.

Nutritional Value Per Serving:

Calories 221, Carbohydrates 18 g, Fats 13 g, Protein 8 g

Vanilla Crème Anglaise

Prep time: 15 minutes, Cook time: 1 hour, Serves: 10

Ingredients:

- 1 cup, whole milk 1
- cup, heavy cream
- ¾ cup, ultrafine sugar
- 5 pieces, egg yolk
- 1 teaspoon, vanilla beanpaste
- Just a pinch, koshersalt

Instructions:

1. Prepare your Sous Vide water bath to a temperature of180°F
2. Transfer ingredients to blender and puree for 30seconds
3. Transfer to zip bag and seal using immersionmethod
4. Cook for 1 hour
5. Remove the bag and transfer to icebath
6. Serve and enjoy!

Nutritional Value Per Serving:

Calories 219, Carbohydrates 2 g, Fats 23 g, Protein 1 g

Crème Fraiche

Prep time: 10 minutes, Cook time: 12 hours, Serves: 10

Ingredients:

- 2 cups, heavy cream

Instructions:

1. Prepare your Sous Vide water bath to a temperature of105°F
2. Add cream and buttermilk in canning jar
3. Submerge and cook for 12 hours
4. Transfer to ice bath
5. Serve once cooled/ store in fridge for 2weeks

Nutritional Value Per Serving:

Calories 219, Carbohydrates 2 g, Fats 23 g, Protein 1 g

Shallot Confit

Prep time: 10 minutes, Cook time: 2 hours, Serves: 8

Ingredients:

- 4 pieces, shallots, peeled and quartered
- 3 tablespoon, extra virgin olive oil
- 3 tablespoons, granulated sugar
- 1 teaspoon, kosher salt

Instructions:

1. Prepare your Sous Vide water bath to a temperature of190°F
2. Add the listed ingredients to zip bag and seal using immersionmethod
3. Submerge and cook for 2 hours
4. Transfer to a storage and use asneeded
5. Enjoy!

Nutritional Value Per Serving:

Calories 116, Carbohydrates 25 g, Fats 0 g, Protein 4 g

Caramel Sauce

Prep time: 5 minutes, Cook time: 2 hours, Serves: 10

Ingredients

- 20 pitted dates
- 1 cup non-dairy milksoy
- 1 teaspoon vanilla
- A pinch of salt

Instructions:

1. Prepare your Sous-vide water bath to a temperature of135°F.
2. Takeyour datesalongside themilk, vanillaand add themto aheavy-duty resealablezip bag.
3. Seal the bag using the immersionmethod.
4. Submerge underwater and cook for about 2hours.
5. Add the mixture to a blender and blend until you have sauce likeconsistency
6. Season with a bit of salt and use asneeded

Nutritional Value Per Serving:

Calories 267, Carbohydrates 28 g, Fats 15 g, Protein 2 g

Cauliflower & Pepper

Prep time: 20 minutes, Cook time: 2 hours, Serves: 2

Ingredients

- 2 cups cauliflower florets, chopped
- 1 medium-sized Yukon gold potato, peeled and chopped
- 1 chopped red bell pepper
- 1 tablespoon extra-virgin olive oil
- 1 garlic clove, crushed
- 1 bay leaf
- Kosher salt as needed
- ¼ teaspoon ground coriander
- ¼ teaspoon ground cumin
- 2 cups chicken broth
- 1 cup whole warmed milk
- Freshly grated parmesan cheese
- Fresh ground black pepper

Instructions:

1. Prepare your Sous-vide water bath to a temperature of185°F.
2. Take a large resealable zip bag and add the cauliflower, bell pepper, olive oil, potato, bay leaf, ½ teaspoon of salt, garlic, ½ teaspoon of cumin, andcoriander.
3. Seal using the immersion method. Submerge underwater and cook for 2hours.
4. Once cooked, remove the bag and transfer the contents to abowl.
5. Add the chicken broth and milk and whisk them using the immersionblender.
6. Season the mixture with pepper and salt
7. Garnish with a bit of parmesan and serve!

Nutritional Value Per Serving:

Calories 201, Carbohydrates 24 g, Fats 9 g, Protein 6 g

Cauliflower Alfredo

Prep time: 5 minutes, Cook time: 2 hours, Serves: 4

Ingredients

- 2 cups chopped up cauliflowerflorets
- 2 crushed garlic cloves
- 2 tablespoons butter
- ½ cup chicken stock
- 2 tablespoons milk
- Salt and pepper as needed

Instructions:

1. Prepare your Sous-vide water bath to a temperature of181°F.
2. Add all the listed ingredients into a resealable zipbag.
3. Seal using the immersion method.
4. Submerge underwater and cook for 2hours.
5. Once done, transfer it to a food processor and puree until you have a smoothtexture
6. Serve!

Nutritional Value Per Serving:

Calories 147, Carbohydrates 21 g, Fats 3 g, Protein 9 g

Strawberry Rhubarb Jam

Prep time: 15 minutes, Cook time: 1 hour 30 minutes, Serves: 4

Ingredients

- 1 cup rhubarb, diced
- 1 cup strawberries, diced
- 2 tablespoons powdered pectin
- 2 tablespoons fresh squeezed lemon juice

Instructions:

1. Prepare your Sous-vide water bath to a temperature of180°F.
2. Add all the listed ingredients to a resealable zipbag.
3. Seal using the immersion method.
4. Cook for 1 ½ hours.
5. Serve as needed.

Nutritional Value Per Serving:

Calories 40, Carbohydrates 10 g, Fats 0 g, Protein 0 g

Mango Chutney (Indian Mango

Prep time: 10 minutes, Cook time: 6 hours, Serves: 4

Ingredients

- 1 large ripe mango, peeled and cut up into small dices
- ¼ cup Granny Smith Apple, cored, peeled, and cut up into small dices
- ¼ red onion, finely chopped
- ¼ cup packed light brown sugar
- 1 ½ tablespoons malt vinegar
- 1 finely chopped chili
- ½ teaspoon grated fresh ginger
- A pinch of salt

Instructions:

1. Prepare your Sous-vide water bath to a temperature of185°F.
2. Add all the listed ingredients to a resealable zipbag.
3. Seal using the immersion method.
4. Submerge underwater and cook for 6 hours.
5. Transfer to an ice bath and allow it to cool.
6. Transfer the cooled chutney to jars and use as needed, or you can store in containerfor up to 1 week.

Nutritional Value Per Serving:

Calories 464, Carbohydrates 116 g, Fats 0 g, Protein 0 g

Mezcal Cream

Prep time: 15 minutes, Cook time: 30 minutes, Serves: 8

Ingredients

- ½ cup heavy cream
- ½ cup mezcal*
- ½ cup ultrafine sugar
- 4 large egg yolks
- 1 teaspoon vanilla extract
- A pinch of kosher salt

Instructions:

1. Prepare your Sous-vide water bath to a temperature of 180°F.
2. Add everything to your blender and puree for 30 seconds.
3. Then, transfer the mixture to a large resealable bag.
4. Seal using the immersion method and cook for 30 minutes.
5. Transfer to an ice bath and serve once cooled.

Nutritional Value Per Serving:

Calories 749, Carbohydrates 101 g, Fats 33 g, Protein 12 g

Béarnaise Sauce

Prep time: 20 minutes, Cook time: 45 minutes, Serves: 10

Ingredients

- ¼ cup white wine vinegar
- ¼ cup white wine
- 2 tablespoons chopped freshtarragon
- 1 tablespoon scallion, chopped
- Salt as needed
- Fresh ground black pepper as needed
- 4 large egg yolks
- 6 tablespoons unsalted butter

Instructions:

1. Prepare your Sous-vide water bath to a temperature of174°F.
2. Add the vinegar, wine, tarragon, and scallion to a largesaucepan.
3. Sprinkle some salt and pepper to the mixture and bring it to a boil over highheat.
4. Lower down the heat to medium-low and allow it to cook for 5 moreminutes.
5. Once done, strain the mixture through a fine metal mesh and allow it to cool for5 minutes.
6. Mix the egg yolks in a medium-sizedbowl.
7. Add the cooled vinegar mixture andmix.
8. Keep mixing constantly and drizzle in the melted butter. Keep mixing untilsmooth.
9. Transferthemixturetoaresealable zipperbag and sealusing the immersion method.
10. Cook for 45 minutes.
11. Once cooked, take the bag out from the water bath and transfer to amedium-sized bowl, blend using immersion blender.
12. Stir in tarragon and serve!

Nutritional Value Per Serving:

Calories 1353, Carbohydrates 5 g, Fats 145 g, Protein 7 g

Champagne Citrus Vinegar

Prep timc: 10 minutes, Cook time: 3 hours, Serves: 8

Ingredients:

- Peels, 2 lemon
- Peels, 2 orange
- 17 oz. champagne vinegar
- 1 thick sliced, lemon
- 1 thick sliced, orange
- 1 tablespoon granulated sugar

Instructions:

1. Prepare your Sous-vide water bath to a temperature of153°F.
2. Twist the citrus peels.
3. Add the lemon slice, vinegar, sugar, orange slice and peels to your resealable zipbag.
4. Seal using the immersion method. Cook for 3 hours
5. Once done, take the bag out from the water bath and strain the contents througha cheesecloth into a storing jar with lid.
6. Serve as needed or you can store in a fridge for up to 6weeks.

Nutritional Value Per Serving:

Calories 61.4, Carbohydrates 10 g, Fats 0.6 g, Protein 4 g

Lemon Ginger Vinegar

Prep time: 15 minutes, Cook time: 3 hours, Serves: 10

Ingredients

- Peel, 1 lemon
- 17-ounce white wine vinegar
- 1-inch piece, fresh ginger root peeled up and sliced into ¼ inch 1
- thick slice lemon
- 1½ tablespoon granulated sugar

Instructions:

1. Prepare your Sous-vide water bath to a temperature of153°F.
2. Twist the lemon peels.
3. Add the vinegar, lemon peel, lemon slice, ginger, sugar, and seal using theimmersion method.
4. Submerge underwater and cook for 3 hours.
5. Strain through cheesecloth into a jar withlid.
6. Serve as needed.

Nutritional Value Per Serving:

Calories 328, Carbohydrates 55 g, Fats 4 g, Protein 18 g

Blackberry Lavender Balsamic

Ingredients

- 17 oz. balsamic vinegar
- 2 cups fresh blackberries
- 5 sprigs lavender
- 1 tablespoon granulated sugar

Instructions:

1. Prepare your Sous-vide water bath to a temperature of153°F.
2. Add all the listed ingredients to Sous Vide zipper bag and seal using the immersion method.
3. Submerge underwater and cook for 3 hours.
4. Halfway through your cooking, make sure to squeeze the bag to soften themup
5. Once cooked, strain the contents through a cheesecloth into a cleanbottle.
6. Serve as needed!

Nutritional Value Per Serving:

Calories 347, Carbohydrates 30 g, Fat 15 g, Protein 23 g

Garlic Confit

Prep time: 10 minutes, Cook timc: 2 hours, Serves: 8

Ingredients

- 1 cup peeled garlic cloves
- ¼ cup extra-virgin olive oil
- 1 tablespoon kosher salt

Instructions:

1. Prepare your Sous-vide water bath to a temperature of190°F.
2. Add the listed ingredients to a large resealable zip bag and seal using the immersion method.
3. Submerge underwater and cook for 2 hours.
4. Once cooked, transfer to a storage and use asneeded

Nutritional Value Per Serving:

Calories 150, Carbohydrates 28 g, Fats 2 g, Protein 5 g

Apricot Jam

Prep time: 10 minutes, Cook time: 2 hours, Serves: 8

Ingredients

- 12 oz. dried apricots
- 1 ½ cup granulated sugar

Instructions:

1. Prepare your Sous-vide water bath to a temperature of190°F.
2. Add the listed ingredients to your bag and seal using the immersionmethod.
3. Submerge underwater and cook for 2hours.
4. Once done, remove from the bag and transfer to abowl.
5. Smash any large pieces.
6. Serve or you can store up to 3 weeks and use asneeded.

Nutritional Value Per Serving:

Calories 293, Carbohydrates 69 g, Fats 1 g, Protein 2 g

Pineapple Compote with Rum &

Prep time: 10 minutes, Cook time: 1 hour, Serves: 8

Ingredients

- 1 lb. fresh pineapple, peeled, cored,diced
- 1 cup granulated sugar
- ½ cup dark rum
- Zest of 1 lime
- 2 sprigs fresh mint

Instructions:

1. Prepare your Sous-vide water bath to a temperature of190°F.
2. Add all the listed ingredients to a resealable bag and seal using the immersionmethod.
3. Submerge underwater and let it cook for 1hour.
4. Once done, transfer to airtight container and use as needed or you can store for up to2 weeks.

Nutritional Value Per Serving:

Calories 136, Carbohydrates 33 g, Fats 0 g, Protein 1 g

Balsamic Fig-Jam

Prep time: 10 minutes, Cook time: 2 hours, Serves: 8

Ingredients

- 12 oz. dried mission figs
- 1 cup water
- 1 cup granulated sugar
- ½ cup balsamic vinegar
- 2 sprigs fresh rosemary

Instructions:

1. Prepare your Sous-vide water bath to a temperature of190°F.
2. Add the listed ingredients to Sous-vide zip bag and seal using the immersionmethod.
3. Cook for 2 hours.
4. Once done, remove from the bag and transfer the jam to abowl.
5. Smash using a spatula.
6. Serve and enjoy!

Nutritional Value Per Serving:

Calories 272, Carbohydrates 67 g, Fats 0 g, Protein 1 g

Smoked Cranberry Relish

Prep time: 15 minutes, Cook time: 1 hour , Serves: 8

Ingredients

- 17 oz. cranberries
- 12 oz. brown sugar
- Juice, ½ orange
- ½ cinnamon stick
- 3-stars anise
- ½ grated nutmeg
- 150 ml port wine
- 2 cloves

Instructions:

1. Prepare the Sous-vide water bath to a temperature of203°F.
2. Add all the above ingredients to a resealable zipper bag and seal using the immersion method.
3. Submerge underwater and let it cook for 1 hour.
4. Once done, remove the cranberries from pouch and discard the cinnamon, cloves,and star anise.
5. Transfer to an air right container andstir.
6. Serve and use as needed.

Nutritional Value Per Serving:

Calories 525, Carbohydrates 130 g, Protein 1 g , Fat 0 g

Strawberry & Rosemary

Prep time: 10 minutes, Cook time: 2 hours, Serves: 8

Ingredients

- 1 lb. freshly diced strawberries, stemmed,quartered
- 1 cup granulated sugar
- Zest, 1 lemon
- 2 sprigs freshrosemary
- 1 teaspoon koshersalt

Instructions:

1. Prepare your Sous-vide water bath to a temperature of190°F.
2. Add all the listed ingredients to Sous-vide zip bag and seal using theimmersion method.
3. Cook for 2 hours.
4. Once done, remove from the bag and transfer it to abowl.
5. Smash using a spatula.
6. Serve!

Nutritional Value Per Serving:

Calories 141, Carbohydrates 31 g, Protein 2 g , Fats 1 g

Fresh Ginger Syrup

Prep time: 10 minutes, Cook time: 1 hour 30 minutes, Serves: 8

Ingredients

- 13 oz. caster sugar
- 4 cups water
- ¼ cup vodka
- 3-inch fresh ginger root, peeled, grated

Instructions:

1. Prepare your Sous-vide water bath to a temperature of142°F.
2. Add the listed ingredients to the resealable zip bag except for the vodka, seal using the immersion method.
3. Cook for 90 minutes.
4. Strain the liquid of the zip bag through a fine metal mesh into a large bowl, addthe vodka and mix
5. Pop into clean bottle and use asneeded.

Nutritional Value Per Serving:

Calories 292, Carbohydrates 72 g, Protein 1 g , Fats 0 g

Peach Chutney

Prep time: 20 minutes, Cook time: 40 minutes, Serves: 8

Ingredients

- ½ cup granulated sugar
- ½ cup water
- ¼ cup white wine vinegar
- 1 clove garlic, minced
- ¼ cup white onion, finely chopped
- 1 lime juice
- 2 teaspoons grated fresh ginger
- 2 teaspoon curry powder
- Pinch, red pepper flakes
- Salt and black pepper as needed
- 4 large peaches, slice, pitted, and peeled into ¼ inch thick wedges
- ¼ cup chopped fresh basil
- Several whole basil leaves for garnishing

Instructions:

1. Prepare your Sous-vide water bath to a temperature of167°F.
2. Add the sugar, white wine vinegar, water and garlic in amedium-sized saucepan and place it over medium-high heat.
3. Bring the mixture to a boil. Dissolve thesugar.
4. Add the onion, curry powder, lime juice, ginger, red pepper flakes and season withsalt and pepper. Stir well.
5. Add the sliced peaches in a large resealable zip bag and pour vinegar mixture over the peach.
6. Seal using the immersion method. Cook for 40minutes.
7. Transfer to an ice bath and cool.
8. Once done, transfer the contents to a storage container and stir inbasil.
9. Serve.

Nutritional Value Per Serving:

Calories 212, Carbohydrates 42 g, Protein 2 g, Fats 4 g

Hot Pepper Sauce

Prep time: 10 minutes, Cook time: 20 minutes, Serves: 8

Ingredients

- 1 ½ lbs. fresh red jalapeno peppers, chopped
- 9 garlic cloves, peeled, smashed
- 1 teaspoon sea salt
- 1/3 cup rice vinegar
- 3 tablespoons syrup

Instructions:

1. Prepare your Sous-vide water bath to a temperature of210°F.
2. Add the chopped peppers, garlic and sea salt to food processor andpuree.
3. Pour the mixture into resealable zip bag and seal using the immersionmethod.
4. Submerge underwater and cook for 20minutes.
5. Once done, remove from the bag and pour into abowl.
6. Stir in rice vinegar and syrup.
7. Serve as needed

Nutritional Value Per Serving:

Calories 338, Carbohydrates 80 g, Protein 2 g, Fats 0 g

Provencal Tomato Sauce

Prep time: 20 minutes, Cook time: 45 minutes, Serves: 8

Ingredients

- 1-pint cherry tomatoes
- ½ small onion, peeled, chopped up finely
- 1 shallot peeled, minced
- 5-6 large chopped basil leaves
- 2-3 sprigs fresh thyme stripped
- A handful, fresh parsley, fully stemmed, chopped up
- ½ teaspoon sea salt
- ¼ teaspoon ground black pepper
- 1 tablespoon olive oil

Instructions:

1. Prepare your Sous-vide water bath to a temperature of182°F.
2. Add all the listed ingredients to your resealable zip bag and seal using the immersion method.
3. Submerge underwater and let it cook for 30-45minutes.
4. Remove the pouch and knead the sauce through thepouch.
5. Serve as needed.

Nutritional Value Per Serving:

Calories 153, Carbohydrates 26 g, Protein 5 g, Fats 1 g

Chicken Stock

Prep time: 10 minutes, Cook time: 8 hours, Serves: 8

Ingredients

- 10 lbs. chicken bones
- 1 lb. yellow onion peeled, cut in half
- 8 oz. carrots, chopped
- 8 oz. celery, chopped
- ½ teaspoon black peppercorn
- 10 sprigs fresh thyme
- Small handful parsley stem
- 1-piece bay leaf

Instructions:

1. Roast your chicken bones for about 1 ½ hours at 400°F in youroven.
2. Add the roasted chicken bones, onion, and the rest of the ingredients to aresealable zipper bag
3. Add the water (reserve 1 cup) and seal using the immersionmethod.
4. Prepare the water bath to a temperature of 194-degrees Fahrenheit usingyour immersion circulator
5. Submerge underwater and cook for 6-8 hours.
6. Strain the mixture from the zip bag through a metal mesh into a large-sizedbowl
7. Cool the stock using an ice bath and place it in your ovenovernight
8. Scrape the surface and discard fat.
9. Use as needed.

Nutritional Value Per Serving:

Calories 2229, Carbohydrates 31 g, Protein 173 g, Fats 137 g

Cinnamon-Apple Flavored Balsamic

Ingredients

- 17 oz. balsamic vinegar
- 2 medium apples, sliced
- 2 cinnamon sticks
- 1 tablespoon sugar

Instructions:

1. Prepare your Sous-vide water bath to a temperature of153°F.
2. Add all the listed ingredients to your resealable zip bag and seal using the immersion method.
3. Submerge underwater and cook for 3 hours.
4. Once done, strain the contents through a cheesecloth into a cleanbottle.
5. Serve as needed!

Nutritional Value Per Serving:

Calories 220, Carbohydrates 54 g, Protein 1 g, Fats 0 g

Strawberry & Blueberry Coulis

Prep time: 10 minutes, Cook time: 30 minutes, Serves: 8

Ingredients

- 1 cup strawberries, stemmed, washed, quartered
- 1 cup fresh blueberries, stemmed, washed
- ¼ cup granulated sugar
- 1 lemon juice

Instructions:

1. Prepare the Sous-vide water bath to a temperature of180°F.
2. Add the berries, sugar and alongside the lemon juice into a resealable zipper bag and seal using the immersion method.
3. Cook for 30 minutes.
4. Mash through the pouch for a smoother consistency.
5. Once done, transfer it to a food processor and puree until you have a smoothtexture
6. Chill and use asneeded!

Nutritional Value Per Serving:

Calories 141, Carbohydrates 30 g, Protein 3 g, Fats 1 g

Summer Corn Salsa

Prep timc: 10 minutes, Cook time: 30 minutes, Serves: 8

Ingredients

- 4 ears fresh corn, shucked, washed
- Salt, and pepper
- 2 cloves garlic, chopped, peeled
- 1 deseeded, finely choppedjalapeno
- 2 tomatoes, chopped
- 2 limes, juiced
- ¼ cup extra-virgin olive oil
- 2 avocados, peeled, chopped, seeded
- 1 bunch coriander, chopped up
- Tortillas for serving

Instructions:

1. Prepare the Sous-vide water bath using your immersion circulator and raisethe temperature to 182°F.
2. Season the corn with salt and pepper.
3. Place the corn in a resealable zip bag and seal using the immersion method. Cookfor 30 minutes.
4. Take a large bowl and mix the finely chopped garlic, tomatoes, jalapenos, limejuice, avocado, coriander, and olive oil.
5. Once cooked, remove the corn and allow it tocool.
6. Cut the kernels and mix in the salsa. Season.
7. Serve with tortillas.

Nutritional Value Per Serving:

Calories 411, Carbohydrates 77 g, Protein 10 g, Fats 7 g

Grand Marnier Cranberry Sauce

Prep time: 10 minutes, Cook time: 2 hours, Serves: 8

Ingredients

- 1 cinnamon stick
- 1 teaspoon allspice berries
- 3 cloves garlic
- 12 oz. fresh cranberries
- 1 cup granulated sugar
- ¼ cup Grand Marnier Orange Liquor
- Juice and zest of 1 orange

Instructions:

1. Prepare your Sous-vide water bath to a temperature of175°F.
2. Bundle the cinnamon stick, cloves, and allspice in a cheesecloth and tie using astring.
3. Add the sachet of spices, sugar, cranberries, Grand Mariner, orange juice and zest to a resealable zip bag.
4. Seal using the immersion method. Cook for 2hours.
5. Once done, remove the spice sachet anddiscard.
6. Transfer the bag of cranberry sauce to an icebath.
7. Allow it to cool.
8. Enjoy!

Nutritional Value Per Serving:

Calories 212, Carbohydrates 52 g, Protein 1 g, Fats 0 g

Lemon Ginger Marmalade

Prep time: 15 minutes, Cook time: 3 hours, Serves: 8

Ingredients

- 4 pieces thinly sliced Meyer lemons
- 4 cups granulated sugar
- ¼ cup chopped crystallized ginger
- 1 tablespoon grated fresh ginger

Instructions:

1. Prepare your Sous-vide water bath to a temperature of190°F.
2. Add the above-listed ingredients to your resealable zipper bag and seal usingthe immersion method. Cook for 3 hours.
3. Once done, transfer the bag to an ice bath and allow it tocool.
4. You can store in an air tight container and serve asneeded.

Nutritional Value Per Serving:

Calories 480, Carbohydrates 119 g, Protein 1 g, Fats 0 g

Meyer Lemon Infused Olive Oil

Prep time: 10 minutes, Cook time: 3 hours, Serves: 8

Ingredients

- 2 cups olive oil
- Peels, two Meyer Lemon, twisted

Instructions:

1. Prepare your Sous-vide water bath to a temperature of131°F.
2. Add the listed ingredients to your resealable zip bag and seal using theimmersion method.
3. Cook for 3 hours.
4. Once done, transfer the bag to an ice bath and allow it tocool.
5. Discard the peels.
6. Store in airtight container and serve asneeded.

Nutritional Value Per Serving:

Calories 104, Carbohydrates 8 g, Protein 9 g, Fats 4 g

Enjoy your meal and thank you for choosing

Sous Vide Cookbook For Beginners!!

CPSIA information can be obtained
at www.ICGtesting.com
Printed in the USA
LVHW021102211220
674700LV00031B/710

9 781801 442206